SOCIAL ANARCHISM AND THE REJECTION OF MORAL TYRANNY

Outside philosophy departments, most self-identified anarchists are social anarchists who reject both the legitimacy of the state and private property. By contrast, most anarchist philosophers are of the pro-market variety. As a result, a philosopher has yet to write an analytic defense of social anarchism. Jesse Spafford fills this gap by arguing that social anarchism is a coherent philosophical position that follows from a more basic, plausible principle that constrains which moral theories are acceptable. In the process of articulating and defending social anarchism Spafford stakes out a number of bold and original positions (e.g., that people own themselves and nothing else), while providing novel solutions to some of the classic problems of political philosophy (e.g., luck egalitarianism's problem of stakes). His distinctive study offers an overarching, unified political theory while also advancing many of the more fine-grained debates that occupy political philosophers. This title is also available as Open Access on Cambridge Core.

JESSE SPAFFORD is a lecturer at Victoria University of Wellington. His work explores debates between libertarians, socialists, and anarchists over the moral status of the market and the state. He is the author of a number of articles in journals including *Philosophical Studies*, *Synthese*, and the *Journal of Ethics and Social Philosophy*.

SOCIAL ANARCHISM AND THE REJECTION OF MORAL TYRANNY

JESSE SPAFFORD
Victoria University of Wellington

Shaftesbury Road, Cambridge CB2 8EA, United Kingdom

One Liberty Plaza, 20th Floor, New York, NY 10006, USA

477 Williamstown Road, Port Melbourne, VIC 3207, Australia

314–321, 3rd Floor, Plot 3, Splendor Forum, Jasola District Centre, New Delhi – 110025, India

103 Penang Road, #05–06/07, Visioncrest Commercial, Singapore 238467

Cambridge University Press is part of Cambridge University Press & Assessment, a department of the University of Cambridge.

We share the University's mission to contribute to society through the pursuit of education, learning and research at the highest international levels of excellence.

www.cambridge.org
Information on this title: www.cambridge.org/9781009375399

DOI: 10.1017/9781009375429

© Jesse Spafford 2023

This work is in copyright. It is subject to statutory exceptions and to the provisions of relevant licensing agreements; with the exception of the Creative Commons version the link for which is provided below, no reproduction of any part of this work may take place without the written permission of Cambridge University Press.

An online version of this work is published at http://dx.doi.org/10.1010/9781234567890 under a Creative Commons Open Access license cc-by-nc 4.0 which permits re-use, distribution and reproduction in any medium for non-commercial purposes providing appropriate credit to the original work is given and any changes made are indicated. To view this license, visit https://creativecommons.org/licenses/by-nc/4.0

All versions of this work may contain content reproduced under license from third parties. Permission to reproduce this third-party content must be obtained from these third-parties directly. When citing this work, please include a reference to the
DOI: 10.1017/9781009375429

First published 2023
First paperback edition 2025

A catalogue record for this publication is available from the British Library

ISBN   978-1-009-37544-3   Hardback
ISBN   978-1-009-37539-9   Paperback

Cambridge University Press & Assessment has no responsibility for the persistence or accuracy of URLs for external or third-party internet websites referred to in this publication and does not guarantee that any content on such websites is, or will remain, accurate or appropriate.

Contents

Acknowledgments	*page* vii
Introduction	1
I.1 The Boundaries of Anarchism	6
I.2 The Aims of the Book	13
I.3 Something for Everyone	16
1 Social Anarchism	21
1.1 The Consent Theory of Legitimacy	22
1.2 The Lockean Proviso	25
1.3 The Self-Ownership Thesis	32
1.4 The Advantages of Anarchist Self-Ownership	42
1.5 The Rejection of Private Property	49
1.6 Anarchist Claim Rights	49
1.7 Is Anarchist Self-Ownership Too Permissive?	55
1.8 Is Anarchist Self-Ownership Too Restrictive?	59
1.9 Conclusion	65
2 The Moral Tyranny Constraint	68
2.1 The Moral Tyranny Constraint	69
2.2 Explicating the Constraint	70
2.3 Defending the Constraint	74
2.4 Three Implications of the Constraint	80
2.5 Three Objections to the Constraint	87
2.6 Conclusion	91
3 You Own Yourself and Nothing Else	92
3.1 The Proviso and Private Property	93
3.2 The Lockean Proviso and Self-Ownership	97
3.3 Comparing Baselines	103
3.4 Defending and Emending the Nonexistence Baseline	108
3.5 Appropriation and Children	116
3.6 Conclusion	119

Contents

4 Property and Legitimacy — 121
- 4.1 Territorial Legitimacy — 122
- 4.2 A Consent Theory of Territorial Legitimacy — 124
- 4.3 The Absence of Appropriation — 129
- 4.4 Land, Resources, and Artifacts — 130
- 4.5 Initial Appropriation and Obligation Imposition — 132
- 4.6 The Propertarian Objection — 135
- 4.7 Commonsense Distinctions — 138
- 4.8 Consent Theory and Self-Ownership — 141
- 4.9 Philosophical Anarchism and the Anarchist Conclusion — 149
- 4.10 Conclusion — 151

5 Entitlement Theory without Entitlements — 152
- 5.1 Hobbesian Moral Tyranny — 155
- 5.2 The Incompatibilist Argument — 157
- 5.3 The Left-Libertarian Solution — 159
- 5.4 Just Holdings vs. Just Distributions — 161
- 5.5 Is Entitlement Necessary for Justice? — 162
- 5.6 Wilt Chamberlain and the Anarchist Conclusion — 164
- 5.7 Libertarian Egalitarianism — 168
- 5.8 Conclusion — 173

6 Luck Egalitarianism without Moral Tyranny — 174
- 6.1 Three Objections to Prudential Contextualism — 176
- 6.2 Moralized Contextualism — 178
- 6.3 A Theory of Sanctionable Choice — 179
- 6.4 Applying the Theory — 187
- 6.5 Anarchism without Moral Tyranny — 192
- 6.6 Amending the Theory — 193
- 6.7 Additional Advantages of the Theory — 195
- 6.8 The Disadvantage Creation Account — 197
- 6.9 Conclusion — 201

7 A State-Tolerant Anarchism — 203
- 7.1 Two *Desiderata* of Political Anarchism — 204
- 7.2 Twelve Analyses of Statehood — 205
- 7.3 A State-Tolerant Anarchism — 215
- 7.4 In Defense of Philosophical Anarchism — 217
- 7.5 Conclusion — 223

References — 224
Index — 234

Acknowledgments

There are so many people who have contributed to this book in so many ways, either by providing substantive feedback on its arguments, asking helpful questions at conferences, suggesting ways for me to improve my writing, or providing me with the inspiration and material support that I needed to complete the project.

I am indebted, first, to Hilary Gaskin at Cambridge University Press for believing in this project and patiently working with me to get it published. Special mention also goes to Adina Preda for giving me the opportunity to work on the book (and for her many helpful comments). I am also grateful to Peter Vallentyne, Carol Gould, Eric Roark, Kei Numao, Fabian Wendt, Miranda Fricker, Charles Mills, and multiple anonymous reviewers for providing generous, detailed, and constructive feedback on various chapters of the book. I further benefitted from the many helpful comments and suggestions made by participants at the Locke and Lockeanism Working Group Meeting; the Philosophy, Politics, and Economics Society Annual Meeting; the American Philosophical Association Pacific Division Conference; the Georgetown Institute for the Study of Markets and Ethics (GISME) workshop; and the Trinity Centre for Justice and Values Works in Progress Workshop. Chris Fowler provided some much-needed assistance when it came to finding elegant numbers for the tables in Chapter 6. And this book would not have been completed without the outstanding mentoring, advocacy, and emotional support provided to me by my parents, friends, partner, undergraduate mentors (Peter Kung, Susan McWilliams, and Michael Green), graduate advisor (Carol Gould), and postdoctoral supervisor (Adina Preda). I am also thankful to the editors and anonymous reviewers of *Philosophical Studies* for their helpful comments on my paper "Luck Egalitarianism without Moral Tyranny" (published in 2022), which I have adapted into Chapter 6 of this book.

In terms of financial support, this project has received funding from the European Research Council (ERC) under the European Union's Horizon

2020 research and innovation program (grant agreement No. 819043). Some of the ideas in this book also emerged out of my dissertation, which was generously supported by the American Council of Learned Societies and the solidarity and collective bargaining efforts of the Professional Staff Congress.

Finally, I am thankful for all of the countless anarchists, socialists, and other radicals whose writings – in books and zines, on forums and walls – influenced this book. I hope that those reading the book will find its various arguments to be similarly useful.

Introduction

> We are told that the word Anarchy needs constant explanation; that whenever used in its literal sense it must be defined. Is there any other word of which this is not true? The introduction of new ideas into a man's mind is not accompanied by the use of a specially coined word, but by the adaptation of old words to broader uses.
>
> Lucy Parsons, "Anarchism"

This book aims to provide a philosophical defense of egalitarian anarchism, more popularly known as *social anarchism*. It is certainly not the first book to attempt to defend this position; numerous egalitarian anarchists across time and place have already produced something of a canon of works expounding and arguing for the ideology.[1] However, this book stands apart from these prior efforts in that it employs the tools of contemporary analytic philosophy to construct its argument. While popular defenses of anarchism generally seek to persuade through the use of rhetoric and informal argumentation, this book aspires to provide something closer to a *proof* of its thesis, with heavy reliance on logic, the precise definition of terms, and concepts developed by academic philosophers.[2]

This book will also differ from canonical anarchist texts in that it defends a moral position rather than a social arrangement. Typically, anarchist texts present social anarchism as a socialist, stateless political

---

[1] Some influential examples include Mikhail Bakunin (1953), Alexander Berkman (2003), Murray Bookchin (2004), Noam Chomsky (2013), Lorenzo Kom'boa Ervin (2021), Luigi Fabbri (1922), Emma Goldman (1911), Daniel Guérin (1970), Peter Kropotkin (1995), Nestor Makhno (1996), Errico Malatesta (1994), Louise Michel (1896), Ito Noe (2005), Lucy Parsons (2004), Pierre-Joseph Proudhon (1876) (though Proudhon is claimed by many anarchist traditions), Elisée Reclus (1899), Rudolf Rocker (2004), and Charlotte Wilson (2005).

[2] The downside to this approach is that it will make the book less accessible to those who do not have prior philosophical training. However, the hope is that non-philosophers with an interest in anarchism will still be able to follow the broader argument even if some of the details get a bit technical.

system. They then attempt to explain how the system works in practice, appeal to moral principles to justify the system, propose strategies for realizing it, and address various objections that might call into question the viability or general attractiveness of the proposed system. By contrast, this book is strictly concerned with the moral principles that motivate social anarchists to endorse the abolition of the state and capitalism. Thus, when the book talks of "social anarchism" or "egalitarian anarchism," it is using these terms to refer to a specific set of moral principles (to be introduced in the subsequent chapter) as opposed to a way of structuring political institutions, society, and the economy.

In addition to the so-called canonical anarchist texts, there have been a few anarchist philosophers who have employed the tools of analytic political philosophy to either explicate or defend anarchism *qua* moral philosophy. However, this book stands apart from these prior efforts in that it *defends* an *egalitarian* anarchist position. Typically, when philosophers write about anarchism, they are primarily concerned with explicating the anarchist position rather than defending it.[3] While some do attempt to provide a sustained defense of anarchism, they generally argue for a more minimal version of the position that merely maintains that people are not obligated to obey the laws of the state.[4] Or, alternatively, they defend a more expansive *market* anarchist or *anarcho-capitalist* position that assigns each person the power to unilaterally acquire a robust set of property rights over an unlimited quantity of natural resources.[5] This posited power opens the door to a significant degree of licensed inequality, as some individuals might acquire much more property than others. Those with less would then have moral duties to respect the property rights of those with more even though doing so leaves them comparatively worse off.

Notably, this property-friendly anarchist position is not one that most self-identified anarchists would endorse. Rather, the bulk of the anarchist movement is composed of self-identified *anarcho-communists* or *social anarchists* who favor equality and reject capitalism, markets, and the private property rights on which these institutions rest. Indeed, as will be discussed subsequently, a popular opinion among these anarchists is that anarcho-capitalism – and, to a lesser extent, market anarchism – are not even genuine forms of anarchism, as they lack the egalitarian and

---

[3] See, for example, Alan Ritter (1980), David Miller (1984), and Paul McLaughlin (2016).
[4] Robert Paul Wolff's (1970) influential book on anarchism takes this approach. For a more recent defense, see Crispin Sartwell (2008).
[5] See Michael Huemer (2013) and Gary Chartier (2013).

anti-capitalist commitments that are essential to anarchism. While the book will not take a stand on this question, its purpose is to propose and defend a moral position that will be much more amenable to these egalitarian anarchists.

The outline of the book is as follows. The remainder of this introduction discusses the general aims of the book and situates the book within the broader ideological landscape by explaining the relationship between its argument, the anarchist movement, and some of the defended position's philosophical rivals. Specifically, Section I.1 begins by considering the question of what it means for a moral position to be an *anarchist* position and whether the position defended by the book can be reasonably characterized as "social anarchism." Section I.2 then discusses the central aims of the book in a bit more detail, the primary two being (1) showing that social anarchism is coherent (in a sense to be described subsequently) and (2) showing that the position is independently plausible. Finally, Section I.3 argues that social anarchism will be attractive (in at least some respect) to partisans of a number of rival philosophical positions. In this way, the section aims to show that the theoretical costs of accepting the position are not as high for these partisans as it might first appear.

With this introductory groundwork in place, Chapter 1 begins the main argument of the book by introducing the five moral principles that make up the social anarchist position. Specifically, it defines social anarchism as the conjunction of the following five theses. First, there is the consent theory of legitimacy. This thesis holds that persons are obligated to obey the laws of the state only if they have consented to do so. Given that practically no one has consented in this way, this thesis entails the *philosophical anarchist* conclusion that all existing states are illegitimate, that is, they lack the power to oblige. Second, there is the Lockean proviso. This proposition places a constraint on persons' powers to convert unowned natural resources into private property. A defining commitment of *right-libertarianism*, this proviso holds that persons can acquire property rights over some bit of land or natural resource if and only if they leave "enough and as good" for others. The third anarchist thesis is the self-ownership thesis. This thesis asserts that each person has the same set of ownership rights over her body that she would have over a fully owned thing (including a permission to use her body, a claim against others using it without permission, etc.). Fourth, the anarchist position asserts that persons do not have private property rights over any external natural resources. And, finally, the social anarchist position includes an endorsement of luck egalitarianism as the moral principle regulating the permissible use of unowned external objects. (This will be called "the anarchist conclusion".)

Notably, the social anarchist position includes both principles that are standardly associated with libertarianism and egalitarian principles that are widely endorsed by socialist philosophers. This pairing is not without precedent; left-libertarian philosophers have influentially endorsed both varieties of principle and defended their compatibility.[6] However, it will be argued that social anarchism represents a distinctive synthesis of libertarian and egalitarian moral positions, both because of the particular theses that it posits and because of the stronger logical relation that it claims obtains between them (more on this in Section I.2).

The five anarchist theses having been introduced, Chapter 2 argues that these principles can all be derived from a single meta-principle that limits which moral theories qualify as theoretically acceptable. This posited *moral tyranny constraint* holds that a theory of duties is acceptable only if full compliance with that theory (and the demands of morality more generally) would not allow any person to unilaterally, discretionarily, and foreseeably act in a way that would leave others with less advantage – that is, whatever it is that matters morally vis-à-vis distributive justice – than they would have possessed given some other choice by the agent. The chapter then explicates the various components of the constraint, defends the constraint's plausibility, and explains how it entails three of the posited anarchist theses (with subsequent chapters arguing that these theses entail the two remaining anarchist theses). Finally, the chapter addresses three potential objections that might be raised against the moral tyranny constraint.

Chapter 3 begins the process of explicating the logical relations that obtain between the various anarchist theses. Taking the Lockean proviso as its starting point, it argues that this thesis entails two further conclusions embraced by social anarchists. First the chapter argues that, contrary to what

---

[6] Left-libertarians differ from right-libertarians in that, while both endorse the self-ownership thesis and affirm that people can acquire private property, left-libertarians believe that this acquisition is subject to demanding egalitarian constraints. For example, Peter Vallentyne (1998) both posits that people own themselves – a core libertarian thesis (discussed in detail in Chapter 1) – and that a society can justly tax away the full benefit that a person receives from natural resources without violating said self-ownership. Similarly, Michael Otsuka (2003) argues that one might endorse a particular version of the self-ownership thesis while still insisting that justice obtains if and only if the acquisition of private property is constrained such that each person has an equal opportunity to obtain welfare. Hillel Steiner (2000) defends a position wherein he accepts the libertarian right to self-ownership while simultaneously affirming the egalitarian position that each person is entitled to an equal share of external natural resources. And Philippe Van Parijs (2000) posits that self-ownership can be balanced with an egalitarian maximin principle that structures resource ownership in a way that maximizes the opportunities available to the worst off.

Introduction 5

right-libertarians typically maintain, the Lockean proviso implies that no one owns (or could reasonably come to own) any natural resources. This is because any appropriation of such resources would leave others worse off in a way that the proviso does not allow, which, in turn, implies that no such appropriation of natural resources has occurred. By contrast, the chapter argues that the proviso is *necessarily* satisfied when it comes to each agent's own body. Thus, while people do not own any external resources, they can easily come to own themselves via acts of self-appropriation.

Chapter 4 provides an alternative argument for rejecting private property. While Chapter 3 attempts to derive this conclusion from the Lockean proviso, this chapter begins with the consent theory of legitimacy as its starting premise. It then argues that property ownership is a form of legitimate authority. Thus, if one accepts a consent theory of legitimacy, one would also have to maintain that property ownership has consent as its necessary condition. However, given that no one has ever consented to the appropriation of natural resources, it follows that no one owns any such resources. The chapter concludes by considering three objections to this argument. It also discusses what the consent-based argument against private property implies vis-à-vis the self-ownership thesis.

Notably, both Chapter 3 and Chapter 4 begin with a libertarian starting premise. They, thus, put significant dialectical pressure on libertarians to reject their standard conclusion that persons have property rights over land and objects. However, Chapter 5 notes that this result underdetermines which positive position libertarians (or, strictly speaking, any property rights theorist) ought to endorse. One option is to simply concede that people lack any sort of claim rights when it comes to natural resources. The chapter labels this proposal "the *Hobbesian conclusion*" and argues that it must be rejected because it violates the moral tyranny constraint. Given the theoretical unacceptability of this option, the chapter contends that libertarians and property rights theorists should, instead, accept what it calls the *anarchist conclusion*. This thesis holds that persons *do* possess certain claims against others using unowned resources, where these claims correspond to the prescriptions of a luck egalitarian principle of distributive justice. The chapter then argues that libertarians have limited basis for rejecting the anarchist conclusion, as it is compatible with both their favored property-based theories of justice and the arguments that support such theories. Finally, it argues that libertarians' tacit presuppositions also commit them to the egalitarian aspect of the anarchist conclusion.

In short, Chapter 5 suggests that libertarians ought to accept that people have some variety of egalitarian distributive claims vis-à-vis natural resources (as opposed to property claims). While it does not establish that these claims should correspond to a *luck* egalitarian theory of distributive justice, this conclusion follows from Chapter 2's argument that luck egalitarianism satisfies the moral tyranny constraint in a way that strict egalitarianism does not. However, Chapter 6 points out that the dominant interpretation of luck egalitarianism fails to fully satisfy the moral tyranny constraint. To resolve this problem, it offers an alternative interpretation that both eliminates the possibility of moral tyranny and rescues luck egalitarianism from two other prominent objections that have been raised against the position. In this way, the chapter demonstrates that there is a plausible egalitarian distributive principle that follows from the moral tyranny constraint (by way of various libertarian moral theses). This result completes the book's defense of the social anarchist position, with the first six chapters having collectively shown that there is a coherent and plausible set of libertarian and egalitarian theses that all follow from the moral tyranny constraint.

Social anarchism *qua* political philosophy having been presented and defended, Chapter 7 notes that there is a significant lacuna in the posited social anarchist position. One might expect that any view described as an "anarchist" position will include an endorsement of the *political anarchist* thesis that the mere existence of a state is unjust, with some persons thereby having an obligation to abolish any existing states. However, this contention does not appear among the five social anarchist theses defended by the book. Rather, as noted previously, social anarchism includes only the endorsement of the weaker philosophical anarchist thesis that all existing states lack the power to impose obligations on their purported subjects. Chapter 7 defends this choice by arguing that political anarchism is implausible. Specifically, it contends that political anarchists must provide an analysis of statehood that entails that (a) any group that qualifies as a state is unjust in a way that its non-state counterpart is not and (b) there are existing states. It then argues that there is no plausible analysis of statehood that satisfies both of these *desiderata*. Thus, political anarchism fails by its own lights. Finally, the chapter concludes by considering and rejecting a recent argument that philosophical anarchism collapses into either political anarchism or statism.

I.1 The Boundaries of Anarchism

The book aims to defend a set of moral theses that it calls "social anarchism." However, this label raises the difficult question of what counts as an anarchist philosophical position. The difficulty emerges from the fact that many different people have claimed the term "anarchism" for their views despite the fact that those views differ in significant ways and, quite often, conflict with one another. For example, as noted previously, most self-identified anarchists – both past and present – are anarcho-communists or social anarchists who call for the abolition of the state, capitalism, and private property. By contrast, a small but vocal group of anarcho-capitalists argue that the state should be abolished but not capitalism. In their view, each person can rightfully acquire and exchange private property, and they call for market-based services to replace much of the activity typically carried out by states (e.g., private security companies would replace the police and military).[7] Notably, social anarchists often wish to deny the "anarchist" label to anarcho-capitalists, arguing that genuine anarchism is incompatible with an embrace of property, markets, and capitalism.[8] Obviously, anarcho-capitalists disagree. Thus, a question is raised regarding how one might resolve this dispute – and, more generally, how one is to determine whether *any* given position (e.g., the one defended in this book) is a genuine anarchist position.

As a starting point for answering this general question, it is helpful to consider some of the arguments philosophers have advanced to try to resolve the debate over whether or not anarcho-capitalism is a genuine form of anarchism. A popular strategy for denying anarcho-capitalism the "anarchist" label involves arguing that anarcho-capitalism's pro-market commitments contradict an essential anarchist thesis. For example, John Clark posits that "the essence of anarchism is … not the theoretical opposition to the state, but the practical and theoretical struggle against domination" (1984, 70), where inequality and private property are forms of domination (120). Thus, one might appeal to the conjunction of these premises to conclude that anarcho-capitalism is not a genuine form of anarchism, as it licenses both inequality and property.[9] By contrast, Roderick Long argues against this conclusion by noting that there are many influential thinkers who are widely recognized as anarchists by social

---

[7] For some influential defenses of this position, see David Friedman (1989) and Michael Huemer (2013).
[8] Some examples include Alan Carter (2013, 259), Peter Sabatini (1994–1995), and Iain McKay et al. (2008). See also Barbara Goodwin (2007, 143).
[9] McKay et al. (2008) appeal to Clark in this way as part of a lengthy and detailed argument against counting anarcho-capitalism as a genuine variety of anarchism. That said, Clark does not direct his quoted comments directly against anarcho-capitalists, and other remarks of his suggest a willingness to count those who oppose the state but endorse property as genuine anarchists (1978, 19, 21).

anarchists despite holding views that social anarchists otherwise consider disqualifying when it comes to anarcho-capitalists (2018, 287–95). Given that there is no principled basis for denying the "anarchist" label to anarcho-capitalists but not these paradigmatic anarchist thinkers, he concludes that social anarchists should accept that anarchism is a big tent that includes anarcho-capitalists.[10]

The problem with both of these argumentative strategies is that they rest on premises that a critical interlocutor could easily reject. The former argument presupposes that there is some commitment that is essential to anarchism such that any broader anarchist position must be at least compatible with this commitment or, more strongly, must follow from it. While the essentialist claim may not, itself, be terribly controversial – though anti-essentialists might reject it and contend that the various anarchist positions merely bear a "family resemblance" to one another without sharing any single property – there will inevitably be controversy over which commitment is the essential one. Is a rejection of domination the defining feature of anarchism? Why not think, instead, that anarchism's essential feature is a respect for property rights (with opposition to the state following from the fact that states necessarily violate such rights)? It is not clear how one might resolve such disagreement. Thus, the essentialist argument for the claim that anarcho-capitalists are not anarchists seems to rest on an indefensible premise.

Long's argument encounters a similar difficulty. He is right that many social anarchists have been willing to grant the "anarchist" label to thinkers who embrace positions associated with anarcho-capitalism (e.g., Benjamin Tucker and Lysander Spooner). However, suppose that someone insisted that this was a mistake. Such a rejection of Long's starting premise – namely, that social anarchists are *correct* to judge that these thinkers are anarchists – would render his argument unsound. Of course, critics can dispute the core premise of any argument, but, in this case, there is no obvious way to defend the premise in question without rendering Long's argument superfluous. Note that any argument for the proposition that the thinkers in question are genuine anarchists would seemingly have to appeal to some general account of which positions qualify as anarchist positions. However, if one had such a general account, then one could

---

[10] Contra Long's argument, McKay et al. (2020, section G) argue that there are important differences between anarcho-capitalists and the property-sympathetic thinkers that social anarchists recognize as anarchists. Thus, they would insist that there *is* a principled basis for uniquely denying anarcho-capitalists the "anarchist" label.

forego Long's argument and appeal to that account directly to resolve the debate over whether anarcho-capitalism is a genuine variety of anarchism.

The foregoing discussion reveals that both of the prior arguments suffer from a common vulnerability: They each assume as their starting premise that one can uncontroversially apply the "anarchist" label to specific commitments or thinkers. However, in each case, there is no obvious supporting argument for this assumption that does not beg the question. To defend a particular application of the "anarchist" label, one must seemingly posit a general theory demarcating which ideas and/or thinkers are anarchist in character, where this theory will be just as controversial as the particular judgments that it is supposed to support. To see this, consider how one might resolve a disagreement between someone advancing one of the just-discussed arguments and an interlocutor who (a) denied that the posited commitments (or thinkers) were anarchist in character and (b) rejected any general theory of anarchism that had this implication. Given these positions, there is no obvious rejoinder available, as one seemingly needs a general theory to resolve disputes about particular commitments/thinkers but also established judgments about particular commitments/thinkers to resolve disputes about the general theory. Granted, one might accuse the interlocutor of simply not grasping the relevant conceptual truths; however, this reply is implausible given that it seems to be at least an open question whether a given commitment (or thinker) is, in fact, an anarchist position (or thinker). Thus, both arguments about the proper boundaries of anarchism appear to be ultimately inconclusive.

This result might suggest a more general form of skepticism about the book's claim that it is presenting and defending an *anarchist* political philosophy. On this skeptical view, the apparent intractability of debates over what counts as anarchism reveals that one ought to adopt a *non-factualist* understanding of these debates. Specifically, the non-factualist holds that the best explanation of this intractability is that there is simply no fact of the matter as to whether or not a given thinker/social arrangement/philosophical position is anarchist in character. Thus, the proposition that the book presents an anarchist viewpoint is neither true nor false, which is to say that it is lacking in genuine semantic content.

Alternatively, one might adopt a *quietist* view that takes debates over the boundaries of anarchism to be merely verbal rather than substantive. This variety of skepticism begins with the observation that there are millions of distinct ideological positions, where these positions are individuated based upon the particular propositions they affirm. When two people intractably disagree about whether one of these positions is a variety of anarchism, their disagreement results from the fact that they mean different things when they use the term "anarchism," with one person using the term to refer to a particular set of positions while the other uses it to refer to a non-identical set. For this reason, the quietist maintains that the disagreement is apparent rather than genuine, as it can be dissolved through greater verbal precision: the person who says the position is a form of anarchism is really saying that it is a form of anarchism$_1$ while the person who disagrees is denying that it is a form of anarchism$_2$. In this way, the quietist can (i) explain why there is disagreement – namely, the disagreeing parties are using the same word to refer to different things – (ii) resolve the disagreement by showing that the two asserted claims are actually compatible, and (iii) still affirm that there is a fact of the matter when it comes to whether a given position is appropriately classified as anarchism$_1$ (or anarchism$_2$, or anarchism$_3$, etc.).

While the quietist does assign a truth value to the proposition that the book is advancing an anarchist position, her view strips this claim of any philosophical significance. Once her demand for verbal precision has been met, the truth of such a proposition becomes simply a matter of definition: if anarchism$_1$ is defined as including some position p, then it is an analytic truth that p is a form of anarchism$_1$. Thus, the book's assertion that it is defending an anarchist position would either be false or trivial depending on one's stipulated definition of "anarchism." If "anarchism" is defined such that the book's posited position is (part of) its extension, then the book's assertion is true; if "anarchism" is not defined in this way, then the claim is false. Either way, the result is uninteresting, and the assertion does not seem worth making – at least on the quietist view.

So, what, then, should one think of the book's claim that it is presenting and defending an anarchist philosophical position? Against both of the just-discussed skeptical positions, the book's contention is that this claim has both semantic content and philosophical significance. Specifically, the claim has nontrivial semantic content because it is an assertion about the relationship between philosophical ideas and a particular social movement. The task of the remainder of this section is to briefly describe this relation and this movement, beginning with the latter.

As a matter of social fact, there are many people across time and space who have called themselves anarchists. While there is likely no single belief that these people share, there is a constellation of beliefs that they will endorse at much higher rates than will people outside of this group. These beliefs include the contention that the state should be eliminated, that

I.1 The Boundaries of Anarchism

police and prisons should be abolished, that (almost) all wars are unjust, that capitalism and/or markets are morally bad forms of economic organization, that private property rights are unacceptable constraints on freedom, that resources should be distributed from each according to her ability to each according to her need, that production should be managed by trade unions and/or democratically, that centralized state planning of the economy is an unacceptable alternative, that gender norms are objectionable constraints on autonomy, that significant social changes need to be made to eliminate racist and sexist practices that prop up White supremacy and patriarchy, that borders should be open or eliminated entirely, that children have a robust set of rights and should not be subject to expansive parental authority or compulsory education, that consuming animal products is exploitative and immoral, and that humans should significantly limit their activities to preserve and restore natural ecosystems, among others. This group of people also will tend to endorse the views espoused by a particular set of thinkers (e.g., those who produced the so-called canonical texts listed in Footnote 1), champion certain causes (the efforts of the CNT/FAI and the Zapatistas, Bundism, the Rojavan revolution, etc.), and affiliate with certain institutions (antifascist groups, the Industrial Workers of the World, etc.). Call the set of self-identified anarchists who exhibit these tendencies *the anarchist movement*.

So, what is the posited relation between the anarchist movement and the egalitarian philosophical position that the book calls "social anarchism?" Obviously, it will not be the case that every member of the anarchist movement endorses social anarchism. As noted previously, self-identified anarchists regularly disagree about most questions, including the truth of each of the claims listed in the previous paragraph. Indeed, it was for this reason that the movement is specified via reference to self-identification rather than any shared set of beliefs held by its members. Given that there is limited *actual* endorsement of social anarchism by self-identified anarchists, the suggestion here is that a substantial number of anarchists *would* endorse the social anarchist position if given adequate philosophical context (e.g. they were presented with a full slate of rival views and the best arguments for and against those views). In other words, if debate and reflection would lead self-identified anarchists to ultimately converge on the social anarchist position, then the position has a claim to the "anarchist" label. Call this proposal the *social movement approach*.

As an analogy, consider a small planet that forms in a field of smaller matter scattered across space. Over time, the gravity of the planet will pull surrounding material either onto its surface or into its orbit, with the greatest pull being exerted on the most spatially proximate material (holding mass constant for these purposes). One might similarly think of self-identified anarchists as being located at different points in n-dimensional ideological space, where n is equal to the total number of normative philosophical propositions that a person can hold and where an anarchist's location along a particular dimension is determined by whether or not she affirms the particular normative proposition associated with that dimension. Similarly, the social anarchist position sits in this space in virtue of the propositions it affirms.[11] Finally, to claim that social anarchism is a genuinely anarchist view is to assert that it will exert an analogous sort of gravitational pull on the self-identified anarchists surrounding it, steadily pulling a large number of them into its orbit (with greatest effect on those anarchists who sit at the most proximate points in ideological space).

There are a few advantages to this proposal. First, one can endorse the social movement approach while also conceding to the quietist that there are other rival concepts that could equally be called "anarchism." While essentialists must insist that there is a pre-theoretical concept of anarchism whose necessary and sufficient conditions of application can be grasped through intuition, the social movement approach can grant that its proposed account of what qualifies as an anarchist view is merely stipulated. However, this concession does not entail that it is trivial to declare that social anarchism is an anarchist position. Rather, this claim expresses a significant and contestable thesis about the relationship between the posited philosophical position and the anarchist social movement.

The second advantage of using the anarchist label in this way is that it allows for the possibility of revisionary anarchist theories – that is, theories that are anarchist in character despite the fact that they are not endorsed by most self-identified anarchists. On the essentialist view, revisionary accounts of an ideology are rendered paradoxical, as they apply the concept of that ideology to targets that, *by the accounts' own admission*, do not meet the necessary conditions for the application of that concept. Or, to put this point another way, given that revisionary accounts deny some core tenet of the ideology in question, why claim that they are revising that ideology

---

[11] More precisely, it would be a cluster of points, as the egalitarian anarchist position in this context should be understood not merely as a set of propositions, but, rather, a *set of such sets S*, where a set of views V belongs to S if and only if V includes each of the five theses presented in Chapter 1 and no propositions incompatible with the conjunction of these theses. Each member of S would then occupy a point in ideological space. However, it is easier to present the analogy if egalitarian anarchism is taken to occupy a single point rather than many, so this bit of complexity is ignored in the main text.

rather than rejecting it in favor of a rival view? The social movement approach helps to answer this question and thereby make sense of revisionary theories: When someone claims to be positing a heterodox version of some ideological position, she is claiming that proponents of the existing orthodox version would, upon adequate reflection, ultimately endorse her proposed heterodox view.[12]

I.2 The Aims of the Book

The book's position is called "social *anarchism*" because it aspires to present a philosophical position that stands in the posited relation to the anarchist movement. It is certainly not the case that most self-identified anarchists *actually* endorse the position. This is partly due to the fact that the position is stated in terms of concepts and principles that are peculiar to academic philosophy and not widely discussed by actual participants in the anarchist movement. Additionally, the position has some revisionary implications that many anarchists would refuse to endorse (these will be discussed in Chapter 7). So why think that self-identified anarchists would ultimately accept the proposed view? The convenient answer is that anarchists, like all persons interested in identifying the correct moral theory, will be attracted to the position in proportion to its general theoretical virtues. Thus, the aim of the book is to establish that social anarchism possesses these theoretical virtues, thereby simultaneously defending the position *qua* political philosophy and the position's claim to the anarchist label.

That said, the book's argument for social anarchism will appeal to a number of principles that will be particularly attractive to self-identified anarchists. Thus, anarchists will be more likely to endorse the social anarchist position after adequate philosophical reflection relative to non-anarchists. As will be discussed shortly, one aim of the book is to show that social anarchism is coherent in the sense that its five theses are connected via relations of logical entailment. Given that self-identified anarchists

---

[12] For example, G. A. Cohen suggests that a core socialist commitment is eliminating all unchosen disadvantage such that any social differences reflect only "difference of taste or choice" (2008, 18). He recognizes that this is a revisionary view, as it declares unjust certain economic regimes that are widely endorsed by socialists. However, in response to this observation, he states that "I acknowledge that socialists have advocated such regimes, and I have no wish, or need, to deny that those regimes can be called *socialist* . . . . What I do need to insist is that such systems contradict the fundamental principles animating socialists, when those principles are fully thought through" (23). In this way, he seemingly endorses the social movement approach to justify his revisionary account of socialism *qua* political philosophy.

often endorse the theses that function as antecedents in these entailment relations, they will also be disposed to accept the consequent theses as well (after philosophical reflection). Thus, they will be particularly disposed to endorse the social anarchist position.

When it comes to establishing the theoretical virtues of social anarchism, the book will attempt to demonstrate that the position is both coherent and independently plausible. As a rough statement of the former virtue, a *coherent* position is one where the adoption of any additional principles beyond one's starting principle is motivated by that starting principle.[13] The virtue of coherence is particularly important for establishing the plausibility of positions that are composed of unusual combinations of normative theses, for example, social anarchism with its simultaneous endorsement of libertarian and egalitarian moral principles. To see the worry here, suppose that one embraces some libertarian principle L. Given this starting commitment, should one build a political philosophy that endorses not only L as its starting premise but also some egalitarian principle S (assuming that L and S are compatible)? There are two reasons one might have doubts about the wisdom of such a project, each of which can be understood as a kind of coherence worry.

First, the worry about the position's coherence can be understood as a worry about *arbitrariness*. Note that there are numerous alternative principles and combinations of principles that might be adopted as a supplement to L. Why, then, affirm a political philosophy that endorses the conjunction of L and S rather than one that affirms L and some other principle T – or, alternatively, L and S and T? Even supposing that L is compatible with both S and T (i.e., there is no contradiction between L and either of these two latter theses), the fact that these principles *can* be jointly held does not establish that they *should* be so held. By contrast, a coherent political position is one where a stronger logical relation than mere compatibility obtains between L and S, where this relation justifies the particular set of principles chosen.

Note that it is not adequate to simply provide freestanding justifications of L and S, that is, independent reasons why each respective moral principle is attractive. This is because a given principle might be compatible with many other independently plausible principles that are, themselves, incompatible. For example, it might be the case that L is compatible with S and is similarly compatible with T, and there is something attractive

---

[13] This is how Barbara Fried defines the notion when criticizing left-libertarian positions for lacking coherence (2004; 87fn50, 89).

I.2 The Aims of the Book

about both S and T; however, it also turns out that S and T contradict one another. Thus, to embrace L & S requires that one reject L & T, even though all three principles are equally plausible. Given this possibility, one might worry that a theoretical position composed of independently attractive principles bound together only by the very weak compatibility relation is theoretically objectionable due to it being unacceptably arbitrary. At the very least, one might ask of the person who endorses L and S whether she is confident that she has found the optimal combination of moral principles, or whether there might be superior combinations of compatible principles available to her.

Second (and relatedly), one might take the worry about coherence to be a worry about how the posited position would hold up in the context of a debate with those who endorse various rival positions. Specifically, consider the ideologue who endorses L as a core principle but rejects S. Given her rejection of S, a demonstration that L and S are compatible will do nothing to push her away from her position, as she can admit such compatibility while denying that there is any need for her to append S to her already-accepted principle. Of course, one might appeal to various intuitive considerations that favor the adoption of S, but a steadfast ideologue could simply deny that she feels the force of the presented intuition pumps.

This worry about the coherence of a conjunctive position that endorses both L and S, then, can be understood as a worry that L and S fail to adequately hang together in a way that gives the position a dialectical advantage over a position that endorses L but not S. In other words, were the conjunctive position coherent, then there would be a logical relation between L and S such that those who merely embraced L would be rationally compelled to accept the conjunctive position. Specifically, it would have to be the case that either L – when coupled with some conjunction of uncontroversial premises U – entails S, or that the most plausible grounds of L (i.e., the most plausible premise that, together with U, entails L) also entails S when conjoined with U. This book will argue that there are such direct relations of logical entailment that connect the libertarian and egalitarian theses that make up the social anarchist position. In this way, the book aims to establish that social anarchism is coherent in the sense described earlier, with the position thereby capturing the associated dialectical and theoretical advantages.

In addition to demonstrating that the various anarchist theses are logically connected, the book will also argue that they are independently plausible. It will do this in two ways. First, as noted in the opening section, it will argue that the anarchist theses follow from an independent meta-principle that constrains which moral theories are acceptable (the moral tyranny constraint). Insofar as this meta-principle is plausible, it will represent a novel reason for accepting the anarchist position that it entails. Second, the book will show that, once the anarchist theses are suitably adjusted to conform to the moral tyranny constraint, they avoid many of the serious objections that plague their unadjusted counterparts. By negating these reasons for rejecting the anarchist position – in addition to having provided the aforementioned positive reason for accepting it – the book aims to show that the all-things-considered balance of reasons favors accepting social anarchism.

In this way, the book aims to increase the metaphorical gravity of the anarchist position. By revealing the logical connections that render the position coherent, the book will help to pull in anarchists who endorse some of the social anarchist theses but not others. Additionally, by enhancing the independent plausibility of the position, the hope is to attract those whose views place them well outside of the part of ideological space primarily occupied by self-identified anarchists. In particular, the book aims to put dialectical pressure on right-libertarians, who share many of the social anarchist's philosophical intuitions and methodological commitments but reach very different conclusions when it comes to distributive justice. The book will try to show that right-libertarians are mistaken in their conclusions and should, thus, enter the social anarchist orbit.

I.3 Something for Everyone

If the argument of the book succeeds, the resulting conclusion will be of some practical use to those across the political spectrum. For anarchists, the uses of the book are more apparent, but still worth discussing. First, the philosophical position it defends (and the argument for that position) can serve as an intellectual foundation for justifying various anarchist political practices. G. A. Cohen (1994) provides a helpful discussion of this relation between theory and practice when laying out the moral principles he takes to be constitutive of socialism. It is worth quoting him at length on this point:

> An essential ingredient in the Right's breakthrough was an intellectual self-confidence that was grounded in fundamental theoretical work by academics

such as Milton Friedman, Friedrich Hayek, and Robert Nozick. In one instructive sense, those authors did not propose new ideas. Instead, they explored, developed, and forthrightly reaffirmed the Right's traditional principles. Those principles are not so traditional to the British *political* Right as they are to the American, but they are traditional nevertheless, in the important sense that they possess a historical depth which is associated with the conceptual and moral depth at which they are located... The point of theory is not to generate a comprehensive social design which the politician then seeks to implement. Things don't work that way, because implementing a design requires whole cloth, and nothing in contemporary politics is made out of whole cloth. Politics is an endless struggle, and theory serves as a weapon in that struggle, because it provides a characterization of its direction, and of its controlling purpose .... The theories [of Friedman, Hayek, and Nozick] are ... uncompromisingly fundamental: they were not devised with one eye on electoral possibility. And, just for that reason, their serviceability in electoral and other political contest is very great. *Politicians and activists can press not-so-crazy right-wing proposals with conviction because they have the strength of conviction that depends upon depth of conviction, and depth comes from theory that is too fundamental to be practicable in a direct sense* .... The large fundamental values help to power (or block) the little changes by nourishing the justificatory rhetoric which is needed to push (or resist) change. (1994, 4–5, emphasis in the original)

In other words, while it is unlikely that anarchists will ever fully realize their envisioned utopia, there are things that can be done to nudge society in that direction. However, such political action often requires both self-sacrifice and the courage to challenge accepted norms and social expectations. Given the costs of acting on political conviction, one might reasonably want some degree of assurance that one's political views are well-grounded and not the product of mistaken reasoning, unquestioned dogma, and beguiling platitudes. This book aims to provide anarchists with such an assurance, thereby giving them the intellectual self-confidence to go forth and realize a more just world.

Additionally, the proposed position will help egalitarian anarchists to more clearly differentiate their position from rival socialist positions. Typically, the distinction between socialism and anarchism is stated in terms of tactics: While socialists and anarchists endorse a shared end – namely, a stateless, classless, socialist society – socialists want to use the state as a tool to realize that end while anarchists take the abolition of the state to be the first step to achieving that end. However, this characterization suggests that there is no serious philosophical disagreement between socialists and anarchists, as both groups endorse egalitarianism and reject private property. By contrast, the book suggests that even when anarchists and socialists arrive at the same moral conclusions, they reach them via very different starting premises (with anarchists beginning with premises typically endorsed by libertarians). Thus, it provides anarchists with an alternative way of articulating what is distinctive about their viewpoint.

While the book emphasizes this difference between anarchists and socialists, the latter should still find the proposed argument valuable, as it will serve as a useful tool to deploy against anti-egalitarian right-libertarians. The right-libertarian philosophical position has become one of the primary philosophical bases for criticizing egalitarian redistribution, with right-libertarians arguing that such redistribution is unjust because it violates persons' property rights. By contrast, the social anarchist position denies the existence of such property rights and insists that justice requires an egalitarian distribution of advantage. Importantly, as subsequent chapters will discuss, it argues for this conclusion by appealing strictly to premises that right-libertarians would accept. In this way, it seeks to defeat anti-egalitarian libertarianism on its own terms, thereby making the position of interest to egalitarians of all varieties. Even if such egalitarians ultimately reject the libertarian premises in question, they can treat the book as a *reductio ad absurdum* argument against right-libertarianism: It demonstrates that the right-libertarian position is composed of incompatible propositions, and, thus, right-libertarians must abandon least some of their standard commitments (with their anti-egalitarian commitments being the most promising candidates to reject).

The argument of the book will also be useful to left-libertarians, as it provides them with a solution to their coherence problem. As briefly noted earlier, left-libertarians argue that certain core libertarian commitments are compatible with the claim that justice requires an egalitarian distribution of resources. However, left-libertarianism has also come under fire from various critics who argue that the position lacks coherence. Most notably, Barbara Fried (2004, 89) argues that, although left-libertarians may have demonstrated the *compatibility* of libertarian and egalitarian principles, their embrace of the latter is not adequately *motivated by* the former (87fn50, 89).[14]

---

[14] Mathias Risse (2004) has raised a related worry about the coherence of left-libertarianism, while conceding that left-libertarians succeed in demonstrating the compatibility of various libertarian and egalitarian principles.

I.3 Something for Everyone

In a joint response to Fried's objection, Peter Vallentyne, Hillel Steiner, and Michael Otsuka largely concede the charge, admitting that "left-libertarians do not all hold that the egalitarian ownership of natural resources follows from their non-egalitarian libertarian commitments," and, instead, invoke "egalitarian ownership of natural resources as an independent principle" (2005, 208). However, they argue that this concession is of little consequence, for, if "coherence requires that the justification for each of one's principles appeal to the same set of considerations … then there is little reason to require coherence so understood" (2005, 209).

The problem with this reply is that it does not adequately appreciate the theoretical value of coherence. As discussed in the previous section, a philosophical position that lacks coherence is at risk of seeming unacceptably arbitrary. Additionally, it loses much of its dialectical force against those who hold rival views. For these reasons, one should, all else being equal, favor a theory that is coherent over one that is not. Thus, if this book succeeds in demonstrating not only the truth of the left-libertarian thesis – namely, that core libertarian principles are compatible with an egalitarian approach to distributive justice – but also that there is a coherent version of left-libertarianism (namely, social anarchism), left-libertarians would be able to sidestep Fried's criticism by adopting the social anarchist position.

Finally, although the book puts significant dialectical pressure on right-libertarians (as was just noted), they, too, might find its argument useful in at least one respect. Given that social anarchism entails a rejection of private property claims – and, thus, right-libertarian conclusions about distributive justice more generally – one might conclude that social anarchism has nothing helpful to offer right-libertarians. However, two things can be said in response to this conclusion. First, note that the anarchist position includes core libertarian moral principles such as the self-ownership thesis, with the book presenting novel arguments in defense of these principles. Thus, even if right-libertarians reject the book's egalitarian conclusions, they will still find these arguments useful. Second, if the libertarian principles in question are taken to be incompatible with egalitarianism, many philosophers and ideologues will be tempted to reject them simply in virtue of this incompatibility. By contrast, if it can be shown that these libertarian principles are not only compatible with but actually *entail* egalitarian conclusions, then this reflexive hostility might dissipate. In this way, the book could help right-libertarians get a second hearing for some of their favored principles.

Of course, these conciliatory remarks merely aim to show that social anarchism is useful, where usefulness does not imply plausibility. In other words, if anarchism *were* a correct normative theory, some practical advantages would follow from that result. However, it still needs to be shown that the theory is, in fact, correct. This will be the task of the next seven chapters: to demonstrate that social anarchism is a plausible and attractive normative position.

CHAPTER 1

Social Anarchism

> The anarchists are and will be thus always very few, but they are everywhere. They are what I will call the leaven which raises the bread. Already, you see them involved everywhere ... in the Free-thought Movement, in the Socialist Party ... the trade unions, the co-operatives, they are everywhere. ... There are even those who are unaware of it! Because once one explains to them what is anarchism, they say: "But if it is that, I am anarchistic! I am with you!"
>
> Sébastien Faure, "The Revolutionary Forces"

> Her development, her freedom, her independence, must come from and through herself. First, by asserting herself as a personality, and not as a sex commodity. Second, by refusing the right to anyone over her body.
>
> Emma Goldman, "Woman Suffrage"

This chapter will introduce the five theses that the social anarchist philosophical position comprises. No individual thesis is entirely original to the anarchist position; rather, they have been drawn from other philosophical camps, particularly the political philosophies advanced by libertarians and egalitarian socialists. However, the principles have been adjusted in various ways so as to render them more precise and plausible. The subsequent sections will present the five anarchist principles, explain how and why they differ from their more standard formulations, and defend their plausibility. Specifically, the chapter will begin with the principles typically endorsed by libertarians (Sections 1.1–1.3) before turning to the anti-propertarian and egalitarian theses that set social anarchism apart from standard libertarianism (Sections 1.5 and 1.6). It will also devote three sections (Sections 1.4, 1.7, and 1.8) to defending the anarchist interpretation of the self-ownership thesis presented in Section 1.3. The remaining anarchist theses will then be defended in subsequent chapters of the book.

1.1 The Consent Theory of Legitimacy

The first anarchist thesis is the *consent theory of legitimacy*, which holds that a state – or, more generally any agent – is legitimate with respect to its purported subjects if and only if they have consented to its legitimacy. This just-mentioned legitimacy relation can be understood as follows: Some person P is *legitimate* with respect to another person Q if and only if P has the Hohfeldian power to determine what obligations Q has via the issuing of edicts.[1] More specifically, P is legitimate with respect to Q if and only if Q is obligated to obey P's edicts, where "P's edicts" designates nonrigidly. Thus, if a state is legitimate with respect to Q and it enacts some law L at time t that mandates that Q ϕ, then Q is obligated to ϕ at t. By contrast, had the state instituted law M (rather than L) mandating that Q ψ, then Q would have been obligated to ψ at t rather than ϕ. Alternatively, one might say that P is legitimate with respect to Q if and only if when P issues an edict that Q must ϕ, Q is obligated to ϕ *because* P issued the edict. However, the counterfactual analysis of legitimacy is a bit clearer, so it will be favored for these purposes. The consent theory of legitimacy, then, maintains that P is legitimate with respect to Q if and only if Q has consented to being bound by P's edicts in this way (where Q consents to some state of affairs only if she intends to consent to it, is reasonably informed about what she is consenting to, can refuse consent without incurring undue costs, etc.).

There are a few things to note about this account of legitimacy. First, legitimate states possess a Hohfeldian power to impose obligations, where, going forward, the term "legitimacy" will be used to denote this power (as well as the abstract relation that obtains between a legitimate agent and her subject). Second, the notion does not discriminate between states and private individuals: Either kind of agent can possess the power in question and, thus, be legitimate vis-à-vis some person or people. One reason for not distinguishing between state legitimacy and private legitimacy is that it is surprisingly difficult to provide an analysis of statehood that can satisfactorily demarcate states from non-state actors. This point will be discussed in detail in Section 7.2. Additionally, the suggestion here is that it is the power that is of moral significance rather than the bearer of that power, where this implies that the possession of that power is subject to the same theoretical constraints irrespective of who possesses it. In other words, if there is something problematic about a state possessing legitimacy without

---

[1] For an explication of the Hohfeldian incidents, see Section 2.2.

consent – as the consent theorist insists that there is – there will equally be something problematic about a private individual possessing this power without consent, as it is the mere possession of the power that must be justified by consent, not the fact that a *state* possesses this power.

Third, note that agents cannot be legitimate *tout court*; rather, they can only be legitimate *with respect to* some particular person. Thus, when one asserts that a state is legitimate with respect to a group of people, what is being asserted, strictly speaking, is that the state is legitimate with respect to each individual member of the group (unless the group qualifies as a group agent, in which case the state might be legitimate with respect to that agent). One might supplement this notion of legitimacy with a derivative scalar concept designed to capture the broader relation between the state and the aggregation of its claimed subjects. For example, to elaborate on a proposal from John Simmons (2001, 130), one might say that a state is more legitimate *on balance* than another if and only if it is legitimate with respect to a larger proportion of its claimed subjects. However, while this notion might be useful in certain evaluative contexts, it is irrelevant to the consent theory of legitimacy, as consent theory posits a necessary and sufficient condition of the more primitive legitimacy relation obtaining between two agents.

Finally, this analysis of legitimacy differs in various ways from how others have defined the term. On one popular account, a legitimate state is one that has a Hohfeldian permission to make and coercively enforce rules (Wellman 1996, 211–12; Huemer 2013, 5). By contrast, the concept is here defined as the *power* to impose obligations by making rules. It, is thus, closer to what Huemer labels "political authority," where a state possessing this property has both a permission to coerce (what he calls "legitimacy") and a right that its subjects obey its rules (2013, 5). However, note that, if one plausibly assumes that the obligations in question are coercively enforceable, a state's power to impose obligations via edicts will entail that it has a permission to coercively enforce those edicts. Additionally, if one thinks that it is permissible to coerce someone to do something only if she is obliged to do it, then a state will have the power to impose obligations by issuing edicts if and only if it has a permission to coercively enforce those edicts – that is, what Wellman and Huemer call "legitimacy" turns out to be materially equivalent to the notion of legitimacy posited here.

It is also worth contrasting the proposed notion of legitimacy with Simmons' (2001) influential definition of the term. According to Simmons, legitimacy is a "complex moral right ... to be the exclusive imposer of binding duties on its subjects, to have its subjects comply with these duties, and to use coercion to enforce the duties" (2001, 130). This definition is a bit puzzling, as it seems like a category mistake to say that someone can have the right to *be* something rather than *do* something. One might interpret Simmons as suggesting that a legitimate authority has a claim against others imposing binding duties on its subjects – that is, against them exercising their power to oblige others. However, it seems more parsimonious to take Simmons to be simply asserting that if an authority has the power to oblige its subjects, then no other authority has this same power.[2] By contrast, the proposed account of legitimacy does not demand exclusivity in this way, with it being possible for multiple authorities to be legitimate with respect to the same person.[3]

---

[2] It is also slightly puzzling that Simmons takes legitimacy to be a right that "subjects comply with these duties," as this claim seems trivial. If P has a right that Q ϕ, then Q has a correlative duty to ϕ. Thus, to say that P has a right that Q discharge her duty to ϕ is just to say that Q has a duty to discharge her duty to ϕ. And, given that Q discharges her duty to ϕ by ϕ-ing, the proposition that P has a right that Q discharge her duty to ϕ is equivalent to the proposition that Q has a duty to ϕ. Thus, the quoted portion of Simmons' definition of legitimacy does not seem to add any content to the broader definition and should seemingly be discounted for this reason.

[3] Note that the exclusivity component of Simmons' definition is actually incompatible with the consent theory of legitimacy. So long as it is possible that a person might consent to be governed by multiple authorities, then consent theory would entail that all of these authorities would be simultaneously legitimate with respect to this person. Thus, consent theorists have reason to favor the proposed definition of legitimacy that foregoes the exclusivity component. In reply to this point, Simmons might modify the consent theory of legitimacy such that P is legitimate with respect to Q if and only if Q consents to being governed by P *and* Q has not previously consented to being governed by a different authority R. Further, to avoid charges of making *ad hoc* revisions, he could argue that this change must be made to avoid the following *reductio* argument:

1. If Q consents to being governed by P (or R), then P (or R) is legitimate with respect to Q.
2. If P (or R) is legitimate with respect to Q, then if P (or R) orders Q to ϕ (or not ϕ) then Q has a duty to ϕ (or not ϕ).
3. Q consents to being governed by P and subsequently consents to being governed by R.
4. P orders Q to ϕ and R subsequently orders P to not ϕ.
5. Duties cannot conflict: it cannot be the case that P has a duty to ϕ and a duty to not ϕ.

Together, these premises generate a contradiction; thus one of them must be rejected. Simmons might contend that the most plausible candidate for rejection is Premise 1 – that is, the consent theory of legitimacy must be revised in the way suggested previously.

There are two problems with this argument. First, many of the other premises might be equally rejected. For example, one might deny Premise 2 (i.e., revise the proposed definition of legitimacy) by holding that a legitimate authority cannot oblige Q to not ϕ if Q already has a duty to ϕ. Or perhaps the later order to not ϕ negates the previous duty to ϕ. Alternatively, one might reject Premise 5 for reasons such as those discussed by Judith Jarvis Thomson (1990, 87–93). Thus, the proposed revision of consent theory still seems *ad hoc*. Second, note that one could construct a parallel *reductio* argument where there is only a single legitimate authority P who orders Q to ϕ and then subsequently orders her to not ϕ. The fact that the resulting contradiction could not be avoided by rejecting Premise 1 of the original *reductio* suggests that it would be better to reject either Premise 2 or Premise 5 as suggested earlier, as such a rejection would avoid the contradiction generated by the parallel *reductio*. That said, the argument of this book does not depend on accepting the proposed account of legitimacy over Simmons'. For these purposes, all that matters is that consent is a necessary condition of some person having the power to oblige another via the issuing of edicts.

In short, the proposed analysis of legitimacy does not refer to any permission to coercively enforce duties and it also does not entail that only one agent can be legitimate with respect to any particular person (contra Wellman, Huemer, and Simmons). Rather, it limits itself to the assertion that an authority is legitimate if and only if that authority possesses the power to oblige via the issuing of edicts. Thus, the consent theory of legitimacy should be understood as asserting that consent is a necessary and sufficient condition of this moral power obtaining, with the book's subsequent arguments for consent theory (presented in Sections 2.4 and 4.2) supporting this posited interpretation.

The final thing to note about the consent theory of legitimacy is that (practically) no people have actually consented to being governed, either by states or by others.[4] In other words, the necessary condition of legitimacy obtaining is (almost) never satisfied and, thus, there are no existing legitimate states or other authorities – at least, vis-à-vis the vast majority of the human population. This is not to say that there are *necessarily* no legitimate states. In fact, the consent theory of legitimacy entails that a state *would* be legitimate vis-à-vis all of its claimed subjects if, as a contingent matter of fact, they all happened to give it their consent to be governed. However, in the actual world, existing states are not legitimate with respect to practically any of their citizens; that is, they lack the power to impose obligations on their citizens by passing laws or issuing other edicts. This conclusion – a position known as *philosophical anarchism* – is a fitting implication of the anarchist position's affirmation of the consent theory of legitimacy.

1.2 The Lockean Proviso

The second component of the social anarchist position is an endorsement of a particular interpretation of what has become known as the *Lockean proviso*. As a bit of context, libertarian property rights theorists typically maintain that the world starts out unowned such that all persons have a permission to use all things. Persons then carry out acts of initial appropriation whereby they convert those resources into private property – that is, they acquire a robust set of rights and powers vis-à-vis the appropriated objects. These rights include Hohfeldian permissions to use the owned thing; claims against all others using the thing; powers to waive these

---

[4] The parenthetical qualifier is included because there may be some people who have given their free and informed consent to be governed (e.g., patriotic people who signed a loyalty oath of some kind).

claims; immunities against the loss of these claims, permissions, and powers; and powers to transfer all of these listed rights to others.[5] Libertarians also uniformly hold that people can *unilaterally* carry out these acts of appropriation – that is, they do not need others' consent in order to successfully appropriate some unowned resource. That said, many libertarian theories also include a proviso limiting the extent to which any given person can appropriate.[6] Most famously, *right-libertarians* adopt a particular interpretation of Locke's contention that a person can appropriate some resource only if "there is enough and as good left in common for others" (2005, §33). Typically, they interpret Locke's proviso as a non-worsening condition: To be left with "enough and as good" is to be left no worse off than if the act of appropriation had not occurred – or, more permissively, to be no worse off than if *no* appropriation *by anyone* ever occurred (as was proposed by Nozick 1974, 181).[7] Additionally, the proviso is taken to be not only a necessary condition of appropriation occurring via some suitable act but also a sufficient condition of that act successfully appropriating the thing in question.[8] Together, these interpretations yield (a preliminary statement of) the Lockean proviso (or "the proviso" for short): A person is able to appropriate some unowned resource via some suitable action if and only if her doing so does not leave anyone worse off.[9]

Given that the proviso is a signature commitment of right-libertarianism, it may seem odd that it would be included within the social anarchist position, as right-libertarians famously reject the kind of distributive egalitarianism that will be endorsed subsequently. However, the anarchist position will incorporate this proviso for three reasons. First, the proviso's proposed non-worsening condition is independently plausible. Specifically,

---

[5] For a stronger statement of full ownership, see Wendt (2015, 318).

[6] Not all libertarians posit such a proviso. Some prominent examples of such *no proviso* or *radical right-libertarians* include Murray Rothbard (1998), Jan Narveson (1998), and Edward Feser (2005). Eric Mack (1995) also denies that appropriation is constrained by a proviso, but suggests that the interests of latecomers might constrain the use of acquired property.

[7] As noted in the Introduction, there is a rival *left-libertarian* school of thought that seeks to show that self-ownership and private property rights are compatible with egalitarian views about distributive justice. Specifically, it rejects the Lockean proviso in favor of an *egalitarian proviso* that holds that an act of appropriation succeeds if and only if it leaves others with enough unappropriated resources such that they could each appropriate a share of equal value.

[8] It is often maintained that Locke took his proviso to be a necessary condition of appropriation rather than a sufficient one. However, this interpretation has been disputed by Thomson (1976) and Jeremy Waldron (1979), among others.

[9] Which acts qualify as "suitable" – that is, which acts are acts of appropriation – will be discussed in Section 1.3.

it seems plausible that, by improving someone's situation via some action – or, at least, not worsening it – one nullifies that person's grounds for complaint about that action, where such grounds for complaint are both necessary and sufficient for precluding successful appropriation. After all, if no one is affected (on net) by the successful appropriation of some resource, then how could anyone object to that appropriation occurring? Further, if no one can reasonably object, then why should a theory of property disallow such appropriation?

Second, Chapter 2 will argue that the Lockean proviso follows from a plausible meta-principle (the moral tyranny constraint) that constrains which moral theories qualify as acceptable. The aim of this book is to derive the entire anarchist position from this meta-principle; thus, the fact that the principle entails the Lockean proviso is a decisive reason for including the proviso in the anarchist position. Finally, including the proviso in the anarchist position gives the anarchist dialectical leverage against right-libertarians who similarly endorse the proviso. As noted in the Introduction, Chapters 3 and 5 will argue that a commitment to the proviso surprisingly entails that one must deny the existence of external private property and, instead, endorse the egalitarian position presented in Section 1.5. Thus, the inclusion of the proviso in the anarchist position helps to advance an argumentative strategy that aims to challenge right-libertarianism on its own terms.

Developing this argument will be the task of the remaining chapters of this book. For now, though, the aim is strictly to give the proviso determinate content by specifying its multiple ambiguous terms.[10] Some of these terms will be left underspecified such that others can fill in the details with their own preferred theories. For example, one must ultimately specify the respect in which others must not be left worse off by appropriation. The dominant position among the proviso's proponents is that welfare is the relevant metric to employ when making this assessment.[11] However, for the purposes of this book, one can remain neutral on this point and allow that there might be other ways in which a person can be left worse off beyond having her welfare diminished (for this reason, this book uses the placeholder "diminished advantage" to denote a person

---

[10] Daniel Attas (2003) similarly notes that many of the proviso's terms are ambiguous, and he argues at length that there is no acceptable specification of the proviso that also is satisfied vis-à-vis external resources.

[11] For some objections to the welfare specification, see Attas (2003, 358–60) and Bas van der Vossen (2021, 187–9).

being left worse off in the relevant respect).[12] By contrast, the anarchist position *does* endorse a particular specification of the comparison point relative to which persons cannot be left worse off. Specifically, it holds that the appropriation of some resource succeeds if and only if such appropriation would not leave anyone worse off *relative to the closest possible world where the agent never existed to appropriate the resource in the first place*. For example, if person Q enjoys sitting on a stretch of beach every weekend but P appropriates that beach and thereby precludes Q from using it, that appropriation would violate the proviso, as it results in Q ending up worse off than she would have been in the world without P that is most similar to the actual world.

A full defense of this specification will be presented in Sections 3.3 and 3.4. For now, this section will turn to specifying exactly what it is that cannot leave others worse off. The obvious suggestion is that it is the *appropriation* of the resource that cannot leave others worse off, where appropriation is the change in normative fact that occurs when non-appropriators go from having a permission to use the resource to an obligation to refrain from using that resource. However, it will now be argued that this *natural interpretation* of the Lockean proviso is implausible because it is trivially satisfied by all possible appropriations. Note that if initial appropriation makes strictly *normative* changes to the world, altering *moral facts* about what rights people have over objects, then it is unclear how an act of appropriation could have any *causal effect* on people's advantage. Given the physical nature of causation, it is odd to suggest that changes in nonphysical moral fact could cause physical events of the kind presupposed by the natural interpretation of the proviso. Or, to put this point another way, the causal relation has events as its *relata*, where events are best understood as either spatiotemporal things or, more controversially, things that are either spatiotemporal *or* mental.[13] Given that a change in moral fact is neither a spatiotemporal event nor a mental event, it follows that initial appropriation cannot cause people to be worse off.

---

[12] That said, the subsequent argument of this section presupposes a specification of this currency of comparison such that the quantity of this currency possessed by persons is not actually a function of appropriation occurring. The meaning of this assertion will be clarified by the discussion presented just below. However, it is worth noting here that the subsequent argument will not be applicable if, for example, one takes a person to be left worse off if and only if she possesses fewer permissions relative to the baseline for comparison.

[13] Even the claim that events are *things* is not without controversy. For a helpful overview of the debate, see Roberto Casati and Achille Varzi (2020).

1.2 The Lockean Proviso

This, in turn, implies that the proviso is trivially satisfied by any act of initial appropriation.

It might be objected that this account of causation is too stringent. Instead, one might propose the following *counterfactual account* of causation: A fact of any kind C causes some other fact E to obtain if and only if (i) C and E are sufficiently distinct (e.g., they are nonidentical and, insofar as facts have parts, neither is a part of the other) and (ii) if C had not obtained then E would not have obtained.[14] This account would make it metaphysically possible that initial appropriation causally affects others' levels of advantage, as the difference in moral fact between the appropriation world and non-appropriation world might be accompanied by a counterfactual difference in advantage. However, the proponent of this suggestion would still need to provide some argument as to why this is more than a mere possibility. Most plausibly, she might posit that human minds are sensitive to moral facts such that people form beliefs in response to those facts and then act on those beliefs.[15] This would allow her to maintain that if the moral facts had been different due to an act of appropriation not occurring, then people would have formed different beliefs, behaved differently, and thereby had a different effect on others' advantage. Thus, a counterfactual difference in advantage would obtain, thereby giving initial appropriation causal purchase in the physical world.

The problem with this argument is that, even if one accepts this unconventional account of causation, the responsiveness of minds to moral facts is limited at best. If minds were highly sensitive to moral facts, one would expect to see wide and enduring consensus about the truth of most moral propositions. However, there is persistent and widespread moral disagreement across time and region. Thus, at most, there is a highly inelastic relationship between moral beliefs and facts such that *some* people *eventually* come to have beliefs that correspond to the facts. Given the loose connection between moral fact and human action, there is no reason to think that any given act of initial appropriation will entail a counterfactual difference in advantage-affecting behavior.

---

[14] Condition (i) is posited so that the account will not deliver unacceptable results like the affirmation that some event caused itself. For more on the need for cause and effect to be distinct, see David Lewis (1986). To be very precise, one would also want to build in Lewis' (1973) prohibition against considering *backtracking* counterfactuals that fail to hold the past fixed when searching for the closest possible world where C does not obtain. The claim that facts can be causes is defended by D. H. Mellor (1995; 2004), though this does not imply that *moral* facts can be causes.

[15] For a defense of this proposition, see Michael Smith (1994) and Huemer (2016). For recent criticisms of this position, see Patrick Hassan (2019) and Jeroen Hopster (2020).

Appropriation's lack of causal power entails that one must reject any specification of the proviso that holds that it is the appropriation itself that must not leave others worse off. Such a specification would render the Lockean proviso trivially satisfied: Even if one person exhaustively appropriated all existing resources, she would not diminish others' advantage, as the moral change would not have any causal effects whatsoever. Given that such a permissive proviso is both implausible and fails to express the idea that motivates it – namely, that, absent any proviso, certain appropriations *would* leave others worse off in a way that is theoretically problematic – some other specification is needed.

Fortunately, there is an alternative specification of the Lockean proviso that seemingly captures the motivation for building the proviso into a theory of property. This version of the proviso asserts that a person can appropriate some thing via some suitable action if and only if *full compliance with* her established claim rights would not leave others worse off than they would have been had she not existed to establish these claims (assuming that others similarly comply with the other demands of morality). Unlike the natural interpretation of the proviso, this interpretation is not trivially satisfied, as there will be cases where compliance with property claims would leave others worse off in this way. Additionally, it seems to capture the thought that motivates the proviso, namely, that there is something morally problematic about imposing costs on fully compliant people – and, thus, a moral theory should not license the imposition of such costs.[16] The natural interpretation of the proviso errs by articulating

---

[16] An anonymous reviewer suggests an alternative specification of the proviso that asserts that appropriation must not leave anyone worse off conditional on *expected* compliance with the established rights. However, there are three reasons for preferring the full-compliance specification proposed in the main text. First, the expected-compliance proviso would be vulnerable to the same objection raised against the standard interpretation of the proviso: It is trivially satisfied due to appropriation lacking causal power. If appropriation changes moral facts and such changes lack causal power, then appropriation will not change how people behave relative to the world where the appropriation does not occur. Thus, everyone's expected behavior in both cases will be identical, which, in turn, implies that the expected compliance proviso is always satisfied. Second, an expected-compliance proviso would have unattractive implications. For example, consider the case where the first-to-arrive person attempts to appropriate the entire planet. If later arrivals were to fully comply with her property rights, they would be left much worse off; however, suppose that, as a matter of contingent fact, these latecomers have a complete disregard for others' property rights. In this case, the expected compliance specification would entail that the act of appropriation *succeeds*, as no one would be left worse off given expected compliance. More generally, the proposed expected-compliance specification entails that some acts of appropriation succeed if and only if no one actually complies with the established rights – a result that seemingly counts against accepting such a specification of the proviso. Finally, Chapter 2 will argue that the full-compliance specification of the proviso follows from the chapter's proposed moral tyranny constraint. Given the chapter's contention that this constraint is both independently plausible and

1.2 The Lockean Proviso

this thought in terms of the (nonexistent) causal effect of the obligations imposed by appropriation. However, this mistake can be corrected by simply stating the proviso in terms of the costs imposed by full compliance with those obligations.[17]

In addition to these three bits of specification, one further amendment to the standard Lockean proviso is needed to yield the complete anarchist interpretation of the proviso. So far it has been proposed that a suitable act of appropriation succeeds if and only if its established claims do not leave anyone worse off under conditions of full compliance (relative to the world where the appropriator did not exist). However, note that initial appropriation does not just establish claims but also the power to waive the established claims. This fact is significant because those committed to the proviso must seemingly also affirm that the exercise of this power must not leave others worse off under conditions of full compliance. Otherwise, the endorsement of the proviso seems arbitrary: Why would one power to change others' permissions vis-à-vis the use of natural resources (via appropriation) be subject to a non-worsening constraint but not another such power (namely, the power to waive)? In other words, if one holds that a person can appropriate some resource only if no one is left worse off as a result under conditions of full compliance, one should also hold that a person can waive her property rights only if that act similarly leaves no one worse off under conditions of full compliance.[18]

Further, note that initial appropriation is generally taken to establish *both* rights against others using the owned thing *and* the power to waive these rights – that is, appropriation is a sufficient condition of the power to waive. However, if this is correct, then any necessary condition of the power to waive must also be a necessary condition of successful appropriation (for, if p entails q and q entails r, then p entails r). Given that the

---

entails other attractive moral positions, a full-compliance specification of the proviso that follows from this constraint would be more likely to survive a process of reflective equilibrium than the expected-compliance specification.

[17] One could also posit an intermediate version of the proviso where the posited restriction is that each person's compliance with a property owner's acquired rights – but not necessarily full compliance by *all* persons – must not leave her (or anyone) worse off relative to the baseline for comparison. This version of the proviso would still solve the causal problem discussed previously but would not follow from the moral tyranny constraint. Additionally, it is unclear why a moral theorist should be concerned about the effects of one person's compliance but not others'. Rather, insofar as one is concerned with the effects of compliance, it is the full-compliance world that seems relevant when assessing whether or not an act of appropriation succeeds.

[18] To simplify matters a bit, this discussion will ignore the possibility of transfers leaving others worse off under conditions of full compliance. The effects of post-transfer compliance are bracketed in this way so as to avoid unnecessary complexity that does not affect the argument of the book.

owner of some resource can possess the power to waive her rights over that resource only if no act of waiving would leave anyone worse off under conditions of full compliance, it follows that she can appropriate the thing only if no subsequent waiving of her rights would leave anyone worse off under conditions of full compliance. Thus, one must build this restriction into the Lockean proviso by restating it as follows:

> **The Lockean Proviso** – A person appropriates some unowned resource via some suitable action if and only if (a) her established claims would not leave anyone worse off under conditions of full compliance and (b) no subsequent waiving of those claims would leave others worse off under conditions of full compliance (where, in both cases, the baseline for comparison is the closest possible world where the appropriator did not exist).

This statement of the proviso is still in need of slight revision for reasons that will be discussed in Section 3.4. Thus, technically speaking, this is not the official anarchist interpretation of the Lockean proviso. However, it has the virtue of being comparatively straightforward and easy to grasp while still being quite proximate to the final version of the proviso. For this reason, it will be left to stand here as the primary statement of the proviso that is affirmed by the social anarchist position.

1.3 The Self-Ownership Thesis

The third component of the social anarchist position is a qualified endorsement of the self-ownership thesis. This signature libertarian thesis asserts that each person has the same set of rights over her own body that she would have over a fully owned thing, including a permission to use her body, a claim against others using her body, a power to waive this claim, an immunity against the loss of any of these listed rights, and a power to transfer them to others.[19] These rights are then taken to entail a number of attractive moral conclusions. For example, a claim against use implies that a person is wronged if someone harvests her organs and redistributes them to other people. It also implies that persons have correlative duties to

---

[19] One might think that the self is not identical to the body and, thus, that the self-ownership thesis should assert a set of rights over the former entity rather than the latter. For example, one might take the self to be nonidentical with the body because it is either merely a part of the body (e.g., the brain) or includes things outside of the body as well (e.g., the external objects that compose what has been called the "extended mind"). For these purposes, it will simply be assumed that the self is identical to the body in virtue of the close connection between one's agency and one's body. However, one might reject this assumption and thereby create a number of complications for the argument presented in Chapter 3.

refrain from attacking or sexually assaulting self-owners. Additionally, this right to exclude others from using one's body is typically taken to imply the permissibility of abortion, as fetuses who use a pregnant person's body without consent infringe on this right (with abortion then becoming a form of permissible self-defense).[20] Proponents of the self-ownership thesis also maintain that the permissions to use one's body entail the negation of (nonconsensual) moral slavery – that is, when one person possesses the moral rights that correspond to the legal rights of slave owners (including a permission to act on the slave's body in whatever way the owner likes as well as a power to oblige the slave to act in whatever way the owner chooses) – as well as various Millian liberties such as the permission to use drugs or the permission to have consensual but socially disapproved of sex.[21]

The anarchist endorsement of the self-ownership thesis is qualified in two important ways. First, contra the standard self-ownership thesis, it does not hold that all persons possess self-ownership rights (prior to waiving or forfeiting those rights). Rather, it allows that some people might lack these rights without having ever possessed them in the first place. This is because the proposed anarchist position posits that self-ownership is not *native* in the sense that persons start out with self-ownership rights as soon as they satisfy the sufficient conditions for moral personhood. Rather, it holds that persons must *acquire* ownership of their bodies – and must do so in just the same way that they would acquire property rights over any unowned resource, namely, via acts of initial appropriation. Call these acts of *self-appropriation*.

There are two reasons for favoring the view that self-ownership is acquired rather than native. First, the latter view seems unacceptably arbitrary. As the initial definition of self-ownership (at the start of this section) suggests, proponents of the self-ownership thesis take the ownership of one's body to be of a kind with the ownership of any other object or resource. Given this similarity, it is odd to insist (as most self-ownership proponents do) that the ownership of all external things is established via acts of initial appropriation while the ownership of the body is simply a correlate of personhood. This posited difference seemingly demands explanation; however, it is not clear how property theorists can provide

---

[20] While practically all self-identified anarchists (and most liberals) will consider this an attractive implication of the right to exclude, not all proponents of the self-ownership thesis would consider it as such, for example, Feser (2004). There are also some complications when it comes to abortion, famously discussed by Thomson (1971).

[21] On this latter point, see Steiner (2000, 76–7) and Otsuka (2003, 2).

such an explanation while continuing to insist that persons own themselves in the same way that they would own anything else. For this reason, it seems better to treat like things alike by maintaining that self-ownership is acquired via self-appropriation.

The second reason for favoring this approach is that it might help to resolve a worry about the kind of *moral equality* presupposed by the proponents of native self-ownership. Briefly, those who affirm the self-ownership thesis posit that each self-owner starts out with the same set of rights as all other self-owners. At the same time, these rights are denied to all nonpersons including very young children, animals, plants, rocks, photons, etc. Further, the apparent reason that these nonpersons are denied self-ownership rights is that they lack certain cognitive capacities that moral persons possess.[22] However, note that cognitive capacity is scalar, and different people will possess any given capacity to different degrees. By contrast, the self-ownership thesis assigns rights in a binary fashion: An individual either possesses the specified set of rights or she does not. As a result, the proponent of moral equality faces two related challenges. First, she must explain why self-ownership rights are not also assigned in a scalar fashion such that persons who have greater cognitive capacities possess proportionately more rights (or weightier rights). Second, she must (a) posit some specific capacity threshold that divides self-owners from nonpersons where (b) this division is nonarbitrary such that she will be able to justify why two individuals who differ only minutely in cognitive capacity – but who happen to fall on either side of the threshold – have very different rights while two individuals who differ significantly in cognitive capacity but are both above (or below) the threshold possess the same set of rights.

While there have been various attempts to address these challenges, assessing their merits would take things too far afield. Rather, the aim here is merely to show that the proponent of self-appropriation can offer a promising alternative reply to the two challenges and thereby provide a novel reason for thinking that self-owners all have the same set of rights (prior to waiving, transfer, and forfeiture). Specifically, note that the proposed theory of self-appropriation does not appeal to cognitive capacities to

---

[22] It may be that some other property difference that grounds the difference in rights. However, proponents of moral equality are typically skeptical that some non-capacity-based property difference can explain why persons possess rights that non-persons lack. For this reason, it is assumed that self-ownership proponents will appeal to capacity differences to explain why only some entities have self-ownership rights (with differences in *cognitive* capacity being the only plausible candidate explanation).

1.3 The Self-Ownership Thesis

explain why moral persons possess self-ownership rights while nonpersons do not. Instead, it holds that individuals possess these rights in virtue of having exercised their respective powers to appropriate resources. Thus, it sidesteps the first challenge to moral equality because the binary property of possessing self-ownership rights is now a function of another binary property, namely, the property of having performed a suitable act of self-appropriation. Similarly, it resolves the second challenge to moral equality because one can explain why two people might have very similar capacities but only one possesses self-ownership rights: The self-owner has carried out an act of self-appropriation while the other person has not.

Granted, one must still answer the question of why some people have the power to appropriate while others (very young children, cats, etc.) do not. And, given that the answer to this question must seemingly appeal to differences in cognitive capacity, one might reasonably worry that the aforementioned proposal simply passes the buck, as one must still ground a binary normative property (the possession of the power to appropriate) in a scalar property (the degree of cognitive capacity possessed). However, the suggestion here is that it is easier to meet the two previously presented challenges if the normative property in question is possessing the power to appropriate as opposed to possessing self-ownership rights. Recall that the first challenge for proponents of native self-ownership is to explain why ownership should not also be treated as scalar, with persons receiving rights in proportion to their cognitive capacities. While perhaps such an explanation can be provided, the proponent of self-appropriation has an easier response to this challenge: Unlike the possession of ownership rights, the possession of the power to appropriate simply cannot be treated in scalar fashion, as it is strictly a binary property. The reason that ownership can be treated as scalar is because it is really a bundle of distinct rights that can be disaggregated and then assigned in proportion to persons' respective cognitive capacities. By contrast, the power to appropriate is not an aggregate of more basic Hohfeldian incidents that can be unbundled and assigned in a scalar fashion. Thus, the proponent of self-appropriation does not face any analogous challenge of explaining why the possession of the power to appropriate is not proportionate to cognitive capacity.[23]

---

[23] One might reanimate the puzzle by positing that a person has a stronger (weaker) power to appropriate if and only if her appropriation establishes a greater (lesser) number of rights. One would then ask why people with greater cognitive capacities do not also have a proportionately stronger power to appropriate. In answer to this revised challenge, the proponent of self-appropriation can note that there are independent constraints on which ownership rights self-appropriation generates. For example, Chapter 3 will argue that self-appropriation should be

What about the challenge of positing a nonarbitrary capacity threshold that divides those who are able to self-appropriate from those who lack this power? Here, again, the proponent of self-appropriation seems better positioned to resolve this challenge than those who contend that self-ownership is native. Specifically, she can propose a nonarbitrary threshold by appealing to her account of which acts qualify as acts of initial appropriation: A person is able to (self-)appropriate if and only if she has the requisite cognitive capacities to carry out an act of initial appropriation. For example, Carol Rose proposes that persons appropriate unowned resources by asserting that they own the resources in question (1985, 81). Thus, someone would be able to self-appropriate if and only if she both possesses the capacity to make assertions and grasps the relevant concepts of ownership such that she can meaningfully assert that she owns her own body. Such a proposal would simultaneously (a) provide a nonarbitrary threshold demarcating potential appropriators from those who are unable to appropriate, (b) plausibly entail that young children and animals are not able to appropriate, and (c) plausibly entail that practically all human adults are able to self-appropriate. Additionally, given that practically every person has, at some point, asserted that her body belongs to her, the account would entail that all persons have carried out acts of self-appropriation.[24] Thus, assuming that these acts satisfy the Lockean proviso – which, as Chapter 3 will argue, they *necessarily* do – it follows

---

understood as generating all and only those claims whose establishment satisfies the Lockean proviso. Additionally, one might think that the rights established by an act of appropriation correspond to the nature of the act. The subsequent paragraph will suggest that one carries out an act of appropriation when one asserts that one has ownership of the appropriated object. Given this premise, one might further maintain that the appropriator acquires the set of ownership rights that she claims to possess (within the limits set out by the Lockean proviso). If this is correct, then differences in cognitive capacity between two persons will not entail that their respective acts of appropriation generate different sets of rights. Rather, the set of rights established by appropriation is determined by facts about the nature of – and constraints on – acts of initial appropriation.

[24] There is some ambiguity here regarding exactly what one must do to appropriate some resource (in this case, the body). Strictly speaking, the proposed anarchist position is neutral on this point, and it should be taken to incorporate whatever the best account of appropriation happens to be. That said, Rose's account is presented because it both seems plausible and illustrates how near-universal self-ownership might be achieved. However, there are questions about the details of her proposal, namely, what one must assert to carry out an act of appropriation. The suggestion here is that appropriators need to merely assert that they have a right to use and exclude others from the owned thing (e.g., by posting a "no trespassing" sign or saying, "don't touch me!" in a way that implies that it would be wrong for the audience to ignore this command). This proposal seems to capture what Rose has in mind (1985, 76). More importantly, it seems to capture an important milestone in the development of children, when they go from merely expressing aversion to being touched to asserting with moral force that they should not be touched. The proposed account of self-appropriation codifies the moral significance of this developmental moment, as it declares that children become self-owners at this point.

1.3 The Self-Ownership Thesis

that practically all persons own themselves (at least, prior to waiving or transfer), even though it is at least possible that some persons never self-appropriate. In this way, the self-appropriation proponent is able to explain why persons own themselves, explain the moral equality of adult persons, explain why children and animals are excluded from the set of morally equal persons, and explain why the threshold that divides those who can self-appropriate from those who cannot is principled rather than arbitrary.[25]

In addition to making self-ownership an acquired status rather than a native one, the anarchist position further qualifies the self-ownership thesis by endorsing a more permissive interpretation of the concept of self-ownership. As noted previously, one of the core self-ownership rights is a claim against others using one's body. According to the *classical interpretation* of the concept of self-ownership, this claim against use is to be understood as a claim against *trespass* – that is, a claim against any person taking an action that makes unwanted contact with the self-owner's body.[26] By contrast, the anarchist interpretation of self-ownership limits this right to exclude by permitting bodily contact that uniquely generates supplemental benefit:

---

[25] Given that the proposal here is that self-ownership is acquired via initial appropriation like any other resource, one might worry that this allows for parents to appropriate the bodies of their children before the latter develop the agential capacities needed to appropriate themselves. This concern will be addressed in Section 3.5.

[26] This classical self-ownership thesis is defended by a number of prominent libertarians from across the political spectrum. For example, Nozick takes there to be a "line" that "circumscribes an area in moral space around an individual" with infringements occurring when others carry out "actions that transgress the boundary or encroach upon the circumscribed area" (1974, 57). This description of self-ownership suggests that mere trespass, that is, bodily contact, qualifies as an infringement. Similarly, Rothbard takes self-ownership to entail a right against invasion, where this includes trespass (1998, 45). That said, he elsewhere limits the notion of trespass such that it includes only *sensible* bodily contact (where this includes contact made by smoke and odors) (1982). Narveson also seems to endorse the classical self-ownership thesis when he proposes that an agent must seek the permission of self-owners if she is to permissibly "*act upon* or with" their bodies (1988, 67, emphasis added). Vallentyne, Steiner, and Otsuka are particularly explicit on this point, as they define rights against use as including rights against "all the ways that persons can physically impact upon an object, including effects that are unforeseen" (2005, 203). And Jessica Flanigan seems to take self-ownership to include a right against all bodily contact, though she is not fully explicit on this point (2019a, 30). Finally, non-libertarian proponents of the self-ownership thesis (or at least its posited claims against use) often endorse the classical understanding of self-ownership. For example, Thomson argues that each person has a claim against others making contact with her body (1990, 205–7). Similarly, Robert S. Taylor contends that self-ownership includes "the right to forbid trespass on one's own person" (2004, 68). Notably, none of these proponents of the self-ownership thesis limits the right against trespass to a right against *harmful* bodily contact, with some explicitly affirming that trespass is wrongful even when it does not harm (e.g., Thomson 1990, 209). This is to be expected given that libertarians and other self-ownership proponents typically want to give people moral *control* over what happens to their bodies rather than merely make intruders *liable for harm* done to those bodies.

ASO – Each self-owner has a right against any other person taking any action that (a) results in physical contact being made with her body and (b) does not uniquely provide anyone with supplemental benefit on net.

Predicate (b) contains a number of technical terms that are in need of explication. However, before explaining these terms and, by extension, which actions ASO forbids and which it permits, it will be helpful to, first, provide some elaboration of Predicate (a). Specifically, this predicate establishes the first necessary condition of an action infringing upon a person's self-ownership rights: The action must cause physical contact with the self-owner's body. There are a few things to note about this necessary condition. First, the action need not make bodily contact directly as one does with a punch or a kick. Rather, it might simply initiate a causal chain that ultimately results in physical contact being made with the owned body. Second, if that causal chain includes another person acting in a way that causes the contact – where an alternative action by that person would not have caused any physical contact with the self-owner's body – then the condition should be understood as not having been met. In such a case, it is the other person who infringes upon the self-owner's rights, not the original agent. Finally, the infringing agent need not intend that her action results in physical contact; rather, Condition (a) is satisfied by the mere fact that the action does result in such contact.

Predicate (b) of ASO asserts a second necessary condition of self-ownership infringement (where the joint satisfaction of both Condition (a) and Condition (b) is a sufficient condition of such infringement occurring). Specifically, it holds that an action that satisfies Condition (a) infringes upon a self-owner's rights if and only if that action does not *uniquely* provide anyone with net *supplemental benefit* – where both of the italicized terms need to be explicated if this proposition is to have clear content. With respect to the latter notion, consider an action that satisfies Condition (a) because it causes physical contact to be made with a self-owner. This action generates supplemental benefit if and only if it also benefits someone on net *excluding all of the effects caused by contact with the self-owner's body*. For example, an action might generate supplemental benefit because it causes two distinct events, one of which is contact being made with a body and the other of which independently produces benefits for some person. In such a case, the resulting benefits would be supplemental benefits, as they are caused by the agent's action but not the resulting bodily contact.

To make this proposal a bit more precise, let "*A*" stand for the world where the agent carries out some body-impacting action and "*B*" stand for any arbitrary comparison world where she does not carry out the action in

1.3 The Self-Ownership Thesis

question. Finally, let "C" stand for the world where the agent carries out the action but the impacted self-owner never existed (but all of the self-owner's previously imposed costs and benefits still obtained).[27] If some person P is x units better off in A than in B, then the action benefits P relative to B. One can then determine what share of that benefit is supplemental by comparing P's level of advantage in B to her level of advantage in C. Specifically, if P is y units better off in B, that should be taken to imply that those y units of benefit were caused by the bodily contact with the self-owner and, thus, do not count as supplemental. One can, thus, conclude that the action generates $x - y$ units of supplemental benefit relative to B (i.e., it produces supplemental benefit if and only if $x > y$).

This comparison helps to clarify what it means to say that some benefit is caused by bodily contact (and is, thus, non-supplemental). Consider the case where an agent can win a race only by pushing a loiterer out of the way by opening a door. There is a sense in which the bodily contact initiated by the action *causes* the agent to benefit: Absent that contact she would not win the race, where these corresponding counterfactual differences imply that the contact causes her to win the race according to counterfactual theories of causation.[28] However, if one applies the proposed test, one sees that the bodily contact does not cause the agent to benefit in the sense of "cause" being employed here. This is because the agent acquires the same benefit in the world where she shoves the loiterer with the door as she does in the world where she opens the door and the loiterer never existed (i.e., $y = 0$). Thus, no portion of her acquired benefit is caused by the bodily contact, at least in the sense of "cause" that is being employed here; rather, the benefit is entirely supplemental. While this usage of "cause" is perhaps idiosyncratic, this is how the term should be understood in the subsequent discussion of what counts as supplemental benefit.

As we continue with the explication of Condition (b), note that this condition does not merely assert that the absence of supplemental benefit is a necessary condition of self-ownership infringement; rather, it insists that an action infringes on someone's self-ownership rights only if it does not *uniquely* generate supplemental benefit. This notion is defined as follows: An action that satisfies Condition (a) uniquely generates supplemental benefit if and only if it generates benefit for some person and there

---
[27] The reason for including this parenthetical will be discussed in Section 3.4.
[28] See Lewis (1973).

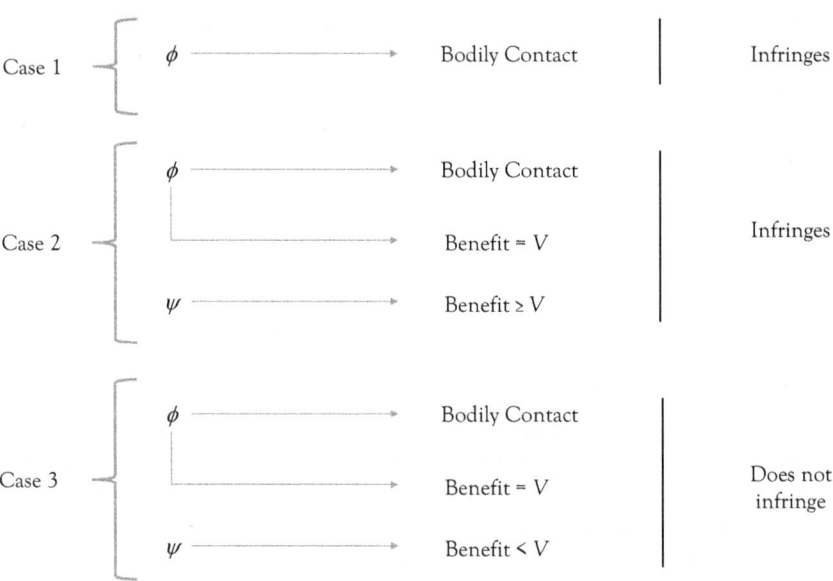

Figure 1.1 Causal chains and rights infringement.

is no alternative action available to the agent that would generate at least as much supplemental benefit for that person without satisfying Condition (a). In other words, if an action makes contact with a body and does not generate supplemental benefit, then it infringes on self-ownership rights. Similarly, if it *does* generate supplemental benefit but that benefit can be equally provided without making bodily contact, then the self-owner has a claim against the action. By contrast, if it generates supplemental benefit *and* there is no way to generate the same (or more) supplemental benefit without bodily contact, then the action in question is permitted by ASO.

This explication of ASO is summarized in Figure 1.1, which schematically illustrates whether an action infringes upon a person's self-ownership rights.

In Case 1, some action φ causes physical contact to be made with some self-owner's body, where this causal relationship is represented by the right-facing arrow. In this case, no supplemental benefit is generated by the agent's φ-ing. Thus, the action straightforwardly satisfies both Condition (a) and Condition (b) of ASO and thereby infringes upon the self-owner's right against others using her body.

1.3 The Self-Ownership Thesis

Case 2 is identical to Case 1 except, in this case, ϕ-ing also causes someone to obtain a supplemental benefit of value V, where this benefit is supplemental in virtue of the fact that it is caused by the ϕ-ing but is not caused by the contact that is made with the self-owner's body. However, in this case, the agent could provide the beneficiary with that same quantity of benefit *and* avoid bodily contact by ψ-ing instead of ϕ-ing. Given these stipulations, the agent's ϕ-ing generates supplemental benefit beyond that caused by bodily contact, but it does not *uniquely* generate this benefit. Thus, ϕ-ing still meets Conditions (a) and (b) and thereby infringes upon the self-owner's rights according to ASO.

Finally, Case 3 modifies Case 2 such that there is no longer any alternative action that can provide the beneficiary with a benefit of equal or greater value to V – that is, the quantity of supplemental benefit generated by ϕ-ing. In this case, it is stipulated that ψ is the action that provides the beneficiary with the greatest quantity of benefit relative to all actions that are not identical to ϕ. Given that this quantity is less than the quantity of supplemental benefit generated by ϕ-ing, ϕ-ing uniquely generates supplemental benefit and, thus, does not infringe upon the self-owner's rights according to ASO.

To make this more concrete, consider the case where P discovers her roommate Q asleep on the kitchen floor. Annoyed, P decides to vent her anger by pouring a glass of water on Q's head. Such an action instantiates Case 1: while P enjoys seeing Q jolted awake, this benefit is caused strictly by the bodily contact that she initiates (as her action of pouring the water would not produce this benefit in the world where Q did not exist). Thus, her action does not generate supplemental benefit and infringes on Q's self-ownership rights. Alternatively, suppose that P decides to take this opportunity to clean the kitchen by starting up her robotic vacuum. P knows that the vacuum will bump into Q's head and thereby wake her up, an outcome that P will enjoy. Additionally, P will derive satisfaction from the kitchen floor being clean. Given this latter stipulation, it follows that P derives supplemental benefit from her action beyond the benefits produced by bodily contact. However, further specification is needed to determine whether starting the vacuum *uniquely* produces this supplemental benefit. Suppose that P could get the same satisfaction by sweeping the floor while avoiding contact with Q. In that case, starting the vacuum would not uniquely produce supplemental benefit; that is, her action instantiates Case 2 and infringes on Q's rights. By contrast, if P has no alternative way of cleaning the floor – for example, because no broom is available –

then starting the vacuum instantiates Case 3, and Q does not have a self-ownership right against P taking that action.[29]

1.4 The Advantages of Anarchist Self-Ownership

The foregoing discussion has attempted to clarify the content of ASO without providing a defense of the principle, that is, explaining *why* one ought to accept ASO over rival versions like the classical concept of self-ownership. While the primary argument for ASO will be presented in Chapter 3, this section will note some attractive implications of ASO, where the fact that ASO generates these implications is one reason to accept the principle. First, note that ASO appears to preserve most of the attractive implications of the classical self-ownership thesis. For example, it would still forbid the involuntary redistribution of kidneys or other organs to needy individuals, as such redistribution initiates bodily contact (thereby satisfying ASO's Condition (a)) without uniquely generating supplemental benefit in the sense defined previously (thereby satisfying Condition (b)). Granted, the organ recipients and their loved ones would benefit from the actions in question; however, because this benefit is caused by the contact made with self-owners' bodies, it would not qualify as *supplemental* benefit. Thus, ASO implies that involuntary organ redistribution infringes upon persons' self-ownership rights. Similarly, ASO forbids agents from slapping someone to blow off steam or drawing crude images on a sleeping person for amusement, as, again, these actions make bodily contact without generating supplemental benefit. Additionally, because fetuses make bodily contact that does not generate supplemental benefits beyond those caused by the contact itself, ASO would entail that pregnant persons have a claim against the fetus using their bodies in this way, thereby opening up the possibility that abortion is permissible.

Second, ASO is able to make sense of many – though, admittedly, not all – of the standard intuitions that people have about Trolley Problem-related cases.[30] Ethicists have now put forward a large number of these cases, but the two paradigmatic ones worth considering here are the switch

---

[29] One might worry that this result reveals ASO to be too permissive, as a self-owner should have a right against being hit with a vacuum in this case. This objection will be addressed in Section 1.7.
[30] The Trolley Problem was introduced by Philippa Foot (1978) and famously developed by Thomson (1985). The following discussion will avoid wading into the voluminous contemporary discussion of the subject, as the aim here is merely to show that ASO can be profitably applied to this problem. For a discussion of the problem cases alluded to by the "not all" qualifier, see Footnote 32.

1.4 The Advantages of Anarchist Self-Ownership

case and the footbridge case. In the *switch case*, a trolley is going to run over five people unless the agent flips a switch and redirects the trolley onto a different track where it will hit and kill one person. In this case, the standard intuition is that it is permissible to redirect the trolley.[31] By contrast, in the *footbridge case*, the only way to stop the trolley from killing five people is to push a person off a footbridge in front of the trolley, thereby making it grind to a halt. In this case, the standard intuition is that it is impermissible to push the person off the footbridge. The problem, then, is trying to explain why there might be this difference in permissibility despite the fact that both flipping the switch and shoving the person amount to killing one person to save five from dying.

The advantage of ASO is that it is able to provide such an explanation. Note that, in the switch case, the benefits that are generated by flipping the switch are all *supplemental benefits*; that is, they are caused by the action but are *not* caused by any bodily contact initiated by that action. Indeed, if the single person on the secondary track had never existed, the five people on the main track would be no worse off than if the trolley hit the person, where this counterfactual comparison reveals that the benefits they derive are supplemental. Further, flipping the switch *uniquely* generates these supplemental benefits, as there is no alternative action that would save the lives of the five people on the track. Given that flipping the switch uniquely produces supplemental benefit, the action does not satisfy ASO's Condition (b) of self-ownership infringement. By contrast, shoving the person from the footbridge does *not* generate any supplemental benefits, as all of the benefits produced are caused by the contact made with her body; absent any such contact, the trolley would not stop and the five people on the track would not survive. Thus, the shove satisfies both Condition (a) and Condition (b) of ASO and thereby qualifies as a self-ownership infringement. In this way, ASO is able to explain why flipping the switch is permissible but shoving the person is not: Only the latter action violates a person's self-ownership rights.[32]

---

[31] While Thomson originally endorsed this judgment (1985), she later argued that redirecting the trolley would actually be impermissible, as it is wrong to sacrifice someone else to save others if one would not be willing to sacrifice oneself in the same way (the presumption being that most people would not flip the switch if doing so would result in their own death rather than the death of the single person on the track) (2008).

[32] It should be noted that ASO does *not* support other intuitive judgments about Trolley Problem-related cases. For example, Foot (1984) suggests it would be impermissible to run over a pedestrian with a car in order to rescue five drowning people. By contrast, ASO would not assign the pedestrian a claim against this action, as driving over her with the car uniquely generates supplemental benefit.

The third advantage of ASO is that it solves what, following Nicola Mulkeen (2019), might be called the self-ownership thesis' *pollution problem*. As noted previously, the classical interpretation of self-ownership assigns each self-owner a claim against others making nonconsensual contact with her body. The problem with this assignment is that it seemingly renders almost all activities impermissible. For example, a claim against all bodily contact would forbid people from protecting their crops with insecticide if the emitted aerosols would drift downwind and make contact with other people's lungs (Railton 2003, 190). People would also be forbidden from operating any sort of vehicle that produces particulates that land on others' skin (Sobel 2012, 35). Rights-infringing particulates would not be limited to exhaust fumes; simply kicking up dust with a car would seemingly infringe on others' self-ownership rights if the dust were to land on them (Brennan and van der Vossen 2018, 205). Even human respiration produces a form of pollution (carbon dioxide) whose contact with others might wrong them (Friedman 1989, 168). Similarly, because sound waves exert force on others' bodies, the classical interpretation of the self-ownership thesis would forbid yelling at someone (Fried 2004, 78) or driving up one's own driveway if others will hear the rumbling (Mack 2015, 196). Further, given that photons are particles, it would be impermissible to turn on a flashlight or start a fire if doing so would slightly illuminate another person's body (Zwolinski 2014, 12). Even walking into another's line of sight would seemingly wrong her, as doing so would bombard her eyes with redirected photons. Thus, the classical interpretation of the self-ownership thesis seems to implausibly entail that a huge portion of indispensable human activity is impermissible.

By contrast, ASO avoids these problematic implications by permitting actions that make bodily contact but also uniquely generate supplemental benefit. For example, when an agent operates a factory that produces particles that land on others' skin, she is also producing material goods that will benefit others – where, presumably, there is no way to produce these goods without emitting pollutants that will make bodily contact. Thus, operating the factory does not infringe upon anyone's self-ownership rights according to ASO. Similarly, while respiration inevitably bombards others' bodies with carbon dioxide molecules, it would be permissible because it

---

Similarly, Thomson argues that it would not be permissible to manufacture a medicine that would save five lives if its production would create a toxic by-product that kills one person (1985, 1407). Here, again, ASO would not assign the person a claim against the production of the medicine, as the production uniquely generates supplemental benefit. Together, these cases might raise the worry that ASO is too permissive. This worry will be addressed in Section 1.7.

1.4 The Advantages of Anarchist Self-Ownership

uniquely generates supplemental benefits for the respirator. And the same goes for actions like driving past one's neighbors, turning on lights, etc. In each of these cases, the agent's action bombards others' bodies with various small particles; however, at the same time, these actions all uniquely produce benefits that are caused by the action and not the bodily contact that it initiates.[33] Given that ASO does not count such actions as self-ownership infringements, it permits the countless indispensable, everyday activities that the classical interpretation of self-ownership forbids.[34]

Fourth, ASO is able to explain a number of other commonsense distinctions that people might be tempted to draw when assessing the permissibility of various activities. For example, one might want to draw a distinction between nudism (where people enjoy being naked for its own sake) and exhibitionism (where people reveal their bodies because they derive pleasure from being seen naked), with the former being judged permissible and the latter wrongful. ASO is able to support this distinction because it entails that sexual exhibitionism infringes on people's self-ownership rights while nudism does not. To see why this is the case, note

---

[33] This claim is overly general, as whether or not these actions *uniquely* generate supplemental benefits will be a contingent matter, varying from context to context. In some cases, it may turn out that there is some alternative way to realize the supplemental benefit without making bodily contact. ASO would, thus, imply that the actions in question infringe on self-owners' rights. However, given that there is an alternative way of realizing the benefits they produce, there seems to be nothing problematic about the fact that ASO forbids such actions.

[34] There have been a number of related attempts to solve the pollution problem by weakening the self-ownership thesis. Some influential proposals include those made by Nozick (1974), Rothbard (1982), Otsuka (2003), Vallentyne, Steiner, and Otsuka (2005), Richard Epstein (2009), and Mack (2015). However, these proposed solutions have been subjected to a number of criticisms such as those raised by Peter Railton (2003), David Sobel (2012; 2013), and Matt Zwolinski (2014). In light of these objections, there has been a renewed effort to revise the thesis with examples including Jason Brennan and Bas van der Vossen (2018), Ben Bryan (2019), and Mulkeen (2019). However, other libertarians have taken the problem to be insoluble, arguing that their fellow libertarians must either bite the bullet (Flanigan 2019a) or give up on the self-ownership thesis altogether (Kukathas, 2019).

While ASO is not free of problems (as discussed in Sections 1.7 and 1.8), the suggestion here is that these are relatively minor when compared to those that afflict the just mentioned theories. Additionally, ASO has the advantage of avoiding Jessica Flanigan's (2019a) objection that attempts to solve the pollution problem by revising the self-ownership thesis are ad hoc in a way that compromises the adequacy of the posited theories. Specifically, she argues that, while it is possible to amend and patch a moral theory until it delivers only intuitively acceptable results, one ought to prefer theories that have unsavory implications but instantiate other theoretical virtues like parsimony and syntactic simplicity. Setting aside the question of whether syntactic simplicity and parsimony are theoretical virtues, ASO seemingly avoids the more general charge of being ad hoc on the grounds that its endorsement follows from a prior acceptance of the Lockean proviso, as will be argued in Chapter 3. This stands in contrast to other revisions of the self-ownership thesis, which are typically posited simply to avoid the thesis' unsavory implications.

that exhibitionists make bodily contact with others because they bombard their victims' eyeballs with photons, thereby satisfying Condition (a) of ASO. Additionally, because exhibitionists derive their enjoyment from perceiving the reaction of their victims – that is, all of the benefit produced by their action is caused by the bodily contact they initiated – their action does not generate any supplemental benefit. Given that exhibitionism also satisfies Condition (b) of ASO, it follows that it infringes upon other people's self-ownership rights. By contrast, nudists, by hypothesis, derive unique pleasure from being naked. Thus, while they also bombard others' bodies with photons, they get unique supplemental benefit from being naked and, therefore, do not satisfy Condition (b) of ASO. As a result, ASO entails that nudism does not infringe upon anyone's self-ownership rights.

ASO also supports a related distinction between speech that is merely blasphemous (e.g., printing a picture of the prophet Muhammad in a history textbook) and speech that is designed deliberately to antagonize religious believers (e.g., distributing rude caricatures of Muhammad). Both kinds of speech satisfy Condition (a), as they bombard people's bodies with photons or soundwaves. However, blasphemous speech, by hypothesis, uniquely generates some other benefit such as educating people about history. It, thus, does not violate anyone's self-ownership rights because it does not satisfy Condition (b) of ASO. By contrast, the benefits of antagonistic speech are produced by a causal chain that passes through self-owners' bodies: Like the exhibitionist, the antagonist gets her satisfaction from perceiving the reaction that her action elicits. In other words, the benefits produced by antagonistic speech are not supplemental benefits, with such speech thereby satisfying Condition (b) and, by extension, infringing on others' self-ownership rights. Admittedly, many liberal and libertarian proponents of free speech will find this result objectionable; however, for those who share the intuition that there is a moral distinction between blasphemy and provocation, this result will count in ASO's favor, as ASO provides a theoretical basis for affirming this distinction.

Finally, in addition to forbidding paradigmatic self-ownership infringements, supporting commonsense moral distinctions, and solving the pollution problem, ASO also solves a less-discussed problem with the classical self-ownership thesis, namely, that the latter fails to adequately differentiate aggressors from victims. To see why this is the case, recall that the classical interpretation of the thesis asserts that an agent wrongs a victim when she touches the victim without consent. For example, a pedestrian who punches a rapidly moving bicyclist wrongs the bicyclist by virtue of

1.4 *The Advantages of Anarchist Self-Ownership* 47

her having made nonconsensual contact with the bicyclist's body. The problem is that, while the classical thesis yields the favorable result that the pedestrian infringes on the bicyclist's self-ownership rights, it also entails that the bicyclist infringes on the pedestrian's self-ownership rights – at least, if one assumes that the concept of touching is analyzed in a reasonably thin way.

To see why this is the case, suppose that one holds that P touches Q if and only if P's body makes physical contact with Q. This very thin physicalist analysis of touching entails that the pedestrian touches the bicyclist, as physical contact is made between their bodies; however, given this contact, the analysis of touching also implies that the bicyclist touches the pedestrian. Further, given that the touching relation is symmetrical on this account, the standard self-ownership thesis would deliver the seemingly incorrect result that the bicyclist infringes on the pedestrian's rights when her face makes unconsented-to contact with the pedestrian's fist.

To correct for this problem, one might insist upon a thicker analysis of touching that makes reference to not only physical contact but also various counterfactual considerations. Specifically, one might suggest that P touches Q if and only if their bodies make contact *and* a different choice by P would have resulted in their bodies not making such contact. This proposal is promising in that it opens up the possibility of the touching relation being asymmetrical, as it possible that only one party could have avoided physical contact by making a different choice. Additionally, one might think that this thicker account supports the intuition that it is the pedestrian (not the bicyclist) who does the touching given that no bodily contact would have occurred had the pedestrian chosen not to punch the bicyclist. However, this proposal does not, in fact, deliver the desired asymmetry, as the bicyclist could equally have chosen in a way that avoided the contact (e.g., she could have ridden in the other direction). Thus, the thicker account still yields the result that the bicyclist touches – and thereby wrongs – the pedestrian.

The general conclusion to draw from this discussion is that proponents of the self-ownership thesis cannot assume that there is some pretheoretical fact of the matter about who touches whom. Rather, they need to either provide an even thicker analysis of touching or adopt the thin analysis and modify the self-ownership thesis to limit which touchings qualify as infringements. Otherwise, they will be unable to correctly differentiate aggressors from victims. ASO represents the latter approach to solving this problem, as it restricts the set of contact-initiating acts that qualify as rights infringements in a way that allows for aggressors to be suitably demarcated from victims. Notably, while mere contact is a symmetrical relation, contact without supplemental benefit can be asymmetric: When two persons come into contact, that contact might be the product of one person acting in a way that generates supplemental benefit while the other's action produces no such benefit. For example, when the bicyclist makes contact with the pedestrian, this contact is the result of her carrying out an action (riding her bike somewhere) that uniquely generates supplemental benefits (getting where she is going in the most efficient way). By contrast, the pedestrian's action does not produce any supplemental benefit, as the only benefit she gets is the satisfaction caused by the physical contact . Thus, ASO entails that the pedestrian infringes on the bicyclist's self-ownership rights by punching but the bicyclist does not infringe on the pedestrian's rights by taking her trip. In this way, ASO is able to adequately differentiate aggressors from victims in a way that the classical interpretation of the self-ownership thesis cannot. This is an additional theoretical advantage for the proposed principle.[35]

This is not to say that ASO does not also have its theoretical drawbacks. For example, Sections 1.7 and 1.8 will consider (and try to ameliorate) worries that it is both too permissive and also too restrictive. However, the hope here has been to show that the anarchist interpretation of self-ownership has much to recommend it, where these advantages must be weighed against the soon-to-be-discussed theoretical disadvantages. Additionally, in Chapter 3

---

[35] Note that this is also a reason for favoring ASO over other proposed solutions to the pollution problem, as they tend to assume a pre-theoretical asymmetry of rights-infringing contact. For example, Nozick (1974) attempts to solve the pollution problem by proposing that self-ownership is a right against boundary crossing *without compensation*. Thus, people are permitted to drive cars, etc., so long as they compensate others for any costs imposed by physical contact. Setting aside the other merits or demerits of this proposal, note that this account assumes that, for any given act of touching, there is some pre-theoretical fact about who is crossing a boundary and whose boundary is being crossed. However, it has been argued that there is no such fact; rather, the asymmetry of rights infringements must be built into a theory of touching/infringement. Thus, Nozick's proposal is inadequate, as is any other attempt to weaken the self-ownership thesis in a way that presupposes that there are pre-theoretical asymmetrical boundary crossings rather than symmetrical touchings.

Admittedly, there are certain alternatives to ASO that might also solve both the asymmetry problem and the pollution problem. For example, a rival revision of the self-ownership thesis might make reference to intentions to determine who wrongs whom, as the pedestrian intends to make contact with the bicyclist while the bicyclist does not intend this contact. This proposal could also help to solve the pollution problem, as a person does not typically intend to make contact with others when she breathes or drives a car. Thus, these actions would be permissible on an intentions-based account of the self-ownership thesis. However, this proposal would have its own drawbacks, most notably that, unlike ASO, it does not avoid Flanigan's (2019a) objection (discussed in the previous footnote) that it is an ad hoc solution to the pollution problem. Additionally, it would not entail that pregnant persons have a right against fetuses using their bodies without consent, as fetuses do not intend to make contact with the bodies in question.

will be argued that there is a supplemental reason for endorsing ASO beyond its attractive implications, namely, that it is the kind of self-ownership that persons can acquire in accordance with the Lockean proviso.

1.5 The Rejection of Private Property

The fourth component of the anarchist position is fairly straightforward, and, thus, requires limited exposition. Specifically, it holds that, while many people own their own bodies in virtue of having self-appropriated, there have been practically no successful appropriations of external unowned resources and nor will there be more than a handful of such appropriations in the future. In other words, practically no one has – or ever will have – any private property rights over any external thing, be it land, objects, or other natural resources.[36]

It is this conclusion that sets social anarchism apart from libertarian views, all of which posit that most things are privately – or, at the very least, collectively – owned.[37] Up to this point, the proposed anarchist theses have all been paradigmatic libertarian positions (albeit with a few heterodox adjustments having been made to them). However, no self-identified libertarians endorse the view that all natural resources are unowned. Rather, the rejection of private property is a signature commitment of socialist philosophical positions, where socialism and libertarianism are generally taken to be diametrically opposed views. One might therefore worry, that the inclusion of this thesis in the social anarchist position renders the view incoherent. The aim of Chapters 3 and 4 is to show that this is not the case and that, in fact, the anarchist denial of property rights follows from the libertarian theses presented previously.

1.6 Anarchist Claim Rights

While the anarchist holds that no one owns – or could come to own – practically any natural resources, this does not commit her to the view that

---

[36] The reason for including these "practically" qualifiers is that there are some very limited circumstances where a person might potentially acquire ownership rights over external objects via appropriation. For example, if scarcity were entirely eliminated, then appropriation would satisfy the Lockean proviso and thereby succeed. The proviso would be similarly satisfied if a person attempted to appropriate resources in a totally isolated location that will never be accessed by others during her lifetime. Thus, strictly speaking, the anarchist allows that there *could* be external private property; however, as a matter of contingent fact, there is practically no such property due to the necessary conditions of external appropriation going unsatisfied.

[37] For a libertarian defense of common ownership, see Billy Christmas (2020; 2021).

persons are free to do whatever they like with these resources. Rather, she insists that a luck egalitarian principle of distributive justice determines which uses of those resources are permissible and which are forbidden. Specifically, she assigns persons *distributive claims* over unowned resources and objects, where these claims correspond to the prescriptions of a luck egalitarian principle of distributive justice. This section will introduce the luck egalitarian theory of justice and then explain what it means to say that persons have distributive claims corresponding to this theory.

To introduce the luck egalitarian theory of distributive justice, it is helpful to contrast it with what might be called a *strict egalitarian* view. According to the strict egalitarian, a distribution of resources is just if and only if everyone has equal advantage, where "advantage" refers to whatever it is that matters as far as justice is concerned.[38] For example, one might implausibly take advantage to be the total number of calories that a person has consumed, with justice obtaining if and only if every person has consumed the same number of calories. More plausibly, one might take advantage to be a quantity of money such that justice requires that all persons have equal wealth. More plausibly still, one might take "advantage" to refer to the amount of welfare that a person experiences either over some specified interval of time or over the course of her entire life. For these purposes, it will be assumed that what is to be equalized – that is, the *equilisandum* or, alternatively, the *currency of egalitarian justice* – is the quantity of welfare experienced across a lifetime. This assumption is made because it seems intuitively plausible and will simplify some of the subsequent discussion (though no derived conclusions depend on it). However, it is worth emphasizing that both strict egalitarianism and luck egalitarianism are neutral with respect to what it is that must be equalized. For this reason, the book will use the ambiguous term "advantage," thereby allowing for those with rival views about the proper currency of egalitarian justice to specify luck egalitarianism as they see fit.

In contrast to strict egalitarianism, *luck egalitarianism* does not insist that justice requires an equal distribution of advantage. Rather, luck egalitarians are willing to declare certain inequalities just if and only if those inequalities correspond to some choice for which the worse-off parties are responsible. For example, Cohen provides a representative statement of the luck egalitarian position when he asserts that "an unequal

---

[38] Note that not everyone uses the label "strict egalitarianism" in this way. For example, Vallentyne, Steiner, and Otsuka use the term to refer to egalitarian theories that prioritize equality over other values such as efficiency or respecting self-ownership rights (2005, 212fn20).

1.6 Anarchist Claim Rights   51

distribution whose inequality cannot be vindicated by some choice or fault or desert on the part of (some of) the relevant affected agents is unfair, and therefore, *pro tanto*, unjust" (2009, 7).[39] As this statement indicates, a defining feature of luck egalitarianism is that it *holds people responsible* for making *sanctionable choices*, where a theory holds someone responsible for a choice if and only if it reduces the size of her just share (but not others') in virtue of that choice.[40] In other words, luck egalitarianism holds that, prior to human action, the distribution is just if and only if everyone possesses equal advantage; however, if people then make sanctionable choices, the distribution will be just if and only if each sanctionable chooser (and no non-sanctionable-chooser) ends up with a smaller share of advantage than she was originally assigned, where the size of this reduction is a function of her past sanctionable choices.[41] Of course, to give this statement of luck egalitarianism determinate content, two further specifications must be made. First, one must provide an account of which choices qualify as sanctionable. And, second, one must provide an account that specifies the extent to which any given sanctionable choice diminishes the size of the chooser's just share.[42] Providing such a specification will be the task of Chapter 6.

To briefly illustrate the difference between strict egalitarianism and luck egalitarianism (setting aside the just-raised question of how to best specify the latter position), consider the case of two equally well-off tennis players, *P* and *Q*, each of whom owns two tennis rackets. At their weekly game,

---

[39] Other representative statements of luck egalitarianism include those made by Arneson (2011a, 243), Cohen (2006, 440; 2008, 17–18; 2011, 13), Lippert-Rasmussen (2015, 1), Temkin (1993, 13), and Vallentyne (2008, 58), among many others.

[40] The notion of responsibility at issue here, then, is what has been alternately called "consequential responsibility" (Dworkin 2000, 287; Stemplowska 2009, 238; Knight and Stemplowska 2011, 13), "substantive responsibility" (Scanlon 1998, 248), and "holding people responsible" (Olsaretti 2009, 167–8). The idea is that the agent's relation to some misdeed (or morally good action) entails that she ought to be left worse off (or better off) than if she did not stand in that relation. That said, not all luck egalitarians think that justice *requires* leaving sanctionable choosers worse off in this way. Rather, they might merely hold that there is no injustice if she is left worse off, though also no injustice if her share is equal to others'. See, for example, Segall (2013, 36).

[41] In addition to the rejection of private property endorsed in Section 1.5, many socialists take luck egalitarianism to be a core socialist commitment, for example, Cohen (2008) and Roemer (2017). However, this claim is disputed by Arneson (2011a).

[42] To request such specification is to ask for what Serena Olsaretti calls a *principle of stakes* – that is, "an account of what consequences can be justifiably attached to features that are the appropriate grounds of responsibility" (2009, 167). Note that this is distinct question from asking which features are such appropriate grounds. Olsaretti focuses only on the former question and brackets the latter; by contrast, Chapter 6 will suggest that the answers to the two questions are linked, as both the grounds of responsibility and their associated stakes follow from the same theoretical constraint, namely, what Chapter 2 calls the moral tyranny constraint.

P gets very frustrated and breaks both of her rackets by throwing them against the court surface. According to strict egalitarianism, justice requires that Q transfer one of her rackets to P, as, absent such a transfer, P would end up worse off than Q due to no longer being able to play tennis. By contrast, according to practically all plausible specifications of luck egalitarianism, P's decision to destroy her rackets qualifies as a sanctionable choice. Thus, her just share would be diminished relative to what it would have been had she not chosen sanctionably, which, in turn, implies that she would not be entitled to an equalizing transfer from Q. Further, if she were to carry out such a transfer herself by seizing one of Q's rackets, the resulting state of affairs would be unjust according to luck egalitarianism, as P's level of advantage would exceed her just share (while Q would end up with less than her just share of advantage due to the loss of her tennis racket).

With an account of luck egalitarianism having been provided, it is now possible to explain the anarchist's contention that persons have distributive claims that *correspond* to its prescriptions. Specifically, the anarchist assigns each person a set of claims such that the luck egalitarian principle would be satisfied if all persons respected the claims of others – that is, any inequality would appropriately correspond to some sanctionable choice on the part of the worse-off individuals. Or, to put this point slightly differently, each person would have a claim against anyone else using an unowned resource in some way if and only if that use would leave her with less than her appropriate share of advantage, where her *appropriate* share is either (a) equal to the respective shares of those who have not yet chosen sanctionably if she has also not yet chosen sanctionably or (b) adjusted downward from this value if she has chosen sanctionably (where the magnitude of this adjustment is specified in Chapter 6).[43] Thus, persons would still have rights vis-à-vis external resources, just not property rights of the kind posited by both left- and right-libertarians. Call this the *anarchist conclusion*.[44]

---

[43] This position is perhaps unnecessarily controversial in that it presupposes that there are claims correlative of persons' duties to realize just distributions. One might equally posit that such distributive duties are non-directed in the sense that no one has a claim that these duties be discharged. However, nothing significant turns on this point, as the entire argument of the book could be restated in terms of non-directed duties.

[44] It is worth briefly noting that, unlike most libertarian theories of property, the anarchist conclusion allows for there to be something proximate to *intellectual property*. Standard natural rights theories of private property are incompatible with intellectual property because the latter places constraints on the use of fully owned things. Suppose that P owns both a factory and some collection of resources. Assuming she fully owns these things, then she has a permission to construct whatever it

1.6 Anarchist Claim Rights

To expand on the contrast between anarchist distributive claims and libertarian property rights, note that the two kinds of rights differ in the following ways. First, distributive claims are not acquired in the historical fashion that characterizes property rights, that is, they are not established via initial appropriation or subsequently acquired via transfer. Rather, moral persons start out with these rights in virtue of the fact that they possess the capacities that make them the appropriate subjects of a theory of distributive justice.[45] In other words, the world comes to persons prepopulated with resource-related exclusionary claims. This stands in contrast to the standard Lockean picture wherein all persons start out with a permission to use all things until acts of appropriation establish property claims that negate some of those permissions.

Second, distributive claims do not come bundled together in the same way that property rights do (at least, according to practically all prominent theories of private property). For example, on almost all accounts of property ownership, if one has a claim against one person using some object in some way — and one has not waived or forfeited any of one's prior claims — then one also has a claim against each other person using the object in this way. Additionally, one would also have a claim against the original person (and all other persons) using the object in all other ways, that is, one would have a general claim against all others including that object in their actions irrespective of what form those actions take. By contrast, a person might have a distributive claim against one person using

---

is that she likes out of these resources and sell the products. However, if Q has a patent on some invention, that implies that P is prohibited from producing and selling that invention using her factory and raw materials. Thus, a contradiction is reached, with most libertarians rejecting intellectual property rather than the premise that persons fully own their property. By contrast, the anarchist conclusion allows that Q might have a distributive claim against P constructing the product. For example, Q might have such a claim if she has developed the socially useful invention at great personal cost and P producing and selling copies of that product would prevent Q from recouping those losses. In such a situation, P's production would leave Q worse off despite no sanctionable choice on her part and, thus, Q would have a claim against P using the factory and resources in this way. In other words, the anarchist conclusion would entail an *egalitarian* variety of intellectual property that would be compatible with practices like patents and copyrights – though, notably, only insofar as those practices aligned with the prescriptions of luck egalitarianism. If one thinks that intellectual property is essential to economic growth and full compliance with the correct moral theory should not dramatically inhibit such growth, then this result represents a reason for favoring the anarchist conclusion over standard libertarian theories of ownership.

[45] Who qualifies as a subject of distributive justice – that is, who can be wronged by the distribution (where the potential to be wronged implies the existence of a distributive claim)? The speculative suggestion here is that the subjects of distributive justice are all and only those persons who are both capable of possessing advantage and able to demand justification from others. Such a suggestion would help establish the kind of moral equality discussed in Section 1.3. However, defending this proposal is beyond the scope of this book.

an object but not another person using it in an identical fashion (e.g., because only the former's use would generate an unjust inequality). Similarly, she might have a claim against a person using the object in one way but not another. Thus, distributive claims are radically unbundled relative to property claims.

Additionally, property theorists uniformly take property claims to come bundled with various other Hohfeldian incidents such as powers to transfer and waive these claims as well as immunities from the loss of these claims. By contrast, while people can forfeit their distributive claims (as discussed in Chapters 2 and 6), they cannot waive them with respect to chosen persons. When P chooses sanctionably, she might forfeit a claim against Q using a resource in a way that disadvantages P (and advantages Q); however, P cannot simply allow Q or some other person R to use the resource, as such use might upset the just distribution. Additionally, the anarchist conclusion entails that persons lack many of the immunities from the loss of their claims that property owners possess. For example, suppose that P has a luck egalitarian distributive claim against Q using a small guest house. Given that this claim is luck egalitarian in character, it must be the case that Q's use of the guest house would generate an inequality such that P ends up comparatively worse off relative to Q (assuming that neither P nor Q has chosen sanctionably in the past). However, suppose that an unforeseeable forest fire burns down Q's home. Given this environmental change, it is no longer the case that Q's use of the guest house would leave her better off than P; rather, Q would be left worse off if she *did not* use the guest house. Thus, P cannot retain her distributive claim against Q, as she can have a claim against some resource use only if that use would leave her with less than her appropriate share of advantage. In other words, the claims posited by the anarchist conclusion are not stable like property claims. As the guest house case demonstrates, people lack an immunity from the loss of their distributive claims, with certain unlucky events negating those claims.[46] The fact that distributive claims are unbundled from the other Hohfeldian incidents of ownership represents another

---

[46] Strictly speaking, the anarchist conclusion underdetermines which claims people forfeit either due to bad luck or sanctionable choice. For example, in the guest house case, P might have many distributive claims against Q, where the negation of any one of these claims would entail that P and Q end up with equal advantage under conditions of full compliance. All that the posited theory entails is that P must be stripped of one of these claims. Thus, to make the anarchist conclusion fully determinate, some supplemental theory would have to be provided that specifies exactly which claims are forfeited when bad luck strikes. Similarly, the anarchist conclusion holds that persons forfeit a claim to a particular quantity of advantage when they choose sanctionably. However, there are many different distributive claims whose forfeiture would realize this outcome. Here again, a

1.7 Is Anarchist Self-Ownership Too Permissive?

significant difference between the anarchist conclusion and the theories of private property posited by libertarians (including left-libertarians).

Finally, having clarified the difference between the anarchist's distributive claims and libertarian private property claims, it is also worth noting how the anarchist conclusion departs from standard luck egalitarianism. The key difference here is that ownership limits the domain of things whose permissible use is regulated by the distributive principle. Standard luck egalitarianism allows that the permission to use any object can be assigned to any person, that is, the right to use P's kidney might be equally assigned to either P or Q in just the same way the permission to use an apple tree might be assigned to either person. Similarly, either P or Q might have a claim against some third party making contact with P's body. By contrast, the anarchist conclusion maintains that if P acquires self-ownership rights over her body via an act of self-appropriation, then others cannot have distributive claims over her body. Rather, they can only have distributive claims over those things that remain unowned (with the theory adjusting these claims in response to P's self-appropriation such that everyone discharging their correlative duties would still produce a luck egalitarian-approved distribution).

1.7 Is Anarchist Self-Ownership Too Permissive?

Now that the anarchist conclusion has been introduced, it is possible to address a potential worry about ASO, namely, that it permits bodily contact that an extensionally adequate moral theory would forbid. While ASO has many attractive implications (as discussed in Section 1.4) and independent theoretical grounding (to be discussed in Chapter 3), it also has some admittedly unattractive implications that have led philosophers to reject similar revisions of the self-ownership thesis.[47] Consider, for example, the case where a thrill seeker decides to throw glass bottles off of the top of a twenty-story building onto the street below. While she knows that some of the bottles will seriously injure pedestrians when they shatter, she derives no enjoyment from this outcome. Rather, she tosses the glass bottles strictly for the thrill of seeing them hit the ground. Given that the thrill seeker derives unique supplemental benefit from this activity – assume she cannot get this same degree of satisfaction any other way – it

---

supplemental theory would be needed to determine exactly which exclusionary claims are forfeited. The subsequent argument will remain neutral regarding which theory one should prefer.

[47] See, for example, Sobel (2012, 56) and Mulkeen (2019, 662–3).

follows that she does not infringe upon their self-ownership rights according to ASO. However, critics of ASO would contend that this result is disqualifying: any acceptable account of self-ownership will entail that the thrill seeker's bottle-throwing infringes on the pedestrians' self-ownership rights.

This objection would be a serious problem for the ASO proponent who takes self-ownership claims to be the only claims that people have against others acting in ways that affect their bodies. Such a position would implausibly entail that the pedestrians have no claim against the thrill seeker throwing bottles at them from the rooftop. However, if one accepts the anarchist position as a whole, then one has the theoretical resources to avoid this conclusion by affirming that the pedestrians *do* have such a claim. Specifically, one can appeal to the anarchist conclusion presented in the previous section to point out that, when the anarchist denies the existence of property rights, she does not thereby conclude that persons are free to do whatever they like with natural resources. Rather, persons have distributive claims against others using resources in a way that would leave them worse off absent any sanctionable choice on their part. For example, if a lumberjack chopping down a tree would block a jogger's path and thereby generate a luck-based inequality, the jogger has a distributive right against the lumberjack chopping down the tree.

By assigning people luck egalitarian distributive rights vis-à-vis objects and resources, the anarchist is able to avoid the objection that ASO entails that the pedestrians have no rights against the thrill seeker bombarding them with bottles. Contra this conclusion, the anarchist can insist that the pedestrians have *distributive claims* against the thrill seeker using the bottles in this way (even if they lack any self-ownership claims against her throwing the bottles). In short, proponents of ASO who take the set of claim rights to be coextensive with property rights (i.e., most natural rights libertarians) would be stuck with a highly implausible result if they endorsed ASO – namely, that the thrill seeker does not infringe upon the rights of the pedestrians. By contrast, anarchists who endorse ASO merely have to maintain that the thrill seeker does not infringe upon the pedestrians' *self-ownership rights*. This is a much smaller theoretical cost to bear than the extensional inadequacy of a theory that affirms that the thrill seeker does not wrong the pedestrians at all. And, given that ASO both follows from Lockean proviso (as will be argued in Chapter 3) and solves the many problems discussed in Section 1.4, it does not seem as though its potential failure to properly categorize certain wrongs warrants its rejection.

1.7 Is Anarchist Self-Ownership Too Permissive? 57

Further, there is reason for thinking that this is not a theoretical cost at all. The claim that ASO delivers bad results presupposes that a pedestrian being hit with glass shards is properly categorized as an infringement of her self-ownership rights rather than an infringement of a distributive right. But why affirm this presupposition? The most obvious reason is that being hit with a bottle *intuitively seems* like a self-ownership-related wrong rather than merely a distributive-justice-related wrong. However, there is reason to doubt the reliability of this intuition. After all, many people would judge things like air pollution, light pollution, or noise pollution to be distributive-justice-related wrongs rather than self-ownership infringements. Given that emitting such pollution is of a kind with bottle tossing, additional argument is needed to establish that one should give up the intuition that pollution is properly categorized as an infringement of distributive rights rather than give up the intuition that bottle tossing is properly categorized as an infringement of self-ownership rights. Absent such argument, the appeal to intuition cannot support the objection that ASO miscategorizes wrongs like the thrill seeker's bottle-throwing (even prior to this theoretical cost being weighed against all of the advantages mentioned in the previous paragraph).

It must be noted that the pedestrians have a distributive claim against being hit by bottles (if and) only if the thrill seeker throwing the bottles would result in an outcome that violates the prescriptions of luck egalitarianism. If the case were reconstructed such that bottle-throwing does not leave the pedestrians any worse off than the thrill seeker (and no one has previously chosen sanctionably), then they would have no right against her throwing bottles. This is, admittedly, counterintuitive. However, this intuitive judgment may reflect the difficulty of properly imagining the case. After all, given the immense pain that would be caused by being hit with shards of glass, it might be challenging to imagine a case where the pedestrians being hit with bottle shards helps to realize an egalitarian outcome. By contrast, if one picks a case where it is easier to imagine how bombardment realizes equality – for example, a person is covered with biting insects and the only way to get them off is to toss them onto others' bodies – it seems less intuitively objectionable to say that others have no right against being bombarded.[48]

---

[48] It was suggested earlier that the relevant currency of egalitarian justice is *lifetime* levels of advantage. Thus, a person has a distributive claim against others impacting her body in a way that leaves her with less lifetime advantage than others absent any corresponding sanctionable choice on her part. However, an anonymous reviewer worries that, because it is difficult to know which actions will leave her worse off in this way – that is, whether any given action will cause her to live a worse life

Finally, note that one should not conclude from the foregoing discussion that the conjunction of ASO and the anarchist conclusion implies that a self-owner has no claim against being slapped or otherwise assaulted by an agent if such an action would realize a luck egalitarian outcome by benefitting the agent. For, in such a case, the action would not generate *supplemental* benefits, as all the produced benefits are caused by the physical contact that the agent makes. Thus, the self-owner would have a claim against such actions per ASO. In other words, the only cases where a self-owner will entirely lack a claim against an action that makes contact with her body are those where the action both uniquely generates supplemental benefit *and* conforms to the prescriptions of a luck egalitarian theory of justice. While there will be some intuitively impermissible actions that meet both of these criteria – for example, the egalitarian bottle-throwing described just prior – the conjunction of ASO and the anarchist conclusion will still forbid the vast majority of intuitively unacceptable uses and abuses of self-owners' bodies.

---

on the whole relative to someone else – it is difficult to know which rights she has. And this, in turn, makes it difficult to assess whether her distributive claims adequately protect her from intuitively objectionable bodily contact.

Against the general epistemic worry that it is hard to determine which rights persons possess, it should be noted that practically all moral theories run into serious epistemic difficulties when it comes to determining what they prescribe in actual-world cases. Thus, this epistemic worry is a problem for moral theorizing in general rather than a specific problem with the proposed anarchist theory.

Turning to the more specific worry that one cannot assess whether ASO is too permissive without knowing which distributive claims persons possess, the suggestion here is that one can consider simplified test cases where (a) no one has chosen sanctionably in the past, (b) bodily contact generates a temporally local (in)equality, and (c) it is stipulated that persons will accumulate equal quantities of advantages across the rest of their lives. Given this latter stipulation, any temporally local (in)equality entails an (in)equality of lifetime advantage. In this way, one can still test whether the proposed distributive claims provide persons with adequate protection. For example, in the insect case, the bodily contact would cause everyone to accrue equal levels of lifetime advantage while the thrill seeker's bottle-throwing would cause the pedestrians to accrue unequal levels of lifetime advantage; thus, the pedestrians have a claim against the bottle-throwing while the bystanders do not have a claim against being bombarded with insects. Further, these results appear to be extensionally adequate, as bottle-throwing seems intuitively impermissible while brushing off biting insects seems permissible. Finally, it seems that these intuitions are best explained by the anti-luck egalitarian versus luck egalitarian consequences of the respective actions under consideration. If this is right, then one can conclude that *any* (ASO-respecting) luck egalitarianism-upholding contact will be permissible while any anti-luck egalitarian contact will be impermissible. Thus, even if one does not know which distributive claims persons have in the actual world, one can conclude that the anarchist's posited distributive claims provide extensionally adequate protection of persons' bodies.

1.8 Is Anarchist Self-Ownership Too Restrictive?

The foregoing section has attempted to address the worry that ASO is too permissive. However, one might also worry that it is also too *restrictive* in that it problematically forbids a number of intuitively permissible actions. To see why ASO invites this objection, begin by noting that one of ASO's advantages over the classical interpretation of self-ownership is that it allows people to go about their business and pursue their independent projects. Because the classical interpretation forbids all actions that result in bodily contact, it ends up prohibiting a huge array of indispensable human activity due to the fact that most human actions generate pollution such as emitted particulates and redirected air molecules and photons that go on to make contact with others' bodies. By contrast, ASO permits these activities because they uniquely produce supplemental benefits that are not caused by bodily contact. Thus, so long as an agent has some purpose that does not crucially involve the bodies of non-consenting self-owners – that is, her action uniquely generates benefits beyond those resulting from physical contact with their bodies – the incidental contact that she makes with them will not infringe upon their self-ownership rights according to ASO.

The problem with this proposal is that there are certain cases where an agent's project *does* crucially involve the bodies of non-consenting others, but her actions seem nonetheless permissible. Specifically, note that *public performances* and *solicitations* make contact with others' bodies, where any resultant benefit is caused by the bodily contact itself (i.e., no supplemental benefit is generated). For example, when a street performer bombards passersby with sound waves, she appears to infringe on their ASO rights – at least, if it is assumed that she does not get any special enjoyment from performing in public that she could not get in a private setting. Similar remarks apply to the person who asks a stranger for the time. In these cases, neither the public performance nor the solicitation uniquely generates supplemental benefit, as any unique benefits are derived from the physical contact the performer/solicitor makes with others' bodies (e.g., a passerby enjoying the show or the solicitor being told the time). Thus, ASO implies that public performances and solicitations infringe upon self-owners' rights. However, the restrictiveness objection contends that not only are such performances and solicitations intuitively unobjectionable, they are also indispensable human activities that are essential to societal functioning. Given that ASO forbids such activities, it is unacceptably restrictive (even if solves the classical self-ownership thesis' pollution problem).

There are a few things that can be said in response to this objection. First, one might contest the intuitive judgment that public performances and solicitations are permissible by appealing to the rival (perhaps curmudgeonly) intuition that such solicitations are a *nuisance*, where this term implies wrongful conduct on the part of those who create the nuisance. After all, it can feel invasive when a street musician comes up and starts performing when one is trying to sit quietly in the park; similarly, catcalling and other aggressive solicitations are often perceived as wrongful incursions by those subjected to these practices. Given this intuition, the defender of ASO might maintain that it is actually a theoretical *virtue* that ASO declares these engagements to be rights infringements. Additionally, note that people often *resent* being asked out on a date by strangers, being called on the phone by telemarketers, or being trapped in a subway car with a particularly annoying busker. Here, again, the conclusion that these engagements infringe upon self-ownership rights both explains and vindicates the natural reactive attitudes that the performances elicit. Finally, at least in the case of solicitations, conscientious people often preface their solicitation with an apology, saying, for example, "Sorry to bother you, but…" before they make their request or proposal.[49] Given that an apology is apt if and only if one has wronged someone, the intuition that an apology is apt in cases of solicitation implies that the solicitor has, in fact, infringed upon a person's rights (and, presumably, her self-ownership rights).[50]

Second, one might complement this reply by suggesting that, while ASO forbids *nonconsensual* performances and solicitations, this merely entails that morally compliant performers and solicitors must seek consent before carrying out their activities. While this requirement is more restrictive than our current norms of social interaction, ASO still allows that people might permissibly carry out the acts in question without incurring serious costs,

---

[49] Apologies seem to be less common in the case of public performances; however, these are often prefaced with something proximate to a request for consent, for example, "If I could just get everyone's attention for a moment" where such a request seems apt if and only if the audience has a right against the performance being carried out.

[50] Note that even a morally conscientious person might solicit and apologize as opposed to refraining from soliciting in the first place, as there might be countervailing moral considerations that justify the rights infringement (i.e., that preclude the rights *infringement* from qualifying as a rights *violation*). For more on this point, see Section 7.4.

1.8 Is Anarchist Self-Ownership Too Restrictive? 61

thereby weakening the force of the restrictiveness objection. However, there is a serious problem with this reply: given that seeking consent is, *itself*, a form of solicitation, there is a regress problem where *P* permissibly solicits *Q* only if *P* has obtained *Q*'s consent to solicit, which, in turn, requires *P* asking *Q* for her consent, where this inquiry is permissible only if *P* has obtained *Q*'s consent to make this inquiry, which, in turn..., etc. Thus, it appears that the reply to the restrictiveness objection cannot be that ASO still allows for performances and solicitations so long as they are consensual, as the regress problem makes it impossible for performers and solicitors to obtain consent.

There are three potential responses to this problem (where one might endorse any or all of these responses). First, one might further emend ASO such that it does not give self-owners a claim against requests for consent. Unfortunately, such an emendation does not follow from the theoretical considerations that support the adoption of ASO to be discussed in Chapter 3. However, there are other justifications that one might give for permitting requests for consent depending on one's preferred theory of rights. For example, one might think that the reason for assigning persons self-ownership rights in the first place is to give them a significant degree of *control* over their lives under conditions of full compliance – that is, giving people such control is a crucial *desideratum* for a theory of rights. Assigning persons claims against bodily contact helps to satisfy this *desideratum* because such claims limit the extent to which fully compliant people can interfere with a self-owner as she directs her life. Similarly, assigning her the power to waive her claims via consent also enhances her ability to direct her life, as she can now allow desired interferences. However, one might also think that, in order to effectively direct her life, a self-owner also needs to be given the *opportunity* to consent to others' proposals. Thus, an adequate theory of rights should not assign her claims against requests for consent, as such claims would deny her this opportunity.

Second, rather than emend ASO to permit consent-seeking, one might alternatively posit an expansive theory of rights waiving. Specifically, one could hold that a self-owner waives her ASO claims not only via explicit consent but also through *hypothetical consent* – that is, her claim against some use of her body is waived if she *would* consent to this use under the appropriate conditions. There is some flexibility here in terms of how one specifies the exact conditions under which persons' rights are waived via hypothetical consent. For example, one might hold that *P*'s right against *Q* ϕ-ing is waived if and only if she (a) would consent to *Q* ϕ-ing were she simply asked if Q may ϕ, (b) would consent to Q ϕ-ing if she were fully informed about all the relevant consequences of Q ϕ-ing, and (c) has not demanded and will not demand that Q not ϕ.[51]

The theoretical motivation for this proposal would have to appeal to one's favored theory of why it is that consent renders actions permissible. For example, one might think that consent to an action expresses a pro-attitude toward that action, where it is actually the pro-attitude that negates the right. To support this latter point, one might appeal to an idea similar to the one posited in Section 1.2's quick justification for including the Lockean proviso in the anarchist position: a pro-attitude about an action nullifies a person's grounds for complaint about that action, where such grounds for complaint are a necessary condition of that action being a rights infringement. After all, if the person has a pro-attitude about the action occurring, how could she object to someone carrying out that action? However, if this is correct, then one might think that hypothetical consent implies the same sort of pro-attitude and, thus, negates a person's claims for the same reason that consent does. That said, this account is speculative and one may need to rebuild the proposed defense of hypothetical consent around some other account of why one is able to exercise the power to waive via acts of consent.

A second reason for endorsing a hypothetical consent view is that it seems to make sense of the rival intuitions presented previously. On the one hand, a street performance might seem permissible, as does asking someone for the time. On the other hand, telemarketing and catcalling seem impermissible. An advantage of the hypothetical consent theory of rights negation is that it can accommodate all of these intuitions without having to declare some ill-founded. Specifically, street performances and asking for the time are actions that people typically would consent to, while telemarketing and catcalling are not.[52] Thus, people waive their rights against the former but not the latter, rendering street performances

---

[51] These additional predicates – that is, Predicates (b) and (c) – are primarily included to help the proposed hypothetical consent theory sidestep various potential counterexamples. That said, it seems plausible that they could be independently justified by appealing to other theoretical considerations beyond the fact that they make the hypothetical consent theory more extensionally adequate.

[52] Granted not everyone would consent to some person P carrying out a street performance. However, so long as (a) there is at least one person Q who would so consent, (b) either P or Q benefits from Q hearing the performance, and (c) this benefit could not be provided in some other way that did not intrude upon other people, then P's performance uniquely generates supplemental benefit (vis-à-vis the bodily contact it makes with other people) and, thus, no one else would have a self-ownership claim against P carrying out this performance.

1.8 Is Anarchist Self-Ownership Too Restrictive? 63

and asking for the time permissible despite telemarketing and catcalling still qualifying as rights infringements. Given the explanatory power of hypothetical consent theory, there is reason to accept it as an auxiliary hypothesis supporting ASO. And, by appending this theory to the anarchist position, one can thereby avoid the objection that ASO is too restrictive, as self-owners' claims against intuitively permissible actions would typically be waived via hypothetical consent.[53]

Finally, one might solve the restrictiveness problem by proposing that, although people cannot permissibly seek consent directly from self-owners under ASO, they can establish conventions that allow self-owners to tacitly consent to being solicited and/or subjected to performances. For example, large public spaces could be designated as cooperation zones with all persons being notified that if they enter these zones, they will be taken to be consenting to solicitation and/or performance.[54] The establishment of such conventions would render ASO compatible with performances and solicitations so long as those solicitations and performances occurred when tacit consent had been given.

This proposal does raise certain questions about how people can establish conventions such that self-owners waive certain claims when their actions fall under a description specified by the convention. For example, one might ask whether anyone can establish such a convention and whether they can do so simply by declaring that some action constitutes tacit consent to some kind of treatment. In response to this question, one might note that consent is a form of communication, and communication often involves audiences declaring how they will interpret certain utterances or actions to facilitate such communication – for example, when a speaker tells an audience, "Raise your hand if you can hear me." Thus, there is no obvious reason for thinking that other people could not similarly specify which actions qualify as consent. That said, such specification will have to meet various conditions

---

[53] One problem with a theory of hypothetical consent is that it raises epistemic challenges for conscientious agents who want to avoid infringing upon others' self-ownership rights. Specifically, it seems more difficult to determine whether an agent *would* consent to something under the appropriate conditions than to determine if she *has* consented to something (though, if one takes genuine consent to imply that the consenting party is fully informed, it might also be challenging to determine whether genuine consent has been given). However, the problem of acting morally under conditions of uncertainty is not unique to hypothetical consent theory; indeed, it is a problem for all moral theories. For some detailed discussions of this problem as well as various proposed solutions, see Michael J. Zimmerman (2014) and Holly M. Smith (2018).

[54] There is a potential worry here that such notifications might, themselves, infringe upon self-owners' rights, as, in order to notify someone, one must make contact with her body (e.g., one must bombard her with sound waves or photons). Fortunately, this worry can be sidestepped if people are notified of the relevant conventions prior to their self-appropriation.

if it is to succeed. For example, if a person asserts that she will take a self-owner to consent to some treatment if the latter blinks at any point in the next twenty minutes, it does not follow that the self-owner consents to the treatment when she blinks. Seemingly, this is because one person can establish a convention for consenting only if consenters have a reasonable alternative to carrying out the act that qualifies as consent according to the convention.

This proposed constraint on the establishment of conventions raises the further question of when a person can be said to have a reasonable alternative to carrying out the action deemed to be an act of consent by the convention. Simmons proposes that the alternative to carrying out the act must be "reasonable and reasonably easily performed" and cannot inflict "extremely detrimental" consequences on the consenting party (1979, 81). However, first, this proposal is underspecified, as a supplemental account must be provided to specify which performances are "reasonably" easy and which consequences are "extremely" detrimental. More importantly, it is not clear why those establishing conventions should be able to make it such that refusing consent comes with any costs at all. Much more will be said about this point in the next chapter, but, for now, the speculative suggestion is that a convention is able to determine what counts as tacit consent if and only if the refusal of consent under that convention would not leave the consenter with less than her appropriate share of advantage as determined by a luck egalitarian theory of justice. Seemingly, so long as this fairly stringent condition is met, there is nothing problematic about persons being able to determine which acts qualify as consent. This, in turn, implies that cooperation zones could be established via convention such that those who enter those zones would thereby be consenting to others' performances and solicitations. In this way, the anarchist could maintain that ASO is not unduly restrictive, as it still allows for performances and solicitations so long as the appropriate conventions have been put into place.

In sum, there is a genuine worry that ASO is too restrictive, as it forbids actions like public performances and solicitations. Further, this problem cannot be solved by appealing to the possibility of consent-seeking, as such consent-seeking is, itself, a form of solicitation. However, this section has argued that the anarchist can both plausibly contest and accommodate this objection. She can contest it by objecting to its foundational premise that there is nothing problematic about performances and solicitations (as these activities are nuisances that render resentment, apologies, and permission-seeking apt). Additionally, she can accommodate the objection by endorsing auxiliary theories of hypothetical and/or tacit consent that allow for people to permissibly perform and solicit under the appropriate circumstances. Thus, like the permissiveness worry, the restrictiveness objection does not seem to be a decisive reason to reject ASO, even if it reveals ASO to be not quite as extensionally adequate as the anarchist might hope.

1.9 Conclusion

This chapter has introduced – and provided a preliminary defense of – the social anarchist philosophical position. Specifically, this position endorses a heterodox combination of libertarian and egalitarian moral principles, namely, the consent theory of legitimacy, the Lockean proviso, a revised self-ownership thesis, a rejection of private property, and the anarchist conclusion's thesis that persons have luck egalitarian distributive claims over unowned objects. In particular, the chapter has focused on defending the anarchist interpretation of the self-ownership thesis, in part because it is a distinctive feature of the anarchist position and, in larger part, because extended defenses of the other anarchist theses will be presented in later chapters. Additionally, these chapters will argue that these theses, despite being drawn from rival philosophical camps, stand in relations of logical entailment with one another in a way that renders the anarchist position coherent. Further, Chapter 2 will argue that the five anarchist theses can all be derived from an independently plausible meta-principle called the moral tyranny constraint.

Before turning to this discussion, however, it is worth making a general point about how one should assess the adequacy of both ASO and the anarchist position more generally. Suppose that one does not find the arguments of Sections 1.7 and 1.8 to be persuasive. In other words, suppose that one still worries that ASO is too permissive, too restrictive, or both. In response to such misgivings, it is worth emphasizing that, whatever ASO's theoretical costs, such costs need to be weighed against its many theoretical advantages. Notably, Section 1.4 has argued that ASO delivers most of the crucial implications that makes the self-ownership attractive while also solving various philosophical puzzles and sidestepping some of the major problems that plague classical accounts of self-ownership. Additionally, Chapter 3 will argue that ASO has the added advantage of being uniquely compatible with the Lockean proviso in the sense that it enables people to easily self-appropriate and thereby become self-owners. In this way, the adoption of ASO produces a novel ground for the self-ownership thesis (while simultaneously avoiding charges that ASO is an ad hoc solution to the problems discussed in Section 1.4, as discussed in Footnote 34 of that section). Thus, any assessment of ASO must be holistic such that the thesis' limitations are not considered in isolation from its advantages when determining whether it should be accepted.

Further, the assessment of ASO – and the anarchist position more broadly – should not only be holistic, but also *comparative*; that is, one must ask whether there are rival positions that are more plausible on the whole once all of their respective theoretical advantages and drawbacks have been considered. For example, while some rivals to ASO might also solve the pollution problem, it is unlikely that they will capture the other four advantages discussed in Section 1.4. And they will likely come with their own set of theoretical disadvantages that must be weighed against their comparative benefits.[55] Indeed, the difficulty of positing an extensionally adequate account of self-ownership is evinced by the challenges raised in the previous two sections: In a world where people perpetually bombard one another with particulates and photons, it will may well be impossible to assign persons rights against bodily incursion in a way that (a) adequately protects them from intuitively wrongful contact and (b) avoids the unacceptable implication that many benign and indispensable human activities are impermissible. The contention here is that while ASO may not perfectly thread this needle, one will be hard-pressed to find an alternative theory that better satisfies these two imperatives.

Of course, one might give up on self-ownership altogether. However, first, Chapter 3 will argue that there is good reason for thinking that people own themselves and, second, such a rejection of the self-ownership thesis comes with its own set of serious theoretical disadvantages. For example, as was briefly noted in Section 1.6, if one abandons the self-ownership thesis in favor of an unconstrained luck egalitarian theory of distributive justice, then one must face the objection that the theory is inadequately sensitive to the difference between people's bodies and natural resources. Specifically, if one rejects the self-ownership thesis and posits that all rights are luck egalitarian distributive rights, then one would seemingly have to deny people any special claim to their own bodies – that is, the right to use P's kidney might be equally assigned to either P or Q. The only constraint imposed by the theory would be that these rights must be assigned in such a way as to forbid acts that would leave one person worse off than another in the

---

[55] For a discussion of the problems that plague other influential attempts to solve the self-ownership thesis' pollution problem, see Zwolinski (2014).

1.9 Conclusion

absence of sanctionable choice. While it may contingently turn out that this constraint entails that each person has a right against others using her body, a more likely outcome is that there will be some cases where one person is assigned a right to use another's body without her consent – a result that many will find intuitively unacceptable. By contrast, the anarchist position avoids this result with its endorsement of ASO.

In short, moral theorizing is a messy process, with complete extensional adequacy generally proving elusive. Too often, the best apparent solution to one problem gives rise to another problem, without there being any way to satisfactorily deliver one's desired results. One should therefore not expect the anarchist position to be an exception to this general rule: While the position has many theoretical virtues, it will almost certainly have some implications that its proponents will be loath to endorse. However, this chapter has tried to demonstrate that the theoretical virtues of the position are numerous while its vices are comparatively minor – where this result both provides reason for accepting the position and supports the hypothesis that it will compare favorably to any rivals that might be posited. The purpose of the remainder of the book is to provide further argumentative support for this contention.

CHAPTER 2

The Moral Tyranny Constraint

> Tyrants: for centuries and centuries, you have sucked our blood. The tears which you have made us spill would be enough to drown you . . . . From today forward, there will not be a man who dares to make others obey him; there will not be a man who exploits the work of another man . . . . Comrades: we must complete social justice. Let us cut off the head of the hydra and take possession of all that exists for the well-being of all. Long live Land and Liberty!
> Ricardo Flores Magón, *Land and Liberty*

A recurrent theme in libertarian thought is that persons should not be allowed to discretionarily impose costs upon others. For example, in an influential polemic, William Sumner objects to publicly funded policing of vagrancy on the grounds that "the industrious workman going home from a hard day's work ... is mulcted of a percentage of his day's earnings to hire a policeman to save the drunkard from himself" (1918, 480). This objection is echoed by Ludwig von Mises' complaint that social insurance for farmers entails that "if they blunder ... the government forces the consumers, the taxpayers, and the mortgagees to foot the bill" (1998, 583). Similarly, Murray Rothbard objects to state-imposed egalitarian redistribution because "others are being forced to pay the cost" of helping the poor (1995, 53). More generally, Eric Mack argues that people must not be granted the "moral liberty to subordinate us to their purposes, that is, to impose sacrifices upon us to advance their ends" (2010, 60).[1] And Jason Brennan has recently argued that democracy is problematic because:

> [In a democracy] some people impose their decisions on others. If most voters act foolishly, they don't just hurt themselves. They hurt better-informed and more rational voters, minority voters ... and foreigners who are unable to vote

---

[1] Mack takes this requirement to follow from the twin libertarian commitments of (a) taking seriously the separateness of persons and (b) affirming that one is "allowed to live one's life in one's own chosen way" (2010, 60).

but still are subject to or harmed by that democracy's decisions .... If the majority makes a capricious decision, others have to suffer the risks." (2016, 9)

The shared presumption of these claims is that there is something objectionable about a social system that allows some people to impose costs on others, either through negligence or malicious intent. The purpose of this book is to explore the consequences of taking this presumption seriously. It will contend that those who are genuinely committed to this libertarian presumption should ultimately endorse the egalitarian variety of anarchism presented in Chapter 1. This chapter will lay the groundwork for this argument by (1) providing a formal statement of the libertarian presumption, (2) explicating that statement, (3) defending its plausibility, and (4) explaining how it both entails two of the core libertarian principles introduced in Chapter 1 and supports a luck egalitarian approach to distributive justice.

2.1 The Moral Tyranny Constraint

To begin, note that the libertarian presumption is best understood as a constraint upon which moral theories count as acceptable. If it is wrong to impose costs upon others, then a moral theory that licenses such cost imposition will be extensionally inadequate. Thus, a moral theory is acceptable only if it does not license such imposition. For these purposes, this general conditional proposition will be restated a bit more narrowly so as to make it as uncontroversial as possible. With the addition of various qualifiers, the posited constraint will be able to sidestep potential counterexamples while still delivering the promised libertarian principles and egalitarian anarchist conclusion introduced in Chapter 1. Call this restatement of the libertarian presumption the *moral tyranny constraint*:

The Moral Tyranny Constraint – A theory of duties is acceptable only if full compliance with that theory would not allow any person to unilaterally, discretionarily, and foreseeably act in a way that would leave others with less advantage than they would have possessed had the agent made some other choice.

There are quite a few qualifying terms packed into this constraint, each of which will be explicated in the subsequent section. Before discussing these details, however, it is worth clarifying the constraint by describing the two ways in which it might be violated by a moral theory. First, a theory violates the constraint if an agent is able to carry out some action that (unilaterally, discretionarily, and foreseeably) worsens another's position and the theory does not give the latter a claim to full compensation. For example, if a theory does not give persons a claim to redress for harm-inflicting actions like assault, then it would run afoul of the constraint. In other words, the constraint is violated by a theory that permits agents to carry out a set of actions that would collectively leave others worse off. Second, a theory violates the constraint if it assigns to any person P a Hohfeldian power to oblige another person Q to do some action ϕ where Q ϕ-ing would leave Q (or some third-party) worse off – for example, if it holds that P can oblige Q to destroy Q's favorite painting. While the mere imposition of the obligation would not leave Q worse off in this case, her compliance with the imposed duties would; thus, the theory violates the moral tyranny constraint.

2.2 Explicating the Constraint

This section will explicate the moral tyranny constraint's many qualifying terms, thereby helping to clarify the constraint and give it determinate content. Specifically, there are six components of the constraint that are in need of explication. First, note that the constraint only applies to theories of duties, that is, theories that assign to every action some deontic status such that the action is declared to be either permissible, impermissible, or obligatory.[2] More precisely, the constraint and the subsequent arguments of the book presume something proximate to Hohfeld's (1913) schema of deontic incidents. According to this schema, *duties* (or, alternatively, *obligations*) are taken to entail the existence of correlative *rights* (or, alternatively, *claims*) possessed by others.[3] A *permission* to do a thing (or, alternatively, a *privilege*) is possessed by a person when no one has a claim that she not do that thing; that is, all others have a correlative *no-claim* with respect to her doing that action.[4] A person possesses a *power* when she is able to alter her own or others' incidents, where the correlative of a

---

[2] Permissible actions might be further divided into those that are permissible *tout court*, those that are supererogatory (Urmson 1958), and those that are suberogatory (Driver 1992). Such theories of duties contrast with *aretaic theories*, which take the primary moral judgment to be assessments of character rather than assessments of actions.

[3] As noted in Footnote 43 of Chapter 1, there may also be *non-directed duties* that do not entail a correlative claim. In other words, people who possess these duties would still be obliged to carry out certain actions, but they would not *owe* such actions to any particular person(s). For a recent critical discussion of the directedness of duties, see Rowan Cruft (2019).

[4] Some people also call permissions "liberties"; however, others such as Thomson use the term "liberty" to refer to the conjunction of a permission to do some action and a claim against all others that they not interfere with that action (1990, 53–4). Thus, the following argument will avoid using this language and will, instead, generally use the term "permission."

2.2 Explicating the Constraint

power is a *liability*. For example, if one person is able to impose a duty on another, the former has a Hohfeldian power while the latter has a liability. Finally, when someone lacks a power to alter an incident, they have a *disability* vis-à-vis that incident, with the possessor of the protected incident having an *immunity* from having that incident negated.

Second, the moral tyranny constraint is stated in terms of diminishing others' *advantage*. "Advantage" here should be taken to have the same referent as the term "advantage" that appeared in Section 1.6; that is, it should be understood to not have any specific content but, rather, function as a placeholder for whatever one takes to be the relevant currency of distributive justice. For example, one might think that what matters is whether a person's welfare is diminished. Alternatively, one might think that the relevant question is whether she is left with fewer goods, where there is some objective list of goods. Or, perhaps, one must consider the output of some function that takes as its arguments a person's objective goods, her welfare, and/or some other property she possesses.[5] Because the argument of the book is compatible with any of these proposals, it will remain neutral regarding which one is best, with the term "advantage" referring to any favored currency of well-being. However, for the book's argument to be valid, the term must have a consistent referent throughout (i.e., it must refer to the same thing when it appears in the moral tyranny constraint as it does when it appears in the anarchist conclusion presented in Section 1.6).

Third, when the constraint asserts that agents must not be able to leave others worse off under conditions of full compliance – or, to introduce a bit of simplifying terminology leave others worse off$_{FC}$/with less$_{FC}$ – it is making a counterfactual claim rather than a temporal one. In other words, when asking whether P is able to act in a way that would leave Q worse off in the full-compliance world, the question is not whether there is some action ϕ that P can take such that the combination of her ϕ-ing and full compliance causes Q to have less advantage than she had before P ϕ-ed. Rather, the question is whether there is some alternative action ψ where (i) ψ-ing is incompossible with P ϕ-ing (e.g., ψ-ing might simply be identical to the omission of not ϕ-ing) and (ii) Q would have more advantage if P were to ψ under conditions of full compliance than she would if P were to ϕ under such conditions.

---

[5] Cohen uses the term "advantage" to refer to some combination of both welfare and resources (2011, 18). However, the term used here should not be understood to be co-referential with Cohen's notion.

The fourth point of clarification pertains to the constraint's qualification that a theory of duties must not license a person to *unilaterally* leave others worse off/with less advantage under conditions of full compliance. The "unilaterally" qualifier should be understood as follows: P unilaterally leaves Q worse off$_{FC}$ by ϕ-ing if and only if (a) Q is unable to avoid being left worse off$_{FC}$ once P has ϕ-ed and (b) Q does not consent to being left worse off in this way. To illustrate, suppose that a moral theory assigns P the power to impose a conditional obligation on Q such that P can make it obligatory that if Q ϕ-s then Q ψ-s. Further, suppose that Q would have just as much advantage if she ϕ-ed as she would if she did not ϕ, but would be left worse off if she were to ψ relative to her not ψ-ing. In this case, Condition (a) is not satisfied, as Q could discharge her obligation by simply not ϕ-ing (as making the antecedent of the conditional false renders the entire conditional true) and be no worse off as a result.[6] Similarly, if P can oblige Q to ψ – but P acquires that power only if she first receives Q's consent – then Condition (b) would not be satisfied and, thus, P would not be able to unilaterally leave Q with less$_{FC}$.

This qualification is included because there is seemingly nothing defective about a theory that permits the imposition of costs that are voluntarily accepted. Indeed, almost all rights theorists would affirm that it is permissible to impose costs upon a person if she consents to that imposition. Granted, the proposed qualification takes an expansive view of what qualifies as voluntary, as it treats a person's response to some action as implying the voluntary acceptance of the consequences of that response. Some might think that this is too permissive and insist that the analysis of "unilaterally" ought to be broadened such that the set of unilateral costs excludes only those costs that were consented to – that is, Condition (a) ought to be removed from the proposed analysis leaving only Condition (b). However, such an adjustment would make the moral tyranny constraint more stringent than it needs to be. As will be made clear in Section 2.5, the moral tyranny constraint still entails two consequential and demanding libertarian principles even assuming the original, narrower specification of what counts as "unilateral." Thus, the proposed constraint is qualified in a way that errs on the side of modesty, avoiding controversy

---

[6] Note that if not ϕ-ing were more costly to Q than ϕ-ing, then P *would* be able to unilaterally leave Q worse off$_{FC}$ by imposing the conditional obligation in question. Thus, while the moral tyranny constraint allows that P might impose conditional obligations on Q, it still imposes strict limits on which conditional obligations P can impose. Specifically, there must always be some option available to Q such that she ends up no worse off$_{FC}$ than if the obligation had not been imposed.

2.2 Explicating the Constraint

by counting more theories as acceptable rather than fewer (while still generating philosophically significant results).

Fifth, the proposition that a person *discretionarily* leaves others worse off$_{FC}$ should be understood as asserting two things. First, it asserts that there was an alternative choice that the agent could have made that would not have resulted in the person ending up worse off$_{FC}$. Second, this alternative choice has to be not merely modally available in the just-mentioned sense but also *morally* available in the sense that the agent has no duty of justice to refrain from making that choice. For example, suppose that a doctor could substantially improve a patient's life by performing an invasive medical procedure to which the patient has refused consent. If the doctor chooses not to perform the procedure, she will leave the patient with worse off$_{FC}$ than if the procedure were performed. However, there is seemingly nothing problematic about a moral theory that countenances this result – that is, that denies that the patient has any claim to compensation. This is because the doctor is simply doing what she *has* to do when she chooses not to carry out the procedure (in the normative sense of "has"). Thus, a theory only seems intuitively unacceptable when it licenses people to act in non-obligatory, cost-imposing$_{FC}$ ways.[7]

Finally, a moral theory only seems unacceptable if it countenances people *foreseeably* leaving others worse off$_{FC}$. For example, consider the case of a hiker who falls into an abandoned well due to the mouth being hidden by moss and leaves. A moral theory that assigns a bystander an obligation to rescue the hiker – where the rescue would be moderately costly to the bystander – does not seem obviously defective. By contrast, if the theory obliged the bystander to rescue a spelunker who decided to

---

[7] This case draws attention to the fact that the moral tyranny constraint *must* include the "discretionarily" qualifier lest it entail that there are conflicting duties in any case where an obligatory action does not maximize others' advantage. To see why, consider the general case where Q has a claim that P ϕ, where P ϕ-ing leaves Q with less advantage than if P did not ϕ. What happens if P ϕ-s? If the moral theory in question does not assign Q some sort of claim to compensation from P, then it would violate the moral tyranny constraint, as P's ϕ-ing would leave Q worse off$_{FC}$ (as full compliance will not offset Q's lost advantage). Thus, Q must have a claim to compensation if P ϕ-s. But what would ground such a claim given that P is merely discharging her duty to Q by ϕ-ing? Seemingly, Q has a claim to compensation only if P's ϕ-ing infringed on some claim of Q's that P not ϕ; that is, P has both a duty to ϕ and a duty to refrain from ϕ-ing. While such a conflict of rights is not a logical contradiction, it is an undesirable thing for a theory of duties to affirm. It would therefore be a significant problem if the moral tyranny constraint entailed that there was a conflict of duties in any case where someone was obliged to act in a way that did not maximize others' advantage. Thus, the "discretionarily" qualifier must be included in the constraint to avoid this implication.

explore the well despite knowing the risks involved, that would seem to be a clear instance of extensional inadequacy. Given that this apparent difference is best explained by the unforeseeability of the former outcome, the moral tyranny constraint must be qualified such that it only rules out theories that license people foreseeably leaving others worse off$_{FC}$.

When a moral theory meets all of the aforementioned conditions – that is, when it affirms that a person can unilaterally and discretionarily act in a way that leaves others foreseeably worse off$_{FC}$ – it seemingly institutes an unacceptable sort of moral tyranny. The hallmark of a tyrant is that she is able to impose discretionary costs on her subjects without any sort of legal restraint. Analogously, a theory that violates the moral tyranny constraint allows people to willfully diminish others' well-being without any sort of normative restraint. It is the licensing of such behavior that the libertarians cited in this chapter's opening paragraph seemingly find so objectionable. Each of their quoted complaints represents an objection to legal systems that license the imposition of costs on others, where such objections seemingly entail a correlative objection to any theory of duties that licenses cost-imposing actions. Thus, the moral tyranny constraint can be understood as giving more precise expression to this persistent libertarian complaint.

2.3 Defending the Constraint

The introduction of this chapter noted that numerous libertarians presume something proximate to the moral tyranny constraint. This section will provide an argument in defense of this libertarian presumption. Specifically, it will present three reasons for accepting the moral tyranny constraint that will appeal to both libertarians and non-libertarians alike. It thereby aims to show that the moral tyranny constraint is an attractive and independently plausible meta-principle.

First, the constraint can be seen as following from the *separateness of persons argument* that liberals advance against utilitarianism.[8] Utilitarians hold that a cost can be permissibly imposed upon one person if the imposition of that cost is a necessary and sufficient condition for providing greater benefit to another. In support of this claim, utilitarians will often present something like the following *argument from prudential choice*. They begin by noting that humans regularly impose costs upon themselves for

---

[8] Notably, versions of this argument have been presented by both John Rawls (1971, 26–7) and Nozick (1974, 32–4), though the two draw very different conclusions about what follows from the separateness of persons (beyond the negation of utilitarianism).

2.3 Defending the Constraint

the sake of obtaining greater benefits in the future – a practice that seems not only morally unproblematic but rationally demanded. Further, they maintain that if there is nothing problematic about a person imposing costs upon herself for greater future benefit, then there is nothing problematic about imposing costs on one person to provide greater benefit to another. Thus, utilitarians conclude that there is nothing problematic about sacrificing one person's well-being for the sake of providing greater benefit to another.[9]

The aforementioned separateness of persons argument is best understood as an objection to this argument from prudential choice. Specifically, it is an objection to the second premise of the utilitarian's argument – that is, the premise that, if it is permissible for a person to impose costs on herself for greater future benefit, then it is permissible to impose costs on one person in order to provide greater benefit to another. The fact that persons are separate rather than some unified social creature renders this inference implausible. The separateness of persons objection points out that there is a crucial disanalogy between prudential sacrifice and utilitarian sacrifice that prevents the permissibility of the former from implying the permissibility of the latter.[10]

---

[9] J. J. C. Smart makes this argument explicitly in reply to Rawls' (1958) suggestion that there is something unfair about imposing costs on some to maximize overall utility:

> [I]f it is rational for me to choose the pain of a visit to the dentist in order to prevent the pain of toothache, why is it not rational of me to choose pain for Jones, similar to that of my visit to the dentist, if that is the only way in which I can prevent a pain, equal to that of my toothache, for Robinson?
>
> (Smart and Williams, 1973, 37)

[10] This way of explicating the separateness of persons argument heads off a potential reply suggested by Mack (2018) in his elaboration of Nozick's version of the argument. Mack posits that the utilitarian might argue that the reason that a person can permissibly impose costs on herself for future benefits is that one ought to maximize utility. As he puts it, "we start with the unrestricted rationality of minimizing costs (or maximizing benefits); and the principle of individual choice is simply the application of that principle of social choice to the special case in which there is only one agent" (2018, §2.2). However, given the chapter's proposed interpretation of the separateness of persons argument, this reply would beg the question, as the general principle that one ought to maximize benefits irrespective of whether there is one person or many is the proposition that has to be demonstrated. Thus, it cannot be assumed as a starting premise.

An additional advantage of stating the argument in this way is that it allows the appeal to separateness of persons to qualify as a supporting argument for liberal deontological positions (as opposed to a mere restatement of those positions). A common tendency in the recent literature is to treat the proposition that persons are separate as merely an alternative way of expressing some other deontological commitment such as the thesis that persons are owed respect and, thus, cannot be treated as a mere means (Zwolinski 2008, 150–2) or the contention that persons have moral authority over their own lives that trumps moral reasons to promote the common good (Mazor 2019, 192–3). However, such an approach strips the separateness of persons argument of its dialectical force. In the debate between utilitarians and deontologists, the former assert that you ought to maximize utility even if that requires treating someone as a mere means or denying her

Proponents of the separateness of persons argument conclude that one cannot permissibly impose costs on some people to benefit others. Admittedly, this conclusion does not strictly follow from the separateness of persons argument, as the utilitarian's conclusion might still be true even if the separateness of persons objection renders her argument from prudential choice unsound. However, one might think that the argument from prudential choice is the only plausible way of justifying something that is *prima facie* unjustified. Thus, if that argument fails due to the separateness of persons objection, then it follows that it is not permissible to sacrifice some to benefit others.

If one accepts this conclusion, then one should also endorse the moral tyranny constraint. Notably, the objection's conclusion condemns utilitarian sacrifice even given the fact that the provision of benefit is at least a plausible candidate for justifying cost imposition. By contrast, there will be many cases of discretionary cost imposition where this is no countervailing moral consideration that might justify the imposed cost. Given that utility-maximizing cost imposition is not permissible even given countervailing moral considerations, it seemingly follows from the separateness of persons argument that discretionary cost imposition (which lacks this justificatory advantage) is also impermissible.

Compare this result with the moral tyranny constraint, which holds that it is not permissible to unilaterally, foreseeably, and discretionarily impose costs$_{FC}$ on a person. The crucial difference between this claim and the conclusion of the separateness of persons argument is that the latter condemns the imposition of actual-world discretionary costs while the former condemns the imposition of full-compliance-world discretionary costs. However, those who hold that it is impermissible to impose actual-world costs are seemingly committed to affirming that it is impermissible to impose full-compliance-world costs. To see why, consider the following case: if P ϕ-s, she leaves Q worse off; by contrast, if P ψ-s, she does not leave Q worse off but *does* leave her worse off$_{FC}$. Further, assume that both actions are discretionary. According to the conclusion of the separateness of persons argument, P's ϕ-ing would be impermissible because it imposes

---

moral authority over how her life goes; by contrast, deontologists assert that you ought not maximize utility under such circumstances. If affirming the separateness of persons merely expresses the proposition that one ought not treat persons as a means and/or individuals' moral authority trumps promoting the common good, then it merely reasserts the deontological position rather than providing a reason for favoring that position over the utilitarian one. By contrast, the proposed separateness of persons argument does provide such a reason.

a cost on Q – where ϕ-ing imposes a cost on Q if and only if Q's loss of advantage is a direct function of P ϕ-ing. In other words, had P not ϕ-ed, then Q would not have lost advantage and *for this reason* P's ϕ-ing is impermissible.

Now, consider the world where P ψ-s and everyone complies with their moral requirements. In such a world, P's action stands in an identical counterfactual relation to Q's loss of advantage. Thus, one might conclude that P's ψ-ing is also impermissible. However, this would be a mistake, as it is actually P's ψ-ing *conjoined* with certain acts of compliance that lead to Q being worse off; absent such compliance, P ψ-ing would not leave Q worse off relative to the world where P does not ψ. In other words, the appropriate conclusion to draw is that *the conjunction of P ψ-ing and the acts of compliance* is impermissible. Given that P ϕ-ing is impermissible because Q's worsened position is a direct function of P ϕ-ing, the fact that Q's worsened position is also a direct function of P ψ-ing plus others' acts of compliance entails the impermissibility of that set of actions.[11] This, in turn, implies that if these other acts are all permissible, then P ψ-ing is impermissible. Further, note that the world of full compliance is, by definition, a world where all other persons act *permissibly*. Thus, it must be the case that P ψ-ing is impermissible. In other words, if one accepts the conclusion of the separateness of persons argument – that is, that it is impermissible to discretionarily leave others worse off – then one should also accept the moral tyranny constraint's implication that it is impermissible to discretionarily leave others worse off$_{FC}$.

A second reason for endorsing the moral tyranny constraint is that it is a less demanding – and, thus, less controversial – version of the popular neo-republican rejection of domination advanced by Philip Pettit (2012). Pettit contends that there is something morally objectionable about a state of affairs where one person has the ability to limit another's freedom by removing one of her options. He suggests that the presence of such

---

[11] One might worry that this argument departs from some of the previous discussion by putting deontic propositions in impersonal terms – that is, there is some action-including state of affairs that is obligatory/permissible – rather than in agential terms such that some agent is said to be obliged/permitted to do a thing. However, first, one could seemingly frame the entire argument of the book in impersonal terms without issue. Any inconsistency in deontic language merely reflects localized stylistic choices that aid in exposition. Alternatively, one might take there to be some way of bridging the agential-impersonal gap, for example, by holding that a person is obliged to act in some way if and only it is obligatory that the person act in that way. This presumption is proximate to what has become known as the "Meinong-Chisholm Reduction" after two early proponents of this view (namely, Alexius Meinong (1972) and Roderick M. Chisholm (1964)). However, this view is not without critics (see, e.g., Jacob Ross (2010)).

domination undermines egalitarian relations between persons, precluding their ability to "look others in the eye without ... fear or deference that a power of interference might inspire; [to] walk tall and assume the public status ... of being equal" (2012, 84). Additionally, beyond this relational egalitarian concern, the objection to domination might be viewed as a natural extension of a more primitive concern with freedom, where the restriction of freedom – and, more strongly, people having the ability to restrict others' freedom – is taken to be objectionable.

To see why the moral tyranny constraint is a weaker version of the republican thesis, it will be helpful to restate the latter in deontic terms. Specifically, a Pettit-influenced republican holds that it is impermissible to realize or preserve a state of affairs where one person has the ability to remove options from another's option set. By contrast, the moral tyranny constraint limits which options it is permissible to remove. Specifically, it entails that an agent is forbidden from carrying out a conjunction of actions that would remove advantage-preserving$_{FC}$ options such that someone is left worse off$_{FC}$. For example, if (a) P ϕ-ing and then ψ-ing would leave Q worse off$_{FC}$ and (b) P ϕ-s, then the moral tyranny constraint would imply that it is impermissible for P to ψ; that is, the moral tyranny constraint implies that it is impermissible for P to remove an option from Q's option set by ψ-ing (namely, the option where Q does her most-preferred action and Q does not ψ). This makes the moral tyranny constraint weaker than the standard republican position in two respects. First, it merely forbids *option removal* rather than forbidding people from having the *capacity* to remove options (where someone lacking the capacity to remove an option entails that they will not remove that option but where the converse of this conditional is false). Second, the republican thesis is concerned with the removal of all options while the moral tyranny constraint forbids only the removal of advantage-preserving$_{FC}$ options, which are a proper subset of all options.[12] Thus, the satisfaction of the republican principle will entail the satisfaction of the moral tyranny constraint but not vice versa. Given this relation, republicans critical of domination should also accept the moral tyranny constraint both because it seems to capture some of the motivating concerns expressed in the previous paragraph and because there is no reason to reject a principle

---

[12] It is assumed here that changing the moral status of some option via the imposition of an obligation also counts as option removal. For example, if P obliges Q to stay out of the park after midnight, P removes an option from Q, namely, the option of going in the park after midnight while discharging her duties. In other words, options are assumed to be individuated in a fairly fine-grained fashion such that actions with different deontic statuses represent different options.

2.3 Defending the Constraint

that is fully satisfied if one's own principle is satisfied. Additionally, because the moral tyranny constraint is less stringent than the standard republican position, it is vulnerable to fewer objections (e.g., that there are cases where having a mere *capacity* to remove some arbitrary option is morally unproblematic).

Finally, one ought to accept the moral tyranny constraint because it would be the result of a process of reflective equilibrium. Most famously championed by John Rawls (1971), the practice of reflective equilibrium involves rendering one's set of normative beliefs coherent, where this set includes one's particular moral judgments, the general moral principles that support those judgments, and the theoretical *desiderata* (i.e., meta-principles) that determine which principles are acceptable. As noted in Section I.2, coherence is an important theoretical virtue of any given normative position, where genuine coherence requires that relations of logical entailment obtain between that position's various propositions. In other words, if one embraces the method of reflective equilibrium – with the associated presupposition that coherence is a theoretical virtue – then one has reason to accept moral principles that entail a large number of one's accepted particular moral judgments or moral principles. Similarly, one has reason to accept those theoretical *desiderata* that entail a large number of one's accepted general principles.

In further defense of accepting theoretical *desiderata* (or moral theories) because they entail many accepted moral theories (or particular judgments), one might draw an analogy between the virtues of normative theories and the virtues of scientific theories. Philosophers of science typically maintain that explanatory power is a virtue of scientific theories: One has more reason to accept a theory that explains a large number of observed phenomena than one that explains fewer, *ceteris paribus*.[13] Analogously, one might think that general normative principles (theoretical *desiderata*) stand in an explanatory relation to particular moral judgments (general moral principles).[14] Together, these claims would entail that one has reason to accept a moral principle (theoretical *desideratum*) in proportion to the number of accepted particular judgments (moral principles) it entails.

If this is right, then there is further reason for accepting the moral tyranny constraint, as it entails a number of influential moral principles.

---

[13] For a defense of this point, see Bas van Fraassen (1980, 98).
[14] For a sustained argument that normative theories are, in important ways, analogous to scientific explanations, see Jesse Spafford (2021a).

Specifically, the next section will argue that the Lockean proviso, the consent theory of legitimacy, and luck egalitarianism's incorporation of responsibility all follow from the moral tyranny constraint.[15] It will thereby show that the moral tyranny constraint has both significant explanatory power – that is, it explains why these various principles obtain – and helps to establish the coherence of a number of attractive views. This makes the moral tyranny constraint a strong candidate theoretical *desideratum* to include in any reflective equilibrium.

In sum, there are a number of reasons for adopting the moral tyranny constraint. Two are foundationalist in the sense that the reason for accepting the constraint is that it follows from some other plausible position, for example, the separateness of persons argument or the republican critique of domination. The third is coherentist in the sense that the reason for accepting the moral tyranny constraint is that the constraint entails – and thereby helps to explain – various other attractive positions (as will be discussed in the subsequent section). Thus, irrespective of which sort of justification one favors, one has reason to endorse the moral tyranny constraint.

2.4 Three Implications of the Constraint

This section will argue that three of the positions introduced in Chapter 1 – namely, the consent theory of legitimacy, the Lockean proviso, and luck

---

[15] Additionally, note that the various claims advanced in the opening paragraph of this chapter also follow from the constraint. For example, von Mises (1998) can be understood as denying that social insurance for farmers is just, as that entails that farmers who make imprudent decisions are *entitled* to the transfers they receive and, thus, can leave others worse off$_{FC}$ when they make such decisions. Similar remarks apply to Brennan's (2016) objection to democracy. If democracy were a just system of government, then hooligans who vote for dangerous policies would have a *right* that those policies be implemented. This, in turn, would imply that these hooligans could, by assembling a simple majority, leave others worse off$_{FC}$. In both cases, the solution is to propose a moral theory that does not license some people to impose costs$_{FC}$ upon others. While this does not stop imprudent farmers or hooligan voters from leaving others worse off as a matter of empirical fact, it does prevent them from leaving others worse off$_{FC}$, which is all that the moral tyranny constraint requires (and all that should really concern those doing normative theorizing). Admittedly, it is unlikely that non-libertarians will find Brennan's or von Mises' positions attractive. For such skeptics, the fact that the moral tyranny constraint entails a rejection of democracy or social insurance will count *against* including the constraint in the ultimate reflective equilibrium. However, any coherent normative position will likely entail some unfortunate conclusions; thus, the question is whether its desirable implications outweigh the undesirable ones and how this net assessment compares to the assessment of other rival positions. The hope is that non-libertarians will find the implications discussed in the subsequent section to be more attractive (particularly the luck egalitarian implication) to the point where they might be willing to accept the moral tyranny constraint even if that means that they have to accept some of its less attractive implications as a consequence.

2.4 Three Implications of the Constraint

egalitarianism's responsibility component – follow from the moral tyranny constraint. To begin, consider the consent theory of legitimacy's assertion that a state or person can impose obligations on others (if and) only if the latter have consented to being morally bound in this way. While there have been many arguments presented in defense of this position (see, e.g., Simmons 2001), it also follows from the moral tyranny constraint's contention that moral theories cannot license persons to unilaterally, discretionarily, and foreseeably leave others worse off$_{FC}$. Recall from Section 2.1 that one way in which a person might leave others worse off$_{FC}$ is by imposing obligations on them that would be costly to discharge. Thus, the constraint entails that any power to impose such obligations must be restricted such that the imposition cannot be carried out foreseeably, discretionarily, and unilaterally.

This result entails that the moral tyranny constraint is incompatible with any theory of legitimacy that does not have consent as its necessary condition. As noted in Section 1.1, a legitimate authority has the power to oblige others via the issuing of edicts, where this power is *content independent* in the sense that the authority can oblige others to act in some way irrespective of the properties of that act (with the possible exception of the act being morally prohibited). Thus, a legitimate authority has the power to impose obligations irrespective of whether or not the obligor would be worse off if she discharged the obligation; that is, she has the ability to leave others worse off$_{FC}$. Further, there is seemingly no way to either eliminate the discretionary character of legitimacy or make it such that legitimate authorities can impose only those obligations that do not foreseeably leave others worse off$_{FC}$. Note that the latter restriction would negate the content-independent character of legitimacy: The proposition that an agent can impose only those obligations that do not foreseeably leave obligors worse off$_{FC}$ is just the kind of content-based restriction that legitimacy lacks as a matter of definition. Similarly, limiting legitimacy such that it becomes a power to *non-discretionarily* impose costly obligations (i.e., impose such obligations only when there is no other permissible option available) strips the power of its essential character. While perhaps there may be such a power, it would only loosely resemble the power that is at issue when philosophers debate whether states are legitimate.

Given that legitimate authorities necessarily have the power to discretionarily and foreseeably impose costly obligations on others, there is only one way to make the power of legitimacy compatible with the moral tyranny constraint: Make others' consent a necessary condition for legitimacy obtaining. If consent is a necessary condition of legitimacy, then legitimate authorities cannot *unilaterally* impose costly obligations on others, as those others will be able to fully control whether the authority leaves them worse off$_{FC}$. By contrast, the absence of this necessary condition entails that legitimate authorities can unilaterally, foreseeably, and discretionarily leave others worse off$_{FC}$.[16] Thus, the moral tyranny constraint entails the consent theory of legitimacy.[17]

A similar argument can be given for why the Lockean proviso – or, more precisely, its posited necessary condition of initial appropriation – follows from the moral tyranny constraint.[18] Note that, much like legitimate authorities, those who appropriate natural resources and convert them into private property impose obligations on others (namely, obligations to refrain from using or making nonconsensual contact with the appropriated thing).[19] Thus, the moral tyranny constraint entails that one must posit some necessary condition of initial appropriation to preclude appropriators from unilaterally, discretionarily, and foreseeably leaving others worse off$_{FC}$ via this obligation imposition. One option is to adopt the consent theorist's approach and make consent a necessary condition of appropriation, thereby precluding appropriators from *unilaterally* leaving others worse off$_{FC}$. However, almost all proponents of initial appropriation reject this option on the grounds that it is too stringent. Given the difficulties of

---

[16] As noted in Section 2.2, it is possible to nonconsensually and non-unilaterally impose costly obligations on others if those obligations have the right sort of conditional structure. However, an authority whose normative power is limited to imposing such obligations cannot qualify as a *legitimate* authority, as such a restriction contradicts the content independence that is an essential characteristic of legitimacy. Only consent can render content-independent obligation imposition non-unilateral.

[17] This is a slight overstatement of what has been demonstrated. Strictly speaking, there is a stronger and weaker version of consent theory, where the former holds that consent is a necessary *and sufficient* condition of legitimacy while the latter holds that it is merely a necessary condition. The preceding argument shows only that the weak version of consent theory follows from the moral tyranny constraint. One might thereby endorse both the moral tyranny constraint and hold that even consent does not allow authorities to impose obligations on others via edict (perhaps for reasons such as those advanced by Robert Paul Wolff (1970)). However, insofar as one takes consent to be a promising ground for obligation imposition (e.g., in the case of promissory obligations), then one should take consent to be a sufficient condition of legitimacy – and, thus, accept the strong version of consent theory in light of the moral tyranny constraint's implication that consent is also a necessary condition of legitimacy. For a quick argument along these lines against Wolff's position, see Simmons (1987, 269fn2).

[18] Note that there are also stronger and weaker versions of the proviso analogous to the stronger and weaker versions of consent theory discussed in the previous footnote. And, just as was true of consent theory, the moral tyranny constraint implies only the weaker version of the proviso that makes non-worsening a necessary – but not sufficient – condition of successfully appropriating unowned resources.

[19] Much more will be said about the relationship between legitimacy and initial appropriation in Chapter 4.

2.4 Three Implications of the Constraint

obtaining universal consent, this standard would unacceptably preclude the establishment of any private property.[20] Thus, a less controversial way to satisfy the moral tyranny constraint is to permit unilateral appropriation but hold that such appropriation cannot leave others worse off$_{FC}$ – that is, affirm Chapter 1's interpretation of the Lockean proviso.

As was noted in Section 2.2 of that chapter, the Lockean proviso is typically presented as asserting that an act of initial appropriation succeeds if and only if it does not leave anyone worse off *tout court*. However, it was argued there that this interpretation of the proviso is unacceptable because it is trivially satisfied by every act of appropriation. Thus, the section concluded that the proviso is better understood as asserting that it is *full compliance with the established claims* that must not leave others worse off (where this thesis can now be stated using the "worse off$_{FC}$" shorthand presented earlier). What is now hopefully apparent is that this adjustment makes the proviso an application of moral tyranny constraint to the appropriation of private property: The constraint insists that moral theories cannot allow persons to leave each other worse off$_{FC}$, and the proviso makes it such that the posited theory of property rights complies with this restriction.

Further, one can now see that the moral tyranny constraint also entails the final adjustment that Section 1.2 made to the Lockean proviso. The proposal there was that it is not just appropriators' established claims that must not leave others worse off$_{FC}$; rather, any potential waiving of the established claims must also not leave others worse off$_{FC}$. The justification for this adjustment appealed to a premise about arbitrariness: Given that the power to establish property claims is constrained by a non-worsening condition, it seems unacceptably arbitrary to not impose this same constraint on the power to waive these claims. However, now that the moral tyranny constraint has been introduced, the appeal to arbitrariness is no longer needed, as the constraint directly entails that people cannot have any normative power that enables them to leave others worse off$_{FC}$. Given that initial appropriation entails the existence of powers to waive the established claims, it follows that initial appropriation can succeed only if any subsequent exercise of these powers would not leave anyone worse

---

[20] See van der Vossen (2019, § 3) and Mack (2010). For an early and influential rejection of consent as a necessary condition of appropriation, see Locke (2005, §28). That said, Chapter 4 will raise some complications for those who want to reject consent as a necessary condition of appropriation without accepting the broader moral tyranny framework presented in this book.

off$_{FC}$. In this way, the moral tyranny constraint entails the revised Lockean proviso presented in Section 1.2.[21]

So far it has been argued that two prominent libertarian theses follow from the moral tyranny constraint: the consent theory of legitimacy and the (slightly adjusted) Lockean proviso. However, there are also influential non-libertarian positions that follow from the moral tyranny constraint. Most notably, luck egalitarianism presupposes the constraint, as the primary reason for accepting the luck egalitarian position over strict egalitarianism is that the latter allows for moral tyranny in a way that the former does not. Recall from Section 1.6 that the signature feature of luck egalitarianism is its incorporation of responsibility into an otherwise strict egalitarian theory of justice. There it was noted that strict egalitarian theories are, by definition, insensitive to responsibility, demanding an equal distribution of advantage regardless of anyone's past actions. By contrast, luck egalitarians are willing to declare certain inequalities just if and only if those inequalities correspond to some sanctionable choice for which the worse-off parties are responsible. And, as it turns out, there is good reason for moderating strict egalitarianism in this way: Absent this responsibility condition, strict egalitarianism is vulnerable to a species of *reductio* argument that renders the position implausible. Consider, for example, how a principle that demands strict equality of advantage would handle the case of a spiteful person who maliciously destroys any advantage she receives. In this case, a strict egalitarian would demand that advantage continually be reallocated to this person such that her share remains as great as everyone else's – a demand that is sustained even as she destroys each bit of advantage that is transferred to her until, eventually, no one has any advantage left to transfer. This result is an apparent *reductio* of strict egalitarianism.

Other examples popularly cited by luck egalitarians can be substituted into the *reductio* to reach the same conclusion. For example, consider Cohen's Aesopian case of the ant who assiduously works all summer storing up food while a neighboring grasshopper lounges idly – a decision the grasshopper makes even while recognizing that she will end up worse off when winter comes (2008, 27–8). In this case, a strict egalitarian

---

[21] If the foregoing argument is correct and both the consent theory of legitimacy and the Lockean proviso follow from the moral tyranny constraint, this would reveal a little-discussed coherence in Locke's *Second Treatise on Civil Government*, which endorses both positions. Similar remarks apply to Nozick's *Anarchy, State, and Utopia*, as he defends both the Lockean proviso (1974, 178) and, in the first section of the book, something proximate to a consent theory of legitimacy, though he is not entirely consistent on this point (see Simmons 2005, 334–6).

2.4 Three Implications of the Constraint

principle of justice would demand that the ant redistribute some of her food to the grasshopper; however, there is something seemingly unfair about the ant having to make do with less because of the grasshopper's choice not to work. Thus, insofar as justice is supposed to track fairness, a strict egalitarian principle must be rejected, as it declares an unfair outcome just.[22]

Why would redistribution in these cases be unfair? Cohen has suggested that such redistribution is a form of exploitation (e.g., of the assiduous ant), where exploitation runs contrary to egalitarianism (Cohen 2011, 8). However, as Michael Otsuka notes, it is unclear in what respect such exploitation can be *inegalitarian* given that the redistribution is equalizing by definition (Otsuka 2010, 223). Rather, Otsuka plausibly argues that what is unfair about such redistribution is that it forces some people to "pick up the tab" for the poor choices of others (2010, 229).

While Otsuka does not provide any analysis of what it means for someone to "pick up the tab" for someone else's choices, a natural way of specifying this notion is in terms of the moral tyranny constraint: A person has to pick up the tab for another's actions when the latter foreseeably, discretionarily, and unilaterally leaves her worse off$_{FC}$. Indeed, this specification explains why strict egalitarianism's prescriptions in the spiteful destroyer and lazy grasshopper cases seem intuitively unacceptable. In both cases, a strict egalitarian theory of justice licenses one party to leave others with less advantage in the counterfactual world where everyone complies with the demands of morality. Note that the spiteful destroyer and grasshopper might not, as a matter of empirical fact, leave others with less, as those others might refuse to transfer any of their advantage-producing resources. Rather, both the spiteful destroyer and the grasshopper strip others of a claim to advantage according to the strict egalitarian theory – while simultaneously acquiring a claim to that stripped advantage – such that others *would* transfer resources to these parties if the former were to fully comply with the latter's claims. Thus, the worry that motivates luck egalitarianism is that there is something problematic about a theory that allows people to leave others worse off$_{FC}$.

As noted in Section 1.6, the luck egalitarian solution to this problem is to *hold people responsible* for making *sanctionable choices*, where a theory

---

[22] For similar motivating cases, see Kymlicka (2002, 73) and Stemplowska (2009, 241, 252–3). Note that such cases seem to count against Segall's (2016) thesis that there is nothing morally objectionable about any equal state of affairs. Contra Segall, the luck egalitarian theory posited by this paper will entail that equal distributions generated by sanctionable choice are unjust. Any theory that does not have this implication will problematically allow for moral tyranny.

holds someone responsible for a choice if and only if it maintains that she forfeits a claim to some quantity of advantage in virtue of that choice. By holding people responsible for their choices, luck egalitarianism is able to avoid granting the spiteful destroyer (or grasshopper) the Hohfeldian power to discretionarily, unilaterally, and foreseeably acquire a claim to others' holdings, thereby leaving them with less$_{FC}$. According to strict egalitarianism, when the spiteful destroyer diminishes her own advantage, she acquires a claim against others that they make equalizing transfers to her. By contrast, luck egalitarianism treats her act of destruction as a sanctionable choice in virtue of which she forfeits a claim to advantage. Specifically, there is some quantity of advantage A such that the conjunction of the destroyer having a claim to A and her act of destruction entails that others are obliged to give her some of their holdings. Luck egalitarianism holds that the destroyer forfeits her claim to A in virtue of her act of destruction, thereby precluding her from acquiring a claim to others making equalizing transfers. This, in turn, implies that fully compliant people would not make any transfers to the spiteful destroyer and, thus, no one else ends up with less$_{FC}$ as a result of her actions. Luck egalitarianism thereby satisfies the moral tyranny constraint in a way that strict egalitarianism does not – which is to say that the constraint entails that an egalitarian theory must include a responsibility component.[23]

Note that the foregoing discussion does not demonstrate that the moral tyranny constraint entails luck egalitarianism. Rather, it entails that egalitarians must endorse the luck egalitarian incorporation of responsibility, that is, the proposition that inequality is just if the worse-off party has chosen sanctionably (more on this in Chapter 6). What it does not entail is the luck egalitarian presumption that persons are entitled to equal shares of advantage absent such sanctionable choice. In other words, unlike the consent theory of legitimacy and the Lockean proviso – each of which merely constrains the kinds of claims and correlative obligations that persons can establish given any arbitrary initial set of claims/obligations – luck egalitarianism also asserts that persons start out with a claim to an equal share of advantage. Chapter 5 will argue that this thesis also

---

[23] This conclusion helps to elucidate Cohen's famous assertion that luck egalitarianism incorporates "within it the most powerful idea in the arsenal of the antiegalitarian Right: the idea of choice and responsibility" (2011, 32). Specifically, the moral tyranny constraint is the foundational principle of the "antiegalitarian Right" as it both entails core theses endorsed by right-libertarians and entails the unacceptability of strict egalitarianism. Luck egalitarianism then incorporates the constraint by ensuring that it is satisfied while still articulating a highly demanding form of egalitarianism (i.e., a position that entails that a large portion of existing inequality is unjust).

ultimately follows from a libertarian *desideratum* for moral theories (albeit not the moral tyranny constraint). For now, though, the argument will pause at the conclusion that the responsibility component of luck egalitarianism follows from the moral tyranny constraint. Such a result is seemingly sufficient for establishing the point that the constraint entails a number of influential and attractive philosophical theses and, thus, ought to be included as part of one's ultimate reflective equilibrium.[24]

2.5 Three Objections to the Constraint

Having discussed some reasons for accepting the moral tyranny constraint, it is worth addressing three objections that might be raised against this meta-principle. The *stringency objection* posits that the moral tyranny constraint is implausible because the constraint entails that persons have a number of excessively demanding duties. For example, suppose that P would have married Q but for the fact that Q fell in love with R and got married to R instead. In this case, Q's choice to marry R seemingly leaves P worse off$_{FC}$ than she would have been otherwise. Thus, according to the moral tyranny constraint, a moral theory is acceptable only if it does not license Q's choice to marry R rather than P, where this might be taken to require assigning Q a duty to marry P. However, given that no acceptable theory will restrict Q's moral freedom in this way, a contradiction is reached. Similarly, T might leave S worse off$_{FC}$ by opening a rival business that drives down S's profits. Here, again, one might worry that the moral tyranny constraint unacceptably entails that T has a duty to refrain from competing with S. If the constraint restricts persons' moral freedom in this way, it must seemingly be rejected despite its virtues (as described in Section 2.3).

Alternatively, one might raise a *laxity objection* against the constraint. According to this objection, the constraint entails that persons do not acquire duties in cases where an adequate moral theory would assign them such duties. Consider, for example, the case where A and B are standing on

---

[24] An additional advantage of the moral tyranny constraint is that it precludes certain varieties of moral blackmail. For example, Johan E. Gustafsson (2022) notes that a committed act utilitarian (or rule utilitarian) can be successfully extorted if other agents commit to bringing about a non-utility-maximizing outcome if and only if the utilitarian does not give them money. As Gustafsson notes, "A plausible moral theory shouldn't lay one open to that kind of exploitation" (2022, 388) and the moral tyranny constraint formalizes this contention: Utilitarianism is defective because a moral theory should not allow would-be extorters to unilaterally, foreseeably, and discretionarily leave others worse off under conditions of full compliance.

the shore of a pond where a child is drowning. Assume that B (and not A) has an obligation to rescue the child, as B is better positioned to carry out the rescue and could do so costlessly while A would incur a modest cost if she were to rescue the child. Further, suppose that B refuses to assist the drowning child. Given B's refusal to assist, it seems that A acquires a remedial duty to rescue the child. However, the acquisition of such a duty would violate the moral tyranny constraint, as B would have thereby left A worse off$_{FC}$ with her choice not to rescue. Thus, the moral tyranny constraint appears to deliver the wrong results in this case.

The reply to the first objection begins with the observation that, for any given action ϕ, the moral tyranny constraint does not imply that a moral theory must declare ϕ-ing to be either permissible or impermissible. Rather, it implies that the moral theory's *entire set of posited claims* must adjust in response to an agent ϕ-ing such that no other person ends up worse off$_{FC}$ than she would have been had the agent not ϕ-ed. Thus, the constraint does not entail that Q has a duty to marry P; rather, it entails that any loss$_{FC}$ of advantage that P incurs in virtue of not marrying Q must be offset by some other advantage-conferring$_{FC}$ rights assigned by the theory (where P would not be assigned these rights if she married Q). By assigning rights in this way, the posited theory of duties avoids moral tyranny by precluding Q from leaving P worse off$_{FC}$ via her choice to marry R – and, crucially, it achieves this without assigning Q a duty to marry P. Similarly, the constraint does not entail that T has a duty to refrain from competing with S's business; rather, it mandates that the theory of duties in question must preclude T from disadvantaging$_{FC}$ S by assigning S other compensatory claims that, if respected, would offset any loss of advantage imposed by T's choice. Thus, the stringency objection does not succeed, as the moral tyranny constraint does not entail the posited unacceptable duties.

The laxity objection poses a greater threat to the moral tyranny constraint, as it begins with the recognition that the constraint sets limits on which duties and permissions persons can have conditional on the choices that agents make. Specifically, it contends that the constraint entails an improper restriction on which remedial duties can obtain when B fails to discharge her duty to rescue a drowning child (namely, that A cannot acquire a duty to rescue the child, as such a rescue would leave A worse off$_{FC}$ relative to the world where B chose differently). However, this objection incorrectly assumes that one must hold all other permissions and duties constant when assessing whether A acquires a duty to rescue the child. Were this the case, then the constraint would, indeed, imply that A

2.5 Three Objections to the Constraint

cannot acquire such a duty. Fortunately for proponents of the constraint, there are many alternative patterns of remedial duties that both satisfy the constraint and assign A a duty to rescue the child. For example, a moral theory might maintain that A acquires a duty to rescue the child *and* that B acquires a duty to compensate A such that A ends up no worse off$_{FC}$ in virtue of B's choice not to rescue the child.[25] In fact, one might take this conjunction of duties to be a more plausible result than simply holding that A has to rescue the child and must shoulder the associated costs without any compensation from B. If so, this putative counterexample to the moral tyranny constraint is transformed into additional reason for favoring the constraint, as the constraint can explain why it is that B must compensate A (despite the fact that her undischarged duty was owed to the *child*). Thus, the stringency and laxity objections fail to undermine the plausibility of the moral tyranny constraint.

Finally, the *paternalism objection* contends that the moral tyranny constraint is incompatible with any claim against paternalistic interference (including so-called hard paternalism that is explicitly unwanted by the beneficiary).[26] While not everyone believes that people have claims against paternalistic interference, such claims are widely endorsed by anarchists, libertarians, and liberals of all stripes – that is, those who would be most naturally attracted to the position advanced by the book. Thus, if the

---

[25] What if B is unable to compensate A? If one thinks that a person can still have a duty even if she is unable to discharge that duty, then B's inability does not pose any special problem for the compensation solution proposed in this section. However, given that the constraint is concerned with the world of full compliance, it may well presuppose that persons can have a duty only if they are able to discharge it. If duties imply "can" in this way, then B's inability to compensate A makes moral tyranny *inevitable*: either one assigns A a duty to rescue the child thereby enabling B to leave A worse off$_{FC}$ or one does not assign A this duty thereby enabling B to leave the *child* worse off$_{FC}$. Given this predicament, the suggestion here is that the moral tyranny constraint should be understood to declare a moral theory unacceptable only if it violates the constraint *and* there is some rival theory that does not violate the constraint. In other words, if all possible theories entail that a person has the ability to foreseeably, discretionarily, and unilaterally leave someone worse off$_{FC}$ by making a particular choice, then no theory should be taken to violate the constraint in virtue of that person's ability. Suppose, for example, that a nuclear-weapon-possessing villain has the ability to destroy the planet. If she makes this choice, everyone will be left worse off and there will be no way for her to compensate them. This, in turn, implies that no moral theory will be able to assign duties in such a way as to preclude her from leaving others worse off$_{FC}$. And, given that *no* theory can satisfy the constraint vis-à-vis this choice, it seems like the fact that some particular theory does not satisfy the constraint vis-à-vis that choice does not count against the theory. For this reason, the moral tyranny constraint should be understood to be satisfied in both this case and the aforementioned rescue case where no compensation is possible.

[26] In fact, one might even think that it entails that agents are *obliged* to paternalistically interfere with others, as this is the only way for a theory to avoid licensing those agents to leave others worse off$_{FC}$.

moral tyranny constraint implies that paternalism is acceptable, that would represent a serious theoretical cost.[27]

The quick reply is that this objection mistakenly presupposes that persons must be assigned the set of duties such that each person ends up with the maximum possible quantity of advantage conditional on full compliance with those duties. However, the constraint merely insists that persons must *lack the ability to diminish others' advantage* conditional on full compliance. While a theory that assigned a person a claim against paternalist interference would fail to maximize her advantage$_{FC}$ relative to an otherwise-identical theory that did not assign that claim, it does not give others any greater ability to *choose* how much advantage she ends up with under conditions of full compliance. Thus, the moral tyranny constraint does not entail that persons lack a claim against paternalistic interference.

This reply is "quick" because it does not adequately address an interesting complication that arises when the moral tyranny constraint is applied to theories that include claims against such interference. Consider an arbitrary moral theory that assigns Q a claim against P ϕ-ing where ϕ-ing is an act of paternalistic interference. Because ϕ-ing is an act of paternalism, P ϕ-ing will leave Q better off than if she discharges her duty and does not ϕ – which is to say that she leaves Q better off in the actual world A than in the world of full compliance F_1. However, her choice to ϕ also changes what the full-compliance world looks like because P will acquire remedial duties in virtue of her failure to discharge her duty to not paternalistically interfere with Q (call this adjusted full compliance world F_2). Specifically, one might think that P will acquire a new duty to *compensate* Q for failing to discharge her duty to Q, where this compensatory remedial duty entails that Q is better off in F_2 than she is in A. Further, given that Q is better off in A than she is in F_1, transitivity implies that Q is better off in F_2 than she is in F_1. Thus, Q is better off$_{FC}$ if P ϕ-s than if P discharges her duty and does not ϕ. This result may seem like a problem for the moral tyranny constraint because it appears that the moral theory – which is to say, any moral theory that includes a claim against paternalistic interference – violates the constraint, as P can unilaterally leave Q worse off$_{FC}$ by doing her duty and refraining from ϕ-ing. One might therefore conclude that the constraint does, in fact, problematically imply that there are no claims against paternalistic interference.

Against this worry, note that the moral tyranny constraint does not merely hold that a theory cannot license a person to leave others worse

---

[27] For a recent defense of paternalism, see Jason Hanna (2018).

off$_{FC}$. Rather, it maintains that the theory must not license her to *unilaterally, foreseeably, and discretionarily* leave others worse off$_{FC}$. For these purposes, the last qualifier is the crucial one, as P discharging her duty to refrain from ϕ-ing would not qualify as discretionary in the sense described in Section 2.2. There it was stipulated that a person acts discretionarily only if she does not *have* to carry out that action, where "have" can be interpreted either in terms of ability – that is, there is no other option physically available to the agent – or normatively, which is to say that the agent lacks a permission to carry out any rival action. Because P's duty to refrain from ϕ-ing entails that she lacks a permission to ϕ, it follows that she does not discretionarily leave Q worse off$_{FC}$ by declining to ϕ (although she does, in fact, leave Q worse off$_{FC}$). Thus, the posited theory does not violate the moral tyranny constraint, which, in turn, implies the more general conclusion that the constraint is compatible with duties against paternalistic interference.

2.6 Conclusion

This chapter has taken the first steps toward demonstrating the coherence of social anarchism. Specifically, it has argued that three of the position's theses follow, either in part or in whole, from a more general constraint on which normative theories are acceptable, namely, the moral tyranny constraint. The chapter has thereby demonstrated that these theses are neither incompatible nor an arbitrary set of views conjoined together without reason. Rather, they are logically connected in a way that renders the social anarchist position coherent in the sense defined in Section I.2. Additionally, this chapter has argued that the moral tyranny constraint is independently plausible. Given its plausibility, the fact that the constraint entails consent theory, the Lockean proviso, and luck egalitarianism's incorporation of responsibility is a reason to accept these positions. The task of the next three chapters is to show that the remaining anarchist theses – namely, the self-ownership thesis, the anarchist rejection of private property, and the anarchist conclusion – similarly cohere with the other components of the anarchist position.

CHAPTER 3

You Own Yourself and Nothing Else

> The granary is full; the national treasury is substantial. But the starving and frozen are everywhere. It is the result of the private ownership of property.
>
> Chu Minyi, "Universal Revolution"

Chapters 1 and 2 have introduced the social anarchist position and the moral tyranny constraint. Chapter 1 proposed that social anarchism should be understood as a set of theses that includes (i) the consent theory of legitimacy (which, in turn, implies philosophical anarchism), (ii) the Lockean proviso, (iii) the anarchist self-ownership thesis, (iv) the denial that there is any existing private property, and (v) an endorsement of luck egalitarianism as the moral principle regulating the permissible use of unowned external objects (what was there called "the anarchist conclusion"). Chapter 2 then introduced the moral tyranny constraint and argued that this theoretical *desideratum* entails the first and second anarchist theses as well as luck egalitarianism's responsibility component. This conclusion represents the first step in the book's broader project of demonstrating the coherence of the social anarchist position – that is, that the position's posited theses are not a set of arbitrarily selected (and potentially conflicting) moral principles, but, rather, stand in relations of logical entailment to one another. However, even if both the consent theory of legitimacy and the Lockean proviso follow from the moral tyranny constraint, that still leaves three additional theses that do not obviously stand in any logical relation to these aforementioned propositions.

This chapter will demonstrate that both the self-ownership thesis (as articulated by ASO in Section 1.3) and the rejection of private property follow from the Lockean proviso (and a few other plausible premises). This argument turns conventional libertarianism on its head in two respects. First, libertarian philosophers generally take the self-ownership thesis to be a foundational commitment while viewing the proviso as an auxiliary thesis that one might adopt to avoid the unsavory implications of unlimited appropriation. This prioritization is evidenced by the fact that natural rights libertarians universally endorse the self-ownership thesis but only a proper subset endorses the proviso, with many rejecting it as an ad hoc restriction on the power to acquire property.[1] However, this chapter suggests that the proviso should be treated as the more basic commitment with self-ownership ultimately following from the proviso. Second, it is typically assumed that the Lockean proviso allows for the appropriation of a significant quantity of natural resources.[2] Against this assumption, the chapter will argue that the proviso actually *precludes* almost all appropriation of resources (while still allowing people to appropriate their own bodies). The chapter will thereby take a right-libertarian premise and use it to derive a conclusion favored by social anarchists, namely, that people own themselves and nothing else.

The argument proceeds as follows. Section 3.1 argues that the Lockean proviso entails the social anarchist rejection of private property. Specifically, it argues that the proviso, at least as is has been specified in Section 1.2, is stringent to the point where it will not be satisfied by practically any act of initial appropriation, thereby precluding the conversion of natural resources into property. Section 3.3 then argues that, although the proviso is almost never satisfied when it comes to natural resources, it is *necessarily* satisfied when it comes to each person's own body – at least, if appropriation is taken to only establish the weaker ownership rights posited by ASO. Thus, the section concludes that the proviso entails that persons own themselves, but only in the sense specified by ASO. Given that much of the chapter's argument rests on the specific interpretation of the Lockean proviso provided in Chapter 1, Sections 3.3 and 3.4 will provide an extended defense of this interpretation. Finally, Section 3.5 will discuss what the chapter's conclusion implies vis-à-vis the rights of children.

3.1 The Proviso and Private Property

To see why the proviso entails the rejection of external private property, recall how it was interpreted in Section 1.2:

---

[1] Recall from Chapter 1, Footnote 6 that these "radical right-libertarians" include Rothbard (1998), Narveson (1998), Feser (2005), and Mack (1995) (though he qualifies his radicalism).
[2] One of the few exceptions is Attas (2003) who argues that any plausible specification of the Lockean proviso will entail that no appropriation has occurred. This chapter will provide slightly different, complementary reasons for accepting the conclusion that no appropriation of external natural resources has occurred.

The Lockean Proviso – A person appropriates some unowned resource via some suitable action if and only if (a) her established claims would not leave anyone worse off under conditions of full compliance and (b) no subsequent waiving of those claims would leave others worse off under conditions of full compliance (where, in both cases, the baseline for comparison is the closest possible world where the appropriator did not exist).[3]

At first glance, the proviso might seem to preclude practically all appropriation, even without the additional restrictions that Condition (b) places on appropriators. This is because most unowned resources are both useful and scarce; that is, a non-appropriator would benefit from the use of those resources and there is not an available substitute that would allow her to acquire that same benefit at an equal or lower cost.[4] Seemingly, the appropriation of such resources would leave others worse off$_{FC}$, as they would now be unable to obtain the benefit in question without incurring a greater cost under conditions of full compliance. Thus, any appropriation of these resources would violate the Lockean proviso.

However, in response to this suggestion, proponents of the proviso will note that one must consider the *net effects*$_{FC}$ of appropriation, not just the costs$_{FC}$ that it imposes on non-appropriators. To do this, one must attend to the various ways in which appropriation *benefits*$_{FC}$ non-appropriators. For example, by precluding fully compliant non-appropriators from using a resource, a person's appropriation might enable her to improve the resource in a way that is ultimately to their benefit (Schmidtz 1994). Or, alternatively, appropriation can prevent fully compliant people from destroying some resource, thereby allowing future non-appropriators to use and benefit from it (Schmidtz 1990). In such cases, although appropriation imposes certain costs$_{FC}$ on others by forbidding their free use of the resource, it will actually leave them better off$_{FC}$ on net, with this fact undermining the prior quick argument that most appropriation violates the Lockean proviso.

There are two things to be said in response to this defense of appropriation. First, even when one factors in the conservation and improvement of resources that appropriation enables$_{FC}$, there will still be many cases

---

[3] This chapter will make use of the strong version of the proviso discussed in Footnote 18 of Chapter 2. While the moral tyranny constraint only implies the weaker version (as discussed in that footnote), it is assumed here that it is independently plausible that non-worsening$_{FC}$ is a sufficient condition of the successful appropriation of unowned resources in addition to a necessary condition.

[4] Note that even if two useful resources are qualitatively identical, the fact that one is closer to an agent than the other will render former scarce, as the agent will have to travel further to benefit from the resource and will thereby incur a slightly higher cost to obtain that benefit.

3.1 The Proviso and Private Property

where appropriation harms$_{FC}$ people on net. For example, the appropriation of beaches and other scenic locations will often violate the proviso, as fully compliant people will suffer due to not being able to access these spaces and will not benefit from any development made possible by compliance with the established rights. More generally, the proviso precludes the appropriation of *any* land if there is a single person who would both benefit from moving across that land and would not benefit from the development of that land. Similar remarks apply to consumable resources: While appropriation might leave many excluded parties better off$_{FC}$ (because appropriation would allow for these resources to be either preserved or improved in the full-compliance world in ways that are ultimately to these non-appropriators' benefit), appropriation will not occur if there is at least one person who would not benefit$_{FC}$ in this way and, instead, incurs a net cost$_{FC}$ in virtue of the owner's claim against her using the resource. For example, suppose that the appropriation of a fishpond prevents full compliers from overfishing and depleting the fish stock (as they otherwise would have). Such appropriation might leave most people better off$_{FC}$, as they are better off purchasing fish from the owner for years than eating for free for a few weeks but running out of fish later. However, if there is even one person who does not benefit$_{FC}$ in this way – for example, because she only wants to consume fish in the short term – then the appropriation of the pond will not satisfy the Lockean proviso.

Additionally, the proviso entails that one could not appropriate any object where a person would provide some benefit to another in exchange for the latter not using the object in question. In such cases, the appropriation of the object would strip$_{FC}$ this second person of her bargaining power, as she would no longer be able to use the object in the world of full compliance. She would, thus, end up worse off in this world because she would not receive the benefit that she would have been paid absent appropriation.[5] In this way, the proviso entails that a significant portion of natural resources cannot be appropriated *even if* one considers only Condition (a)'s contention that the claims established by appropriation must not leave others worse off$_{FC}$.

To arrive at the anarchist's conclusion that *practically all* appropriation fails to satisfy the Lockean proviso, however, one must appeal to Condition (b) of the proviso. This condition asserts that, in addition to the established claims not leaving anyone worse off$_{FC}$, it must also be the

---

[5] For a relevant discussion of a bargaining situation where people trade away the permission to use natural resources in exchange for benefits, see Alan Gibbard (1976, 78–82).

case that no subsequent waiving of those claims would leave anyone worse off$_{FC}$. To see why this condition precludes almost all appropriation, consider the case of an explorer who discovers a waterfall and attempts to appropriate it. A few days later, a hiker arrives who wants to spend every morning swimming at the base of the waterfall. If the explorer's act of appropriation succeeded, then she has a set of claims against the hiker swimming, where it is assumed that each day's swim is a distinct action, and the explorer has a distinct claim against each. As it turns out, full compliance with these claims would actually be to the hiker's benefit: Although not swimming each day imposes a cost upon the hiker, it also keeps her from unknowingly polluting the only available water source with her sunscreen, thereby making the water forever taste of soap. Because the hiker prefers never swimming to drinking soap-flavored water, she would end up better off on net if she were to fully comply with the explorer's full set of (hypothetical) claims. Thus, the explorer's appropriation would satisfy an unamended statement of the Lockean proviso that merely asks whether the explorer's full set of established exclusionary claims leaves others worse off$_{FC}$ (i.e., a proviso that includes Condition (a) but not Condition (b)).

However, Condition (b) of the proviso holds that one must ask whether the hiker would be left worse off given *any possible pattern of waiving* of the explorer's posited claims. Suppose, for example, that the hiker wanted to take a post-arrival swim and the explorer decided to waive her claim against this one action. Such waiving would leave the hiker worse off in the full-compliance world, as she would end up with soapy tasting water (due to her swim) and would not get to swim on any of the other days. Given that a possible pattern of post-appropriation waiving would leave the hiker worse off$_{FC}$, the explorer's attempted appropriation of the waterfall does not satisfy the restated Lockean proviso and, thus, does not succeed.

This case helps to illustrate why the proposed interpretation of the proviso entails that practically all purported appropriations of external resources violate the proviso. Note that, for any posited appropriation of a resource, there is a possible world where the appropriator waives all her posited claim rights – functionally treating the resource as though it were still unowned – *except* for those claims that would impose the greatest costs on full compliers. For the proposed specification of the proviso to be satisfied, it must be the case that every non-appropriator is no worse off$_{FC}$ in this world than she would be in the world where the appropriator did not exist to appropriate the resource in question. Given that the appropriation of practically any resource would violate this constraint, this specification of the proviso entails the anarchist thesis that practically no one has acquired – or will acquire – private property over external things via acts of initial appropriation.[6] Specifically, Condition (b) of the proviso undermines the previous libertarian reply that appropriation often benefits$_{FC}$ non-appropriators by enabling the improvement and preservation of natural resources. For, even if appropriation does establish claims that have this beneficial$_{FC}$ effect, it also gives appropriators the power to waive these claims while leaving in place only those claims that impose costs$_{FC}$ on non-appropriators. Given that an appropriately specified proviso must preclude the possibility of appropriators acting in this way, even much beneficial$_{FC}$ appropriation will violate the proviso. Thus, one arrives at the anarchist contention that there has been (practically) no successful appropriation of external resources.[7]

3.2 The Lockean Proviso and Self-Ownership

Section 3.1 has argued that the Lockean proviso, as specified in Section 1.2, entails the absence of private property rights.[8] This section will argue that, while the proviso may entail that there is no ownership of external

---

[6] The "practically" qualifier is included because it is at least possible that the appropriation of certain resources will satisfy the proviso. For example, in a world without scarcity even the most disadvantageous pattern of compliance will not leave others worse off, as they would have equally good resources available to them to use as a substitute.

[7] It should be noted that the foregoing argument assumes that initial appropriation of external things establishes *full* private property rights including both claims against others using the owned thing in any way and the power to waive any of these claims. However, one might maintain that appropriation establishes a weaker set of rights, where a suitably weak set might satisfy the proviso. For example, a theory of ownership might narrow the set of established property rights by limiting owners' power to waive those rights. That said, this move is not available to will theorists, who maintain that a person possesses a claim (e.g., a claim against others using an owned thing) only if she has a power to waive that claim. Additionally, those who wish to restrict the power to waive must provide some explanation of why the owner's consent is not a sufficient condition for waiving the claims that are declared unwaivable – a task that will be difficult due to the many reasons for thinking that a rightholder's consent is sufficient for waiving any of her rights (see, e.g., Hurd (1996)). Given these difficulties, one might, instead, posit that appropriation establishes a more limited set of claims against use. Specifically, one might hold that it establishes *whichever* maximal set of rights satisfies the proviso, that is, the strongest set of claims against use such that compliance with any post-waiving pattern of those rights would not leave anyone worse off (where this set might include only a single right). The problem with this proposal is that the set of claims that would not leave anyone worse off$_{FC}$ irrespective of whether or not they are waived might be extremely small to the point where it no longer satisfies any of the theoretical *desiderata* that motivate libertarians to endorse private property-based theories of justice in the first place.

[8] The Lockean proviso does not entail the supplementary anarchist contention that rights vis-à-vis external resources are determined by an egalitarian principle of distributive justice (i.e., what Section 1.6 calls "the anarchist conclusion"). However, the conclusion that there are (practically) no existing property rights makes this contention much more attractive, as it allows for proponents of the proviso to avoid the conclusion that the world is in a state of moral free-for-all where any person can permissibly use any resource at any time, no matter how that use affects others. Rather, she is able to maintain that people still have distributive claims against others using resources in various ways. A full defense of the distributive component of the view will be provided in Chapter 5.

things, it entails that persons can easily acquire ownership of the self – and, more specifically, self-ownership of the kind articulated by ASO. In this way, it aims to provide a novel ground for the self-ownership thesis while simultaneously demonstrating the coherence of the anarchist position (by showing that its various theses stand in the appropriate relations of logical entailment to one another).

So why does the proviso allow for ownership of the self when it also entails that there is no ownership of external natural resources? To answer this question, recall that the proviso holds that an act of appropriation succeeds if its established claims – and any possible subsequent waiving thereof – would not leave others worse off$_{FC}$ *relative to the world where the appropriator did not exist to appropriate*. Further, note that the truth of the antecedent of this conditional can be determined by applying the following *nonexistence test* to the various costs$_{FC}$ incurred by non-appropriators: such costs$_{FC}$ *pass* the nonexistence test if and only if they obtain in the appropriation world but not the counterfactual world where the appropriator did not exist. For example, if P's appropriation gives her a claim against Q eating some fruit that Q would have enjoyed in the world where P never existed, then Q suffers a cost$_{FC}$ that passes the nonexistence test. This, in turn, implies that P's appropriation leaves Q worse off$_{FC}$ relative to the nonexistence baseline (assuming that there are no offsetting benefits$_{FC}$ that similarly pass the nonexistence test) and, thus, P's appropriation violates the proviso.

By contrast, an imposed cost$_{FC}$ *fails* the nonexistence test if and only if it *would* equally obtain in the nonexistence world. For example, if P's appropriation establishes a claim against Q eating some fruit, but Q would not have been able to eat that fruit in the nonexistence world due to it being out of her reach, then the costs$_{FC}$ of non-enjoyment fail the nonexistence test. And, crucially, because costs$_{FC}$ that fail the nonexistence test obtain in both the appropriation world and the baseline for comparison, they will not contribute to non-appropriators being worse off$_{FC}$ in a way that would violate the proviso.[9] Thus, an act of appropriation will satisfy the Lockean proviso if all of its imposed costs$_{FC}$ (and all incurred costs$_{FC}$ more generally) fail the nonexistence test. Or, to slightly restate this point, an act of appropriation satisfies the Lockean proviso if its

---

[9] Note that it does not matter whether the act of appropriation *imposes* costs$_{FC}$ in the sense that those costs$_{FC}$ would not have obtained *absent appropriation*. Because the proviso's baseline for comparison is the nonexistence world rather than the non-appropriation world, any actual-world costs$_{FC}$ that do not obtain in the non-appropriation world but still obtain in the nonexistence world will not contribute to non-appropriators being worse off$_{FC}$ in the relevant sense. More will be said to defend the proviso's specified baseline in Section 3.4.

3.2 The Lockean Proviso and Self-Ownership

established claims – and any possible waiving of these claims – would not impose costs$_{FC}$ that pass the nonexistence test.

This test has little bearing on the appropriation of external natural resources, as there does not appear to be any case where the costs$_{FC}$ imposed by exclusionary claims would equally obtain in the world where the appropriator never existed. In other words, when it comes to external appropriation, the imposed costs$_{FC}$ – that is, all of the various costs$_{FC}$ discussed in the previous section – still pass the nonexistence test, with the associated acts of appropriation thereby violating the Lockean proviso. Thus, the nonexistence test does not undermine the previous section's denial that people have acquired or will acquire external property.

By contrast, when it comes to people appropriating *their own bodies*, the nonexistence test entails that the proviso is *necessarily* satisfied – at least, if self-appropriation is taken to establish the claims posited by ASO (i.e., claims against any actions that initiate bodily contact without generating unique supplemental benefit). To see why this is the case, consider the scenario where *P*'s body is unowned (due to her never having previously appropriated it) and *Q* is in desperate need of a new kidney. Suppose that *P* then self-appropriates, thereby acquiring a claim against *Q* that *Q* not take one of her kidneys. In this case, *P*'s self-appropriation leaves *Q* worse off$_{FC}$ relative to the world where *P* has no such claim: Absent such a claim, a fully compliant *Q* would have taken one of *P*'s kidneys, thereby avoiding the pain and suffering of kidney failure (while a fully compliant *Q* would now suffer these costs given *P*'s claim against this action). However, as far as the Lockean proviso is concerned, the question is not whether *Q* is left worse off$_{FC}$ relative to the world where some alternative moral facts obtain. Rather, the question is whether *Q* is left worse off$_{FC}$ relative to the world where *P* did not exist – that is, whether the costs$_{FC}$ she incurs pass the nonexistence test. And, notably, these costs$_{FC}$ *fail* this test, as in the counterfactual world where *P* never existed, a fully compliant *Q* would be just as disadvantaged as she would be in the self-appropriation world where she complies with *P*'s established claims. Specifically, in both worlds, she does not get the kidney and suffers the associated costs. Thus, these costs$_{FC}$ do not count when assessing whether *P*'s self-appropriation leaves *Q* worse off$_{FC}$ in a way that would violate the Lockean proviso. This, in turn, implies that the establishment of a claim against kidney harvesting via self-appropriation does not entail a violation of the proviso.

One might be tempted to conclude that this result generalizes such that a person establishing *any* right to exclude others from her body does not leave others worse off$_{FC}$ in a way that violates the Lockean proviso. Were this the case, then self-appropriation that generated the classical self-ownership right against all bodily contact would satisfy the proviso. However, this is a bit too quick, as there are many cases where establishing a general right against contact *will* impose costs$_{FC}$ that pass the nonexistence test. For example, consider the case where P's unowned body stands blocking the only entrance to Q's office. Further, suppose that if Q is late for work, then her wages will be docked. Given that P's body is unowned, Q can permissibly shove it to the side, thereby allowing her to enter the building and be on time for work. But what happens if P suddenly self-appropriates? Assuming that self-appropriation establishes a classical right against nonconsensual contact, it follows that P now has a claim that Q not shove her aside. This, in turn, entails that a fully compliant Q would be unable to access her office and would incur the associated cost. Thus, P's self-appropriation leaves Q worse off$_{FC}$ than she would have been otherwise.

Further, P's appropriation leaves Q worse off$_{FC}$ *even after one applies the nonexistence test.* In this case, the test asks whether a fully compliant Q would equally suffer the costs of being late for work if P did not exist. And, unlike in the kidney case, the answer here is no: While Q would be late for work in the full-compliance world, she would not be late in the full-compliance world where P does not exist (as there would be no one blocking her path). Thus, the costs imposed by P's self-appropriation pass the nonexistence test, which, in turn, entails that P's self-appropriation leaves Q worse off$_{FC}$ relative to the nonexistence baseline; that is, P's self-appropriation violates the Lockean proviso.

Why is it that the costs$_{FC}$ imposed in the kidney case fail the nonexistence test while the costs$_{FC}$ imposed in the doorway case pass this test? The explanatory difference here is that, in the kidney case, the cost of compliance for Q is limited to the loss of benefits derived from bodily contact *without any loss of supplemental benefit.* Note that, in this case, the only reason that Q is worse off$_{FC}$ in the appropriation world relative to the nonappropriation world is that, absent appropriation, she would benefit$_{FC}$ from the contact that she would make with P's body (specifically P's kidneys). When P then makes it such that a fully compliant Q cannot touch her body, that leaves Q worse off$_{FC}$ than she would have been otherwise. However, the nonexistence of P equally makes it such that a fully compliant Q cannot touch P's body and derive the associated benefits. Thus, Q is no worse off$_{FC}$ in the appropriation world than she is in the world where P does not exist, with the costs of P's self-appropriation thereby failing the nonexistence test.

By contrast, in the doorway case, Q shoving P to the side would *uniquely generate supplemental benefit* not caused by the physical contact

3.2 The Lockean Proviso and Self-Ownership

itself, namely, Q getting paid her full wages. P's self-appropriation then denies Q this supplemental benefit$_{FC}$ (by giving P a classical self-ownership claim against Q shoving her), thereby imposing costs$_{FC}$ on Q.[10] Further, because the benefit is supplemental – that is, it is not derived from contact made with P's body – the nonexistence of P would not equally impose these costs$_{FC}$, which is to say that these costs$_{FC}$ would *not* have obtained in the world where P did not exist. Thus, they pass the nonexistence test, with P's appropriation thereby leaving Q worse off$_{FC}$ in a way that violates the Lockean proviso.

In other words, the costs$_{FC}$ imposed by a claim against kidney harvesting fail the nonexistence test because they are correlative of a denial of a benefit$_{FC}$ that is solely derived from bodily contact (i.e., non-supplemental benefit$_{FC}$). By contrast, the costs$_{FC}$ imposed by P's claim against being shoved in the doorway case pass the nonexistence test because they are correlative of a denial of unique supplemental benefit$_{FC}$. And, importantly, this result generalizes: The costs$_{FC}$ imposed by an agent's act of self-appropriation will fail the nonexistence test – that is, her self-appropriation will satisfy the Lockean proviso – if and only if her self-appropriation does not establish a claim against any person taking an action that uniquely produces supplemental benefit beyond those benefits that result from contact with the self-appropriator's body.

There are two different conclusions that one might draw from the preceding discussion. First, one might conclude that the proviso largely precludes the possibility of self-appropriation. Those who favor this approach would insist that self-appropriation establishes the classical right against any nonconsensual bodily contact. They would then concede that the Lockean proviso is not satisfied in the countless cases where compliance with (any post-waiving pattern of) the established exclusion rights would preclude the realization of unique supplemental benefit. This, in turn, would imply that very few – if any – persons possess the self-ownership rights established by initial appropriation.

Fortunately for those attracted to the self-ownership thesis, one can reach an alternative conclusion by rejecting the classical assumption that self-appropriation establishes rights against all bodily contact. Instead, one would posit that appropriation only realizes the weaker exclusion rights referenced by ASO, that is, rights against all and only those actions that both result in bodily contact and do not uniquely produce supplemental

---

[10] Note that if Q pushing P did not *uniquely* generate supplemental benefit, then P's self-appropriation would not deny Q these benefits, as she would still have an alternative way of securing them.

benefit. Thus, when assessing whether *P*'s self-appropriation satisfies the Lockean proviso, one only needs to consider whether *P* establishing these more limited ASO rights would impose costs$_{FC}$ that pass the nonexistence test. Further, given that *P* imposes such costs$_{FC}$ on *Q* if and only if she establishes claims against people acting in ways that *do* uniquely produce supplemental benefit for *Q*, it follows that *P*'s self-appropriation *necessarily* satisfies the proviso. This, in turn, implies that all persons can freely self-appropriate and establish self-ownership rights of the kind articulated by ASO.[11]

Of course, this result does not entail that one *must* accept ASO. As just noted, one could still choose to endorse the classical interpretation of self-ownership so long as one is willing to accept the conclusion that practically all acts of self-appropriation violate the Lockean proviso and, thus, almost no one owns themselves. However, first, it is unclear why self-appropriation must be taken to establish the classical set of rights against all bodily contact. Second, one might contend that which rights self-appropriation establishes is, at least in part, a function of which rights satisfy the Lockean proviso. On this approach, one does not start with a particular interpretation of self-ownership and then hope that self-appropriation satisfies the proviso; rather, one affirms a particular interpretation of self-ownership in virtue of the fact that such self-ownership could be established in accordance with the Lockean proviso. In other words, the reason for thinking that self-owners possess ASO rights is because these are the only rights that persons could come to possess. Such a supplemental premise would render the anarchist position coherent, as ASO would then follow from the Lockean proviso.

Finally, note that the foregoing argument does not entail the truth of the self-ownership thesis – that is, the proposition that all persons own themselves in the sense articulated by ASO. Rather, assuming that one accepts ASO, it merely demonstrates that a person owns herself if and only if she has carried out an act of self-appropriation (as all acts of self-appropriation succeed in virtue of the fact that they necessarily satisfy the Lockean proviso). However, if one accepts an account of appropriation

---

[11] This argument from the Lockean proviso provides support for something proximate to what Kasper Lippert-Rasmussen calls the "Asymmetry Thesis: Ownership of external resources is intrinsically different, morally, from ownership of one's mind and body" (2008, 88). Lippert-Rasmussen rejects this thesis and one can see why he might be skeptical that there is something special about the ownership of bodies. However, the foregoing argument has demonstrated why bodies are, in fact, special such that all persons might own their bodies even as they are precluded from owning external resources.

such as that proposed in Section 1.3 – namely, that persons appropriate unowned resources by asserting that they own the resources in question (following Rose (1985, 81)) – then it follows that practically all persons own themselves, as almost everyone has, at some point, asserted that they own themselves (e.g., by saying "don't touch *my* body!"). Thus, the foregoing proviso-based argument for ASO also provides a novel explanation of why people own themselves: They have successfully appropriated their own bodies in accordance with the proviso. This supplemental justification puts the self-ownership thesis on firmer philosophical footing, albeit at the cost of weakening the rights it assigns to each person.[12]

3.3 Comparing Baselines

The arguments of Sections 3.1 and 3.2 have leaned heavily on the specification of the proviso in Section 1.2. In particular, both arguments rely on its proposed baseline for comparison, that is, its contention that appropriation must not leave others worse off$_{FC}$ relative to the world where the appropriator did not exist. Chapter 1 did not provide a defense of this specification, as it was primarily concerned with explicating other aspects of the anarchist position. However, now that the specified baseline has been shown to have significant implications, it is worth defending it at some length. Specifically, this section will defend the specification from the objection that it is unduly restrictive, where a more appropriately permissive specification might avoid the conclusion of Section 3.1 that practically no appropriation satisfies the Lockean proviso. To do this, it will consider the most promising alternative specification of the proviso – one famously endorsed by Nozick – and argue that this rival view is implausible. Further, this section will argue that the reasons for rejecting Nozick's specification also support the anarchist's proposed nonexistence baseline. It will, thus, conclude that one ought to favor the proposed baseline.

According to Nozick's specification, an act of appropriation satisfies the proviso if and only if no one is left worse off – or, presumably, for the reasons discussed in Section 1.3, worse off$_{FC}$ – than they would have been *in a world without any appropriation at all.*[13] This specification is attractive

---

[12] This weakening is characterized as a "cost" for the reasons discussed in Section 1.7. However, Section 1.4 has argued that ASO's weakening the classical self-ownership thesis gives it a number of important theoretical advantages relative to the classical interpretation of self-ownership.

[13] Nozick's interpretation of the proviso is actually a bit ambiguous. On the one hand, his explicit statement of the proviso puts things in terms of whether or not the appropriation of a particular

to those who want a more permissive proviso that allows for appropriation precluded by the anarchist's proposed specification, as it licenses appropriation in the many instances where non-appropriators would be harmed$_{FC}$ by an individual's appropriation but would still benefit$_{FC}$ on net from the system of established private property as a whole. For example, suppose that peanut farmer P appropriates some unowned field, where this appropriation enables her to produce a large amount of peanuts. Further, suppose that this appropriation will worsen$_{FC}$ the position of neighbor Q, as Q both previously enjoyed using the field and is allergic to peanuts (i.e., she has no interest in consuming the produced crops). In this case, P's appropriation leaves Q worse off$_{FC}$ than she would have been had P never existed to appropriate the field. However, it does not leave her worse off$_{FC}$ than she would have been in the world where no appropriation ever occurs, as she benefits$_{FC}$ extensively from others' appropriation. For example, she benefits$_{FC}$ when *other* farmers appropriate land and thereby become able$_{FC}$ to grow crops without interference. Thus, P's appropriation would satisfy Nozick's specification of the proviso but not the proviso as it has been interpreted here. Given this result, some proponents of the proviso might contend that Nozick's specification is superior to the anarchist one, as the former allows for appropriation in cases such as the one just described.

The problem with this contention is that the purpose of the proviso is to ensure that appropriation is justified; however, it does not appear that Nozick's specification is able to play this justificatory role. This point has been expressed by Daniel Attas, who argues that specifications like Nozick's – that is, specifications that compare how *the entire established set private property rights* affects Q to how she fares in a world without

---

thing (in his words, the "process giving rise to a... property right" over that thing) worsens others' position (1974, 178). However, he also asks whether their position is "worsened by a system allowing appropriation" and devotes much more space to explaining the advantages of systems of private property than the benefits of particular acts of appropriation (177). Additionally, while Nozick initially sidesteps the question of how to specify the baseline for comparison (177), he later suggests that the relevant comparison world is the world where *no appropriation takes place* (181). Given that it is more natural to compare a world with property to a world without property than it is to compare a world with a particular act of appropriation to a world without property, Nozick's choice of baseline additionally supports reading him as endorsing the interpretation of the proviso attributed to him here. This interpretation of the proviso has also been explicitly endorsed by David Schmidtz (1994, 49–50), and it is also seemingly presupposed by proviso proponents who justify private property by appealing to the benefits of private property systems. See, for example, Loren Lomasky (1987) and an earlier statement of the proviso posited by van der Vossen (2015). Brennan (2014) similarly appeals to the benefits of a system of property, though he does not explicitly endorse the Lockean proviso.

3.3 Comparing Baselines

appropriation – are "completely off the point. The proviso is a requirement of *particular* appropriations. Particular appropriations have to involve counterbalancing gains in order to be justified . . . . [Thus,] a promise of increased benefits of the *general* system. . . . cannot justify [*P*] owning [an appropriated resource]" (2003, 359). However, while Attas is right to assert that it is the particular act of appropriation that must be justified, Nozick's defenders might counter that systemic benefits$_{FC}$ *do* justify particular appropriations. It is, thus, worth considering why one might think that the entire system plays this justificatory role. It will then be argued that these apparent grounds for affirming Nozick's specification are philosophically untenable.

The suggestion here is that defenders of Nozick might advance the following *baseline argument* to defend the idea that systemic benefits justify individual appropriations:

1. If an action – in tandem with various other actions – brings about a state of affairs that is non-inferior to the relevant baseline for comparison, then that action is justified.
2. If an appropriation satisfies Nozick's proviso, then it (in tandem with various other actions) brings about a state of affairs that is non-inferior to the relevant baseline for comparison.
3. Thus, if an appropriation satisfies Nozick's proviso, then it justified.

Admittedly, Premise 1 does not fit easily with Nozick's signature view that the justice of a state of affairs is a function of the justice of the actions that bring it about, as it reverses the dependency relation between the justifiability of states of affairs and the justifiability of the actions that bring them about. However, without this premise, it is not clear how one could establish that appropriations are just by appealing to the harmless$_{FC}$ effects of the entire established system of private property. Additionally, the premise can be supported by appealing to cases where the comparative non-inferiority of a resultant state seemingly justifies the actions that brought it about. Consider, for example, the case where a surgeon saves a patient's life by a process that includes cutting open her chest. In this case, the incision seems justified because it, in tandem with other actions, brings about a state of affairs – namely, the patient continuing to live – that is non-inferior to the relevant baseline, namely, her death. This result seems to support the general claim asserted by Premise 1. One could then apply this general claim to the analogous case where a proviso-satisfying act of appropriation, in tandem with other appropriations, brings about a system of property rights that is non-inferior to the absence of such a system.

The defense of Premise 2 would then point out that Nozick's specification of the proviso ensures that the entire set of private property rights does not harm$_{FC}$ anyone – where the absence of harm$_{FC}$ renders that system non-inferior to the relevant baseline for comparison (namely, the world where no appropriation occurs). Specifically, Nozick's proposal would preclude any appropriation that tipped the balance such that the entire system of property rights worked to some person's detriment$_{FC}$. Thus, his specification of the proviso ensures that all appropriations preserve the comparative non-inferiority of the system of property rights relative to the absence of any such rights.

The problem with the baseline argument is its assumption that the world without any appropriation is the relevant baseline for comparison to the appropriation world. Notably, the argument glosses over the question of which alternative state of affairs is the relevant comparison point when making judgments of non-inferiority. To answer this question, consider a modification of the surgery case where a nurse embeds a small metal sphere inside the patient's chest during the operation. In this case, the action of inserting the sphere brings about a state of affairs (the patient living with a sphere in her chest) that is non-inferior to the alternative baseline where no surgery occurs and the patient dies. However, given that inserting the sphere into the chest was clearly not justified, Premise 1 will be false if this no-surgery state of affairs is the relevant baseline for comparison. Thus, to preserve the soundness of the baseline argument, one should seemingly hold that the relevant baseline state of affairs is one where the surgery occurs but no sphere is inserted into the chest – perhaps because the surgical nurse never existed carry out this action. Such a proposal delivers the correct result by blocking the implication that the sphere insertion was justified.

Similarly, consider the case where two parents throw their child a birthday party but a rude guest shoves birthday cake in her face. While this action upsets the child, suppose that she is glad that she got to have the party on net, even factoring in the cake incident (though she would have preferred a party where the incident did not occur). In this case, the guest brought about an outcome that is non-inferior to the comparison world where no party ever took place. Thus, if this is the baseline for comparison, then Premise 1 entails that her action is justified. However, given that the action is clearly not justified, some other baseline for comparison must be posited. And, again, it appears that the more plausible baseline for comparison

3.3 Comparing Baselines 107

is the counterfactual world where the rude guest did not (exist to) smash cake on the child.

These results can be generalized as follows. When considering whether the actions in the prior cases were justified, the initial assessments employed what might be called a *compensation baseline*, where this baseline was defined by taking the actual world and removing from it some conjunction of actions that, together, benefit a person on net (e.g., the complete surgical procedure or the entire birthday party), even though at least one of those actions actually harms the person (e.g., the sphere insertion or the cake smashing). However, in both cases, it was argued that Premise 1 of the baseline argument ("if an action – in tandem with various other actions – brings about a state of affairs that is non-inferior to the relevant baseline for comparison, then that action is justified") is false if its use of the term "relevant baseline" refers to a compensation baseline. However, note that Premise 2 of the argument ("if an appropriation satisfies Nozick's proviso, then it (in tandem with various other actions) brings about a state of affairs that is non-inferior to the relevant baseline for comparison") is true only if "the relevant baseline for comparison" refers to the world that lacks the entire advantage-generating conjunction of appropriations that have been (and will be) carried out by many people across time. The problem here is that this baseline is a paradigmatic compensation baseline. Thus, barring equivocation, Premise 2 is true only if Premise 1 is false – which is to say that the baseline argument is necessarily unsound and cannot support the contention that appropriations that satisfy Nozick's proviso are justified. This, in turn, implies that Nozick's specification of the proviso cannot fulfill its theoretical function and should therefore be rejected.

By contrast, the following revised version of the baseline argument is seemingly sound:

1'. If an action brings about a state of affairs that is non-inferior to its corresponding nonexistence baseline, then that action is justified.
2'. If an appropriation satisfies the anarchist proviso, then it brings about a state of affairs that is non-inferior to its corresponding nonexistence baseline.
3'. Thus, if an appropriation satisfies the anarchist proviso, then it justified.

Specifically, one could defend Premise 1' by appealing to the sphere and birthday cases, where, in each case, non-inferiority relative to a nonexistence baseline – that is, the baseline where the agent did not exist to carry out the action in the first place – *would* seem to justify the agent's realization of a particular state of affairs. Strictly speaking, the states of affairs produced by *unjustified* actions in these cases were shown to be *not* non-inferior (i.e., inferior) to a nonexistence baseline. In other words, these cases do not function as counterexamples to Premise 1'. Further, if one adjusts these cases such that the action brought about a state that *was* non-inferior to the nonexistence baseline, then the action seems justified as a result. For example, suppose that the sphere prevented blood clots and thereby ensured the patient's survival. Or, in the birthday case, suppose that hitting the child with cake was the only way to keep them from eating it and having a terrible allergic reaction. Together, these results suggest that Premise 1' is true. Given that Premise 2' is true as a matter of definition, one can then infer the proposition asserted by 3' and thereby conclude that the proposed nonexistence specification ensures that appropriation is justified. In this way, the baseline argument ends up supporting the anarchist specification of the proviso rather than Nozick's.

3.4 Defending and Emending the Nonexistence Baseline

The previous section suggested that Nozick's baseline specification is the most obvious more permissive alternative to the proposed anarchist specification of the proviso. It then argued that the best apparent argument for Nozick's proviso actually supports the anarchist specification, with proponents of the proviso thereby having reason to favor this specification despite the fact that it entails surprising conclusions that they would otherwise reject. However, given the importance of the nonexistence baseline, more needs to be said in its defense. Specifically, this section will argue that there is a supplemental reason for endorsing the proposed specification, namely, that it follows from the moral tyranny constraint. Next, it will argue that the nonexistence baseline is superior to an alternative counterfactual inaction baseline. Finally, it will present a slightly technical emendation of the proposed baseline so as to bring the proviso into full compliance with the moral tyranny constraint.

To begin, note that there are many libertarians who reject the Lockean proviso, as they take it to be an auxiliary theory that can be costlessly excised from the core set of propositions endorsed by libertarian property theorists.[14] Given the existence of such proviso skeptics, proponents of the proviso need to provide an adequate justification for building the proviso

---

[14] Recall the radical right-libertarians from Footnote 6 of Chapter 1. That said, the claim that no-proviso libertarians think the proviso can be "costlessly excised" slightly overstates things, as there

3.4 Defending and Emending the Nonexistence Baseline

into a theory of property. Fortunately, Section 2.4 provided just such a justification, namely, that the proviso follows from the moral tyranny constraint. However, whether this conclusion holds depends on how one specifies the content of the Lockean proviso. Thus, there is reason to interpret the proviso in such a way as to ensure that it does, in fact, follow from the moral tyranny constraint.

While Chapter 2 did not specifically demonstrate that the constraint entails the nonexistence specification, that gap can now be filled in here. Or, more precisely, it will be argued that a slight generalization of constraint entails the specification in question, where those who accept the constraint ought to accept the generalization as well. Recall that the moral tyranny constraint holds that a theory of duties is acceptable only if it precludes persons from unilaterally, discretionarily, and foreseeably leaving others worse off under conditions of full compliance. Additionally, recall that these qualifiers were built into the constraint because there is seemingly nothing problematic about a theory allowing persons to unforeseeably, nondiscretionarily, or non-unilaterally leave others worse off$_{FC}$. For example, suppose that a person makes a choice that, as a matter of pure bad luck (i.e., unforeseeably), leaves her much worse off than others. Further, suppose that she would not have ended up worse off had she made a different choice. In this scenario, a luck egalitarian theory of justice holds that she is entitled to equalizing transfers from others – a conclusion that seems unproblematic even though it entails that the person was able to leave others worse off$_{FC}$ than they otherwise could have been. Similarly, there seems to be nothing problematic about the fact that luck egalitarianism entitles her to transfers if her advantage-destroying action was nondiscretionary, for example, because her action was a mere reflexive movement rather than an exercise of agency. Nor is there anything problematic about a moral theory permitting some person P to leave another person Q worse off$_{FC}$ if the only reason that Q ends up worse off$_{FC}$ is that she made a particular advantage-destroying choice in light of P's action (i.e., Q's loss$_{FC}$ of advantage is a function of both P's choice and Q's subsequent choice such that Q is fully able to avoid that loss$_{FC}$).

While Chapter 2 opted for a more modest statement of the constraint that enumerated the qualifications restricting when a theory cannot allow

---

are no-proviso libertarians who recognize that allowing genuinely unrestricted appropriation would entail certain highly implausible conclusions – for example, that a person could acquire the entire Earth and oblige all others to starve to death – and, thus, try to adjust their theory to avoid such implications (see Mack (1995) and Feser (2005, 71–6)). For a critique of their proposed solution, see Peter Bornschein (2018).

persons to leave others worse off$_{FC}$, the posited qualifications suggest a more general statement of the moral tyranny constraint: A moral theory is acceptable only if it precludes a person from taking any action such that (a) this action leaves others worse off$_{FC}$ and (b) the person is *morally responsible* for this action. With respect to Condition (b), note that each of the qualifications listed by the original moral tyranny constraint expresses an apparent necessary condition of moral responsibility. Seemingly, *P* is morally responsible for *Q*'s predicament only if *P* could have reasonably foreseen that *Q* would end up in this predicament. Similarly, *P* is morally responsible for that outcome only if she could have avoided bringing about that outcome (i.e., it was brought about by a discretionary choice). And, if *Q*'s predicament is brought about by *Q*'s own actions carried out in light of *P*'s actions, then that, too, seems to negate the *P*'s responsibility, as *Q* is responsible for her own predicament, with that responsibility exculpating *P*. Thus, it appears that moral tyranny requires moral responsibility – that is, the constraint should condemn a theory that allows *P* to leave *Q* worse off$_{FC}$ in some situation if and only if *P* is also responsible for leaving *Q* worse off$_{FC}$ in that situation.

If one accepts this more general moral tyranny constraint, then one must adjust the proviso if one wishes to sustain the desired entailment relation between the two propositions. Specifically, the proviso must prohibit all and only those appropriations where the appropriator is *responsible* for leaving others worse off$_{FC}$. And this, in turn, requires adopting the posited nonexistence specification of the proviso. To see why the proviso must be specified in this way, consider the case where person *O* both watches person *B* pour a bucket of sand in *H*'s house and declines to do anything to help clean up the sand. In this case, it is *B* who is responsible for leaving *H* worse off rather than *O*. But what explains this fact? The answer cannot appeal strictly to counterfactual choices that *B* and *O* could have made, as *H* would have been better off had either of the two chosen differently (i.e., had *B* not dumped the sand or had *O* not declined to clean it up). Rather, it seems that the best way to determine who is responsible for leaving *H* worse off is to compare the world where *H* incurs this cost to the world where various agents never existed. Given that *H*'s house would still have had sand in it had *O* not existed, *H*'s predicament cannot be attributed to *O* or her choices. By contrast, the proposed comparison would not vindicate *B* in this way. Thus, the nonexistence comparison appears to adequately demarcate when a person is responsible for someone else incurring a cost: *O* is responsible for imposing a cost on *H* only if *H* is better off in the closest possible world where *O* does not exist.

3.4 Defending and Emending the Nonexistence Baseline

In short, the moral tyranny constraint insists that theories of duties not enable people to both leave others worse off$_{FC}$ and be responsible for leaving them worse off$_{FC}$ in this way. It, therefore, entails the Lockean proviso if and only if the proviso strictly precludes each agent from being *responsible* for leaving others worse off$_{FC}$ via acts of appropriation. Further, given that an agent is responsible for leaving others worse off$_{FC}$ only if they would be better off$_{FC}$ in the world where she did not exist, the proviso must preclude any and all appropriation that leaves someone worse off$_{FC}$ than she would have been in the closest possible world where the appropriator did not exist. Thus, one arrives at the conclusion that the moral tyranny constraint entails the proviso if and only if the proviso is specified in the way proposed in Section 1.2, namely, with the baseline for comparison being the world where the appropriator did not exist.

There are two objections to this argument that are worth considering. First, one might argue that, when assessing whether an agent is responsible for some cost, the relevant comparison is *not* the world where the agent did not exist but, *rather*, the world where she refrained from carrying out some set of actions that imposed that cost.[15] In other words, O is responsible for a cost incurred by H only if H would have been better off had O refrained from exercising her agency in the situations in question – or, to restate this consequent a bit more precisely, there is some set of actions S such that H would have been better off had O refrained from carrying out every member of S. This proposal has the apparent advantage of comparative evaluative simplicity, as one need only consider a possible world where some set of actions did not occur rather than the more distant possible world where O did not exist at all. Additionally, it seems to equally deliver the correct results in the sand case: H would have been better off if B had refrained from pouring the bucket of sand in H's house, but there is no action on the part O such that H would have been better off had O not carried out that action. Given that (a) the inaction comparison is able to equally demarcate responsible parties from non-responsible parties in this test case and (b) it is easier to apply than the nonexistence comparison, one might conclude that it should replace the latter comparison in the proposed necessary condition of responsibility.[16] And, this, in turn, would entail that the Lockean proviso, if it is to follow from the generalized

---

[15] This point was raised by an anonymous referee for *Ethics* who reviewed an adapted version of this chapter.

[16] Cf. Nozick's (1974, 84–6) discussion of productive exchange wherein he uses the two comparisons interchangeably (or, strictly speaking, something quite proximate to these comparisons).

version of the moral tyranny constraint, must be specified such that the inaction world is the relevant baseline for comparison.

However, there are four reasons for favoring the nonexistence comparison over this proposed inaction comparison. First, it is not clear that the inaction comparison is simpler than the nonexistence comparison. Note that the former comparison is already more syntactically complex than the nonexistence comparison (where syntactic complexity is a standard metric for assessing theoretical simplicity) (Baker 2016). Additionally, contrary to initial appearances, the inaction comparison does not seem to be any easier to apply to specific cases. Note that, in order to exculpate someone, one must consider every possible subset of the actions she has carried out and compare the actual world with the possible world where every member of that subset was not carried out – where this possible world will often be quite distant from the actual one, for example, the world where the agent did nothing at all.[17] Thus, carrying out the rival inaction comparison turns out to be significantly more epistemically demanding than merely comparing the single nonexistence world to the actual world.

Second, the inaction comparison seems to deliver incorrect results in certain cases. For example, suppose that O is moved against her will and placed in a doorway. Minutes later, a fire starts inside the building, but O declines to move, thereby blocking the doorway with her body. This, in turn, results in H sustaining a serious injury due to not being able to escape the fire. According to the inaction comparison, O is not responsible for H's injury: H would not have been better off had O refrained from exercising her agency in this situation, as this counterfactual world is identical to the actual world (due to O not exercising her agency in either). By contrast, the nonexistence comparison delivers the intuitively correct result that O is responsible for H's injury. Given that H can freely pass through the doorway in the world where O does not exist, she will avoid injury and thereby end up better off relative to the actual world. Thus, the nonexistence comparison appears to have greater extensional adequacy than the inaction comparison.

The doorway case suggests a third worry about the inaction comparison, namely, that it may prove difficult to draw a defensible metaphysical

---

[17] One could simplify this procedure my considering only single actions rather than sets of actions. However, this modified procedure would deliver incorrect results in cases where an agent has acted in a way that overdetermines some outcome (e.g., she both poisons and stabs a person). In such cases, there will be no single action such that the victim is better off in the possible world where that action does not occur; however, it seems clear that the agent is responsible for the victim's predicament. Thus, one must consider whether the victim would be better off in worlds where conjunctions of the agent's actions were not carried out.

3.4 Defending and Emending the Nonexistence Baseline

distinction between action and inaction or the exercise of agency and the absence of such exercise. If the comparison is to yield any determinate judgment, each action must have a counterpart *nonaction* (as opposed to some rival action, which might generate confounding effects). However, it is not clear what would count as a nonaction given a natural account of what actions are – for example, intentional positionings of the body across space and time – as standing in one place is equally an intentional spatiotemporal positioning of the body. Absent such an account, the inaction comparison will lack determinate content.

Finally, the inaction comparison does not provide adequate theoretical support for exculpatory judgments relative to the nonexistence comparison. Briefly, the nonexistence comparison supports the conclusion that a person is not responsible for some state of affairs because it functions as a premise in the following argument:

1. A person P is responsible for some state of affairs S only if her choices are part of the explanation of why S obtains.
2. If S would equally obtain absent P making any choices at all, then P's choices are not part of the explanation of why S obtains.
3. If S equally obtains in the world where P does not exist, then S would equally obtain absent P making any choices at all.

   Thus, if S obtains in the world where P does not exist, then P is not responsible for S.

By contrast, the inaction comparison could only be substituted into this argument by changing the argument as follows:

1'. A person P is responsible for some state of affairs S only if her choices are part of the explanation of why S obtains.
2'. *If S would have equally obtained had P not carried out any subset of her actions*, then P's choices are not part of the explanation of why S obtains.

   Thus, *if S would have equally obtained had P not carried out any subset of her actions*, then P is not responsible for S.

While this argument would still be valid, it would be much weaker, as Premise 2' is contestable: P's choices could still explain why S obtains even if S would equally obtain if any conjunction of P's actions were replaced by their inaction counterparts because P's choice *to not carry out some rival action(s)* might explain why S obtains. Indeed, it was just such a choice by O in the doorway case that seems to explain H's injuries.

Premise 2' could be strengthened if one adjusted the argument as follows:

1". A person P is responsible for some state of affairs S only if her *actions* are part of the explanation of why S obtains.
2". If S would have equally obtained had P not carried out any subset of her actions, then P's *actions* are not part of the explanation of why S obtains.

Thus, if S would have equally obtained had P not carried out any subset of her actions, then P is not responsible for S.

The problem with this revision is that Premise 1" is open to contestation by those who contend that P might be responsible for S in virtue of some of her *omissions* explaining S (even if her *actions* do not explain S). By contrast, it seems much harder to dispute Premise 1 (and the identical Premise 1'), as it makes reference to P's *choices* rather than merely her actions. Thus, the nonexistence comparison should be favored over the proposed inaction comparison.

While this first objection to the nonexistence comparison does not succeed, there is a second objection that can only be addressed by emending the proposed comparison and the associated specification of the Lockean proviso's comparative baseline. Specifically, this objection notes that the nonexistence comparison will wrongly exculpate people (i.e., declare them not responsible) in cases where B has provided prior benefit to H. For example, consider the case where wind blows sand into H's house, B cleans it up, but then, a few days later, pours a bucket of sand into H's house. In this case, B seems responsible for H's predicament in virtue of her second action. However, the nonexistence comparison would say that B is not responsible, as H would not be worse off had B never existed. To avoid this bad result, the comparison must be modified such that B is held to be responsible for leaving H worse off via some action only if H would be better off in the world where B never existed *and* all of the costs and benefits that B had previously provided to H – that is, all of the other costs and benefits for which B is responsible – were provided in some other way.[18]

---

[18] Strictly speaking, one would also have to modify the comparison so that it delivers correct judgments in cases of overdetermination – that is, cases where B is seemingly responsible for imposing some cost on H but there is some other person who would impose an equal cost on H if B did not (e.g., suppose a third party T would have dumped just as much sand in the house if B did not do so). In such cases, H would similarly be no better off in the world where B never existed; however, it seems that B *is* responsible for leaving H worse off. Thus, the nonexistence comparison delivers the incorrect result

3.4 Defending and Emending the Nonexistence Baseline 115

In short, when assessing whether B is responsible for leaving someone worse off (or worse off$_{FC}$), one must carry out the more complex comparison presented just prior.[19] Further, given that the proviso must be specified so as to ensure that it only precludes appropriations where the appropriator is *responsible* for leaving others worse off$_{FC}$, it follows that its baseline for comparison must correspond to this emended comparison. Specifically, the proviso must hold that appropriation succeeds if and only if its established claims – or any subsequent waiving of those claims – would not leave anyone worse off$_{FC}$ relative to the world where the appropriator did not exist but all of her prior imposed costs$_{FC}$ and benefits$_{FC}$ still obtained. That said, this emendation does not seem to undermine the arguments presented previously. The establishment of – and most-harmful selective waiving – of claims over external resources will still almost always leave others worse off$_{FC}$ than they would have been in the nonexistence world where they still possessed the prior past benefits$_{FC}$ and costs$_{FC}$ imposed by the appropriator. In fact, this adjustment actually makes the proviso slightly *more* restrictive for reasons that will be discussed in the next section. Similarly, self-appropriation still necessarily satisfies the proviso. The fact that the baseline for comparison now includes all of the costs$_{FC}$ and benefits$_{FC}$ previously produced by the self-appropriator does

---

and is in need of further emendation. That said, because the concern here is specifically whether appropriators are responsible for leaving others worse off$_{FC}$ via appropriation, one need not worry about cases of overdetermination. Note that overdetermination cases arise if and only if one person imposes a cost on someone but another person would have equally imposed that cost had the former acted differently. However, in the case of appropriation, such overdetermination is not possible, as one of its necessary conditions is negated by the Lockean proviso. To see this, consider the case where B attempts to appropriate some resource R, where the appropriation of R would leave H worse off$_{FC}$ relative to the world where R is not appropriated. In this case, B's appropriation would also leave H worse off$_{FC}$ relative to the world where B never existed and, thus, would violate the Lockean proviso. But what if the costs$_{FC}$ imposed on H are overdetermined such that they would obtain even if B did not exist? In order for the costs$_{FC}$ to be overdetermined in this way, it must be the case that there is some other person T who would impose these costs$_{FC}$ if B did not exist – that is, who would appropriate R in the nonexistence world. However, the Lockean proviso entails that there could be no such counterfactual appropriation, as this appropriation, too, would violate the proviso. This is because H would be better off in the world where T never existed relative to the counterfactual appropriation world (as the closest possible world where T never existed is also one where B never existed and, thus, where no appropriation of R occurs). Thus, the costs imposed by appropriation cannot be overdetermined and one need not worry about such overdetermination when specifying the proviso's baseline (even though the aim is to provide a specification that ensures that a person violates the proviso only if she is *responsible* for leaving others worse off, and overdetermination complicates counterfactual analyses of responsibility (as noted by Nozick 1974, 85)).

[19] It was suggested previously that the nonexistence comparison may actually be easier to carry out than the inaction comparison. However, with the emendation it is no longer clear that this is the case.

nothing to change the fact that all costs$_{FC}$ imposed by her self-appropriation will be equally imposed by her nonexistence in that comparison world. Thus, the emended proviso still supports the anarchist contention that people own themselves and practically nothing else (with only those who have yet to self-appropriate being excluded from the set of self-owners).

3.5 Appropriation and Children

With the foregoing argument in place, it is now possible to discuss what the anarchist position entails vis-à-vis children. The primary thing to note is that it implies that children are not self-owners until they self-appropriate, where such self-appropriation requires the cognitive capacities discussed in Section 1.3. Specifically, it was suggested there that persons self-appropriate by asserting that they own themselves. Thus, persons cannot be self-owners if they lack the capacities to make such an assertion (the linguistic capacity needed to make assertions more generally, the cognitive capacity needed to conceptualize ownership, etc.). Given that infants and young children lack these capacities, it follows that they are not self-owners and that their bodies therefore qualify as unowned natural resources. There are two worries that might be raised about this implication.

First, one might worry that the absence of self-ownership unacceptably permits people to mistreat children in various ways, as children lack important claims against bodily contact of the kind possessed by adult self-owners. However, there are three things that can be said in response to this worry. First, practically no theories of rights, libertarian or otherwise, take infants and young children to be self-owners. Thus, it is not a unique problem for the anarchist position that it, too, denies self-ownership rights to young children. Second, as was discussed in Sections 1.6 and 1.7, the fact that someone does not possesses a (self-)ownership claim against a person taking some action does not imply that she lacks *any* claim against the person taking that action. Rather, she might have a distributive claim against that action (or, perhaps, some other variety of claim, though, for the sake of parsimony, no other kinds of claims have been posited here). One can then apply this observation to the case of children who have not yet self-appropriated: although these children lack self-ownership rights, they will still have a robust set of claims against mistreatment, as they will have a claim against any uses of their body that would leave them worse off than others absent some sanctionable choice on their part (where it is assumed that children lack the requisite capacities to choose sanctionably).²⁰ Granted, they have this same claim vis-à-vis all other natural resources and not just their respective bodies; however, given that they will be particularly affected by how people interact with their bodies, their bodily distributive claims will likely be much more restrictive than their other distributive claims (i.e., their claims against uses of their bodies will far outnumber their claims against uses of any other object). One can, therefore, expect that the anarchist position will entail that children have a claim against practically all actions that intuitively seem like child abuse or mistreatment.

There is a third quick reply that can be made to the worry that the anarchist position entails that children lack self-ownership rights. Specifically, one might argue that this result actually counts in *favor* of social anarchism, as it has the intuitively attractive implication that paternalistic bodily contact – that is, contact that benefits the child – is permissible. Note that ASO entails that self-owners have a claim against paternalistic interference with their bodies (so long as that interference does not uniquely generate supplemental benefits). Thus, if children were self-owners, one could not clothe them, for example, without infringing upon their rights. By contrast, if children merely possess distributive claims vis-à-vis their bodies, then it will typically be permissible to make contact with their bodies when that contact is to their benefit.²¹

The second worry that one might have about the proposition that the bodies of young children qualify as unowned natural resources is that it implies that parents can appropriate their children's bodies before the children develop the requisite capacities to self-appropriate. Indeed, this concern is raised by Susan Moller Okin (1989, 79–85) as part of her critique of Nozick's entitlement theory of justice. A quick reply to this concern is that parental appropriation violates the proviso, as there are

---

[20] One might defend this parenthetical assumption by appealing to the generalized moral tyranny constraint in Section 3.4. There it was suggested that moral theories are unacceptable if they allow an agent to leave others worse off$_{FC}$ while also being responsible for leaving them worse off$_{FC}$. Further, Section 2.4 argued that luck egalitarianism holds people responsible for sanctionable choices in order to satisfy the moral tyranny constraint. Thus, it should declare that a person has chosen sanctionably if and only if not doing so would entail that the person is responsible for leaving others worse off$_{FC}$. If one then assumes that young children are never responsible for leaving others worse off$_{FC}$ (because they lack the requisite cognitive capacities to be morally responsible for their actions), it follows that luck egalitarianism should not declare that they have chosen sanctionably or hold them responsible for their choices.

[21] The "typically" qualifier is included because, strictly speaking, other people would have a claim against someone making paternalistic bodily contact with a child if that contact somehow left them with less than their appropriate share of advantage (according to a luck egalitarian theory of distributive justice).

many post-waiving patterns of the established claims that would leave the child worse off under conditions of full compliance. For example, parental appropriation would give parents a claim against the child putting food in her own mouth, where compliance with this claim would leave the child much worse off. However, one might worry that this reply is, in fact, too quick, as it neglects the way in which the proviso's nonexistence baseline interacts with parental appropriation. Note that this specification – at least, the unemended version – entails that parental appropriation violates the proviso if and only if some subset of the established claims leaves the child worse off$_{FC}$ *relative to the world where the appropriating parent did not exist.* However, if a child's parent(s) did not exist, then the child would not exist either, with the cost$_{FC}$ of nonexistence seeming to equal or even exceed whatever costs the child would incur by complying with her parents' ownership rights over her body.

One way of responding to this worry is to argue that parental appropriation actually *does* leave the child worse off$_{FC}$ relative to the nonexistence baseline (i.e., the world where the appropriating parent(s) – and, by extension, the child – did not exist). For example, one might maintain that being a moral slave to one's parents is a "fate worse than death." If it is better to not exist than have to comply with any arbitrary parental ownership claims vis-à-vis one's own body, then parental appropriation still violates the proviso. Alternatively, one might simply respecify the baseline of the proviso to avoid this arguably marginal problematic implication. Specifically, one could hold that the relevant baseline is the closest possible world where the appropriator does not exist but where all of the non-appropriators under consideration do. Thus, the nonexistence world would be one where the child's parents did not exist but she was somehow conjured into existence or engineered in a lab. And, given that the child is worse off$_{FC}$ in the world where her parents own her body than she is in this respecified comparison world, it follows that parental appropriation violates the Lockean proviso.

An easier response, however, is to simply appeal to the more precise formulation of the proviso presented in the prior section. There it was argued that the proviso must be emended such that the comparison world is the one where the appropriator did not exist but all of her previously produced costs$_{FC}$ and benefits$_{FC}$ still obtained. Given that these benefits$_{FC}$ include the child getting to experience life, the relevant baseline for comparison would be the world where the parents did not exist but the child still existed. Thus, parental appropriation of a child's body would violate the emended proviso, as the established claims would leave the child worse off$_{FC}$ than she would be in the appropriate baseline for comparison. This result, in turn, implies that no one can appropriate a child's body prior to her developing the relevant capacities needed to self-appropriate. In this way, the anarchist position avoids the unacceptable implication that adults or parents can come to own a child's body.

3.6 Conclusion

This chapter has attempted to demonstrate that the Lockean proviso simultaneously entails that most people own themselves in the sense articulated by ASO (as it is trivially easy to self-appropriate) and that there is no external private property. In this way, it has attempted to demonstrate the coherence of the anarchist position while also addressing some of the most obvious objections that might be leveled against the foregoing argument. It has also provided an extended defense – and slight emendation – of the Lockean proviso, thereby bolstering the starting premise on which the chapter's argument rests. Finally, it has completed the explication of what anarchism implies vis-à-vis children that was started in Section 1.3. There it was argued that children lack self-ownership rights because they lack the capacities needed to self-appropriate. This chapter has now explained why this lack of self-ownership does not leave them vulnerable to permitted mistreatment or the appropriation of their bodies. In this way, it has demonstrated that the anarchist position can be employed to provide a well-grounded and extensionally adequate account of the rights of children.

Finally, it is worth noting that this discussion of children's rights is another illustration of how the component parts of the anarchist position complement each other by jointly entailing attractive results. The anarchist premise that people acquire self-ownership via self-appropriation helped to explain why practically all adults – despite varying cognitive capacities – have the same set of rights while young children do not possess these rights. The anarchist rejection of external property in favor of luck egalitarian distributive claims then helped to ensure that these children still have rights against mistreatment and abuse (while permitting paternalistic bodily contact). And the anarchist interpretation of the Lockean proviso protected children from having their bodies appropriated before they had a chance to self-appropriate. In this way, the distinct components of the anarchist position come together to help answer notoriously difficult philosophical questions about the moral equality of persons and the rights of children.

The fact that the anarchist theses jointly entail attractive conclusions in this way also reveals an additional sense in which the anarchist position is coherent: Its separate theses hang together in the sense that affirming only some of these theses but not others will negate certain attractive implications and often generate unfortunate ones in their place. For example, rejecting the Lockean proviso – as radical right-libertarians are inclined to do – raises difficult questions about why adults are not able to appropriate the bodies of young children prior to their achieving self-ownership.[22] One can perhaps solve this problem by contending that children are self-owners from birth, perhaps in virtue of the fact that they will eventually develop certain capacities later on. However, one must then address the apparent implication that parents are forbidden from making even paternalistic contact with their children's bodies. Additionally, by grounding self-ownership in scalar cognitive capacities, one faces the difficult challenge of explaining human moral equality (as was discussed in Section 1.3). Similarly, if one denies that people possess distributive claims over unowned things while accepting the other anarchist theses, then it is difficult to explain why child abuse and other forms of mistreatment are wrongful, as one can no longer appeal to the anarchist's posited distributive claims as part of this explanation. Thus, there is additional reason to affirm the entire set of anarchist theses as opposed to some proper subset – that is, reason beyond the fact that these theses both stand in entailment relations with one another and are also jointly entailed by the moral tyranny constraint – namely, that these theses jointly deliver favorable results that do not follow from the conjunction of any proper subset of the theses.

---

[22] This objection is directed explicitly at Feser's radical right-libertarian position in Spafford (2021b, 332).

CHAPTER 4

Property and Legitimacy

> But nobody has the right to seize a single one of these machines and say: "This is mine; if you want to use it you must pay me a tax on each of your products," any more than the feudal lord of medieval times had the right to say to the peasant: "This hill, this meadow belong to me, and you must pay me a tax on every sheaf of corn you reap, on every rick you build."
>
> All is for all! If the man and the woman bear their fair share of work, they have a right to their fair share of all that is produced by all, and that share is enough to secure them well-being. No more of such vague formulas as "The right to work," or "To each the whole result of his labour." What we proclaim is the Right to Well-Being: Well-Being for All!
>
> Peter Kropotkin, The Conquest of Bread

Chapter 3 argued that no one has successfully appropriated external natural resources because (practically) no acts of appropriation satisfy the Lockean proviso. This chapter will provide an alternative route for reaching this conclusion by arguing that those who accept a consent theory of legitimacy must also concede that there have been no successful acts of appropriation. Specifically, it will contend that property ownership is a *form* of legitimacy and, thus, has the same necessary conditions as legitimacy, namely, consent. Given that no one has actually consented to the establishment of property, it follows that there is no existing private property, as social anarchists contend.

To reach this conclusion, Section 4.1 will begin by introducing a slightly modified notion of legitimacy called *territorial legitimacy*. Next, Section 4.2 will argue that anyone who endorses a consent theory of legitimacy should also endorse a consent theory of territorial legitimacy. Section 4.3 will then argue that property ownership in land entails territorial legitimacy (and, thus, has consent as its necessary condition). Further, Section 4.4 will argue that there is no relevant distinction between land and objects such that consent becomes a necessary condition of appropriating any natural resource – a result that, in turn, entails that no one has any private property rights over such resources. Sections 4.5–4.7 consider and reject three objections to the proposed argument. However, whereas these objections do not succeed, Section 4.8 will note that a consent theory of property acquisition is in tension with the claim in Chapter 3 that persons can easily appropriate themselves. It will then consider three possible ways to resolve this tension. Finally, Section 4.9 will conclude with a discussion of the relationship between philosophical anarchism and the anarchist conclusion – that is, the conclusion that the permissible use of external resources is governed by distributive claims rather than property claims.

4.1 Territorial Legitimacy

The crucial step in this chapter's argument is to show that anyone who has property rights over some tract of land has the same normative power as a legitimate state, where the term "legitimacy" is used to refer to this power. For, if this is the case, then the consent theory of legitimacy entails that land ownership can only be established with the consent of others – that is, the initial appropriation of land has consent as its necessary condition. To see why property rights entail legitimacy, recall the definition of legitimacy offered in Section 1.1: Person P is a legitimate authority with respect to another person Q when P has the power to determine what obligations Q has via the issuing of edicts. In other words, if a legitimate P at time t issues the edict that Q must ϕ, then Q is obligated to ϕ at t. Additionally, it will be helpful to label the set of duties imposed by a legitimate authority the duty bearer's *political obligations*.

Notably, this account makes legitimacy an interpersonal relation that might obtain between any two agents. Thus, one cannot simply assert that a state is legitimate *tout court*; rather, it must be specified which persons are subject to its legitimate authority. However, this notion of legitimacy is very different from the power that actually existing states claim to possess. As Simmons notes, one of the primary rights claimed by states is the jurisdictional control right to impose and coercively enforce laws upon all people *within its claimed territory* (2016, 4–5). According to Simmons, the legitimacy of states should be understood as *bounded* by the borders of their territory such that "only those persons within a state's claimed territories are claimed as subjects of that state's authority, as bound by its laws" (2016, 31).

4.1 Territorial Legitimacy

Note that this makes the actual power claimed by states both weaker and stronger than *unbounded legitimacy* as defined just prior. On the one hand, it is weaker because states only claim the right to regulate conduct within their territory. By contrast, an unbounded legitimacy relation obtains irrespective of the location of the person(s) subject to the legitimate authority. On the other hand, the power claimed by states is stronger than unbounded legitimacy in that it is the power to specify the obligations of *anyone* who is within their respective territories. An alien – who, by definition, is not a person with respect to whom a state is legitimate in the unbounded sense – is, nonetheless, taken by the state to be obligated to comply with its edicts upon entering its territory. Further, the state takes her to be obliged to comply with edicts that were issued prior to her entry. If the state passed a law in January prohibiting drug use, an alien who enters the territory in February would, in the eyes of the state, be obliged to refrain from using drugs (despite the fact that she was not in the territory when the edict was issued).

To put this point more precisely, states claim the power to specify the *conditional* obligations of others, where such obligations are those that obtain only on the condition that the obliged party is within a given state's territory.[1] This power will be called *territorial legitimacy*, where some person P is territorially legitimate with respect to person Q if and only if there is some bit of territory T such that, if P issues an edict of the form "if Q is within T, then Q must ϕ," then Q is obligated to ϕ if she is within T. States can then be understood as claiming that they possess *universal* territorial legitimacy; that is, they are territorially legitimate with respect to all people.

Section 4.2 will argue that it is *territorial* legitimacy that should concern consent theorists; that is, if one takes consent to be a necessary condition of unbounded legitimacy, then one should also take consent to be a necessary condition of territorial legitimacy. Section 4.3 will then argue that having property rights is equivalent to possessing territorial legitimacy. Thus, consent theorists should also take consent to be a necessary condition of the initial appropriation of private property. The remaining sections will then address some objections to this argument, discuss how it bears upon the self-ownership thesis, and explicate the relationship between philosophical anarchism and the anarchist conclusion.

---

[1] Or, alternatively, conditional obligations might be understood as obligations to make certain conditional propositions true. For example, if a legitimate state passes a law that all those within its territory T must ϕ, then any given Q is obliged to act in a way that makes true the proposition that if Q is within T, then Q ϕ-s. This might be done either by making the antecedent false (i.e., not entering T) or the consequent true when the antecedent is true (i.e., ϕ-ing within T).

4.2 A Consent Theory of Territorial Legitimacy

As noted in Section 4.1, territorial legitimacy is weaker than unbounded legitimacy, as the latter is a power to specify subjects' unconditional obligations while the former is the power to specify conditional obligations (where such obligations obtain conditional on a subject's location). Given this difference, a consent theory of legitimacy does not necessarily entail a consent theory of territorial legitimacy. Indeed, there is no logical inconsistency in simultaneously holding that (a) a person must consent if another is to have the power to specify her unconditional obligations and (b) the weaker power to specify conditional territorial obligations does not require such consent. The question, then, is whether a person who endorses Proposition (a) *should also* endorse a consent theory of territorial legitimacy.

There are a number of reasons to answer this question in the affirmative. First, from a purely dialectical standpoint, proponents of consent theory are typically concerned with the moral standing of actually existing states. Given that such states insist that they have territorial legitimacy rather than unbounded legitimacy, consent theorists will want to make consent a necessary condition of the former as well as the latter. Additionally, consent theorists would not want their thesis to be rendered irrelevant by the conditionalization of an unbounded legitimacy claim. For example, suppose that a monarch denies that she needs consent to oblige others because she is not legitimate in the unbounded sense but, rather, is simply *territorially* legitimate vis-à-vis the entire Milky Way Galaxy. Unless consent theorists are willing to admit that their thesis loses all relevance in this case – that is, when what is asserted is not "Q is obligated to ϕ when P says she must ϕ," but, rather, "Q is obligated to ϕ if she is within the Milky Way and P says she must ϕ while in the Milky Way" – then the consent theorist should also take consent to be a necessary condition of territorial legitimacy.

More importantly, the grounds for adopting a consent theory of legitimacy equally support endorsing a consent theory of territorial legitimacy. Consider, for example, Simmons' prominent argument by elimination for a consent theory of legitimacy (2001).[2] Simmons begins by introducing three possible categories of moral requirement under which political obligations might fall. First, there are *natural duties*, which are

---

[2] Simmons makes this argument across a number of works, beginning with his *Moral Principles and Political Obligations* (1979). However, the cited 2001 text appears to be his attempt at a definitive and condensed restatement of the argument. Thus, the following synopsis largely reconstructs the argument as it is presented there, turning to the 1979 text only to supplement the argument and fill in some minor gaps.

4.2 A Consent Theory of Territorial Legitimacy

"moral requirements which apply to all [persons] irrespective of status or of acts performed" and are "owed by all persons to all others" (1979, 13). Additionally, because the duties are owed to all others, the content of those duties must be general, making no reference to particular persons or institutions (2001, 47).[3] By contrast, *special obligations* are owed by particular people to other particular people and arise from the actions of individuals. For example, the moral requirements generated by acts of promising are special obligations, as (a) only a proper subset of people are obliged to carry out the promised action; (b) only a proper subset of people are owed this action (where the content of the obligation makes specific reference to these people); and (c) the moral requirement to act did not previously exist, but, rather, came into existence via the actions of the involved parties.

Simmons divides special obligations into two subcategories: those that are *voluntary* and arise via intentional acts of consent (e.g., promissory obligations) and those that do not come about via voluntary action (e.g., filial obligations) (2001, 45). Simmons then argues by elimination, arguing, first, that political obligations cannot be natural duties, and, second, that they cannot be nonvoluntary special obligations. He, therefore, concludes that political obligations must be voluntary special obligations, that is, they have consent as their necessary condition.

Simmons makes two arguments to support his claim that political obligations are not natural duties. First, he argues that political obligations are *particular* in a way that natural duties are not: Political obligations are owed to only one state, with the content of one's obligation specifically referencing that state (2001, 47). One might have a natural duty to support states that are just or aid states in desperate need, but one will owe this duty to any state that meets the relevant posited criteria. By contrast, political obligations are owed to only one particular state. Thus, political obligations cannot be natural duties.

Second, Simmons argues that natural duties come in two varieties. *Negative duties* are requirements that agents refrain from acting in certain ways. By contrast, *positive duties* require positive action by the agent. Simmons contends that, while negative natural duties are perfect and, thus, allow for little to no discretion in terms of how they are carried

---

[3] Technically, Simmons claims that the content of duties must be general in this way because "duties are binding on all persons" (2001, 47). However, this seems like a non sequitur, as it seems possible that all persons might have a requirement that specifies a particular person. Rather, it seems generality follows not from all having the duty, but the fact that the duty is owed to all.

out, positive natural duties are imperfect and allow people a degree of discretion over how to discharge those duties (2001, 48). For example, an agent is typically permitted to refrain from discharging positive natural duties if discharging those duties would impose a significant cost on her (47). Given that political obligations do not allow for such discretion – including those that demand the agent carry out some positive action – it follows that they cannot be natural duties and must, instead, be special obligations.

Having shown that political obligations are special obligations, Simmons still needs to show that they are of the voluntary variety as opposed to the involuntary variety. Here, again, he employs an argument by elimination, considering the most plausible theories of involuntary special obligation and rejecting each in turn. While Simmons' arguments against these theories are too numerous to reconstruct here, he provides sufficient conceptual resources for constructing an abbreviated version of his argument that eliminates whole classes of theories without having to consider them individually.[4] Specifically, nonvoluntary special obligations can be divided into two kinds: those that are grounded in the provision of benefits – that is, have the provision of benefits as their necessary condition – and those that can obtain even absent any such benefit being provided. Simmons rejects the possibility of the latter, contending that it is implausible to hold that anyone might owe involuntary duties to an agent from whom they receive no benefit (1979, 158).[5] As a supporting example, he considers the case of a fur trapper living in isolation so deep within the interior of a territory that the state is not able to provide her with any benefits such as security or defense (159). Simmons contends that, given her circumstances, the trapper is not obligated to comply with the laws of the state (e.g., its gun control laws) (159). Further, if one accepts that the trapper has no such obligation *because* she does not receive any benefits from the state, then it follows that receipt of benefit is, at least partially, a ground of having a (nonvoluntary) special obligation.

This leaves only one remaining competitor to voluntary special obligations: the class of nonvoluntary special obligations grounded in the

---

[4] For Simmons' discussion of various specific proposals, see Simmons (1979, ch. 6; 1996; 2001, 50–5).

[5] In the context where he advances this claim, Simmons speaks specifically of political obligations having receipt of benefit as a necessary condition, but, presumably, this claim would generalize to all special obligations, or, at least, special obligations of the kind under consideration here (namely, political obligations and territorial obligations).

4.2 A Consent Theory of Territorial Legitimacy

provision of benefits. These obligations purportedly arise when the receipt of benefits leaves the recipient indebted to the provider. However, Simmons argues that the receipt of benefits fails to give rise to such special obligations. First, he notes that the mere receipt of benefits (as opposed to the *acceptance* of benefits) cannot ground obligations, as it is implausible to think that a person who explicitly refuses some benefit but has it forced upon her owes a special obligation to the provider of that benefit (2001, 56). Further, even when benefits have been accepted, Simmons insists that this acceptance still cannot ground special obligations. Specifically, he argues that, even insofar as an indebted person owes some return to her benefactor, she does not owe *whatever the benefactor demands* (56). Rather, she merely owes some "fitting return" that is adequately "responsive to the benefactor's needs" (56). Thus, benefaction cannot generate political obligations, as such obligations are "content-specific," that is, they demand specific performances over which the obligor has little to no discretion (56–7). In this way, Simmons rules out the possibility of any sort of nonvoluntary political obligations; that is, one must be a consent theorist about political obligations/legitimacy.

Does this argument for a consent theory of legitimacy also commit its proponent to a consent theory of *territorial* legitimacy? The answer to this question will depend on whether any of the premises or inferences described previously would be compromised if one were to replace all references to the political obligations of unbounded legitimacy with references to the conditional obligations of territorial legitimacy. To put the question a bit more precisely: Must such conditional obligations also fall under the category of voluntary special obligations? Or could they be natural duties or involuntary special obligations? The answer to these questions appears to vindicate a consent theory of territorial legitimacy. Quick consideration of each step of Simmons' argument suggests that, just as political obligations are voluntary special obligations, so, too, are the conditional obligations established by territorially legitimate authorities. Thus, territorial legitimacy has consent as its necessary condition.

First, note that, like political obligations, territory-specific conditional obligations are special obligations, as they are owed only to some person(s) rather than to all persons. There is a slight disanalogy between political obligations and territorial obligations, as the former are typically thought to be owed to a single political authority (the state) while the latter can be owed to multiple authorities, each corresponding to some distinct bit of territory. However, as with political obligations, territorial obligations are owed to a proper subset of people rather than being owed to all people.⁶ Additionally, the territorial obligations that states claim to impose are both perfect and often demand positive actions – a conjunction of properties that is incompatible with an obligation being a natural duty. Thus, Simmons' argument that the obligations associated with unbounded legitimacy cannot be natural duties applies equally to the conditional obligations established by territorially legitimate authorities.

Similarly, the fact that the obligations associated with territorial legitimacy are conditional fails to exempt them from the second step of Simmons' argument, which denies that there are nonvoluntary special obligations grounded in something other than the receipt of benefit. Given that territorial obligations are special obligations, Simmons' conclusion implies that they also cannot be both nonvoluntary and grounded in something other than benefit receipt. This implication can be further supported by appealing to a modified version of Simmons' fur trapper case. Simmons' contention is that the state is not legitimate with respect to the trapper because it does not provide her with any benefits. However, suppose, instead, that the state merely asserts that it is *territorially* legitimate such that the trapper must comply with its laws *if* she is within its territory. Such a weakening of the state's asserted power does nothing to make it more plausible that the trapper must comply with its gun control laws. Thus, if territorial obligations are to be nonvoluntary, they must be grounded in the receipt of benefits.

Finally, consider Simmons' rejection of the receipt of benefits as a ground for political obligation. Simmons suggests that benefaction cannot generate moral requirements that have the kind of specific content that characterizes political obligations. Similarly, the specificity of territorial obligations precludes them from being grounded in the receipt of benefits: They are requirements to act in the specific way(s) dictated by the territorially legitimate authority (when one is within the territory) without any of the discretion characteristic of benefaction-grounded obligations. Thus, the conditional obligations imposed by territorially legitimate authorities must

---

⁶ There is some oversimplification here. Strictly speaking, natural duties would be owed to a proper subset of persons if some people were to waive their correlative claims. Inversely, a special obligation would be owed to all persons if a single person made an identical promise to each of them (as noted by Diane Jeske (2014, fn1)). Thus, the distinction between natural duties and obligations is better put in terms of *achievement*: All persons *start out* owing a natural duty to all persons, though a state of affairs might be *achieved* where these duties are only owed by some to some (e.g., due to the waiving or forfeiture of claims). By contrast, no one starts out owing a special obligation to all persons; rather, such a state of affairs can only be achieved through human action. However, the main text opts for the simpler statement of the distinction, both for ease of exposition and because this is how it is articulated by Simmons.

4.3 The Absence of Appropriation

be special obligations of a voluntary kind. Given this result, any consent theorist who bases her view on Simmons' argument by elimination should also accept a consent theory of territorial legitimacy.[7]

Sections 4.1 and 4.2 introduced the concepts of legitimacy and territorial legitimacy and argued that, if one is a consent theorist about the former, one should also be a consent theorist about the latter. The current section builds upon this conclusion by arguing that the holder of private property rights in land is territorially legitimate with respect to all other persons. Thus, consent theorists are committed to the conclusion that the establishment of property rights in land has consent as its necessary condition.

To begin, note that to have a private property right over some tract of land is to have a bundle of rights including the right to use the land, the power to transfer the land (i.e., all of the listed rights and powers), the right to exclude others from that land, and the power to waive these rights.[8] This last-mentioned power is notable because, when paired with the right to exclude others from the land, it follows that the right-holder has the power to determine the conditions under which others are permitted to use the land. If P has property rights over some tract of land, then P has a waivable right to exclude Q from that land, where she can specify the conditions under which the right is waived. Thus, P has the power to make it such that Q rightfully occupies and/or uses that land if and only if Q complies with some edict issued by P. For example, P might declare that anyone who wishes to use the land – where such use includes standing/walking upon the land – must wear red. She would then have a conditional right against Q that Q wear red if Q is on the land. Further, because this conditional right has a correlative conditional obligation, it follows that Q is obligated to wear red if she is within P's property. Thus, P has the power to establish conditional obligations for Q via the issuing of edicts, where the antecedent of the obligation is Q being within the bounds of some

---

[7] Indeed, Simmons appears to tacitly accept the arguments of the preceding section, as he takes control rights over territory – which is seemingly implied by territorial legitimacy – to be grounded in the legitimacy of the governing authority (2016). Given that he takes legitimacy to have consent as its necessary condition, he is seemingly committed to the conclusion that territorial legitimacy has consent as its necessary condition.

[8] The following discussion will focus exclusively upon land. However, Section 4.4 will contend that the argument generalizes to *all* property.

geographic territory. In other words, *P* has the power of territorial legitimacy described in Section 4.1.

Given that the consent theorist is committed to the proposition that territorial legitimacy has the consent of all claimed subjects as its necessary condition, she is consequently committed to the proposition that property rights in land have the consent of all claimed subjects (namely, all other people) as their necessary condition. This, in turn, implies a commitment to the proposition that the acts of initial appropriation that establish such property rights have the consent of all others as their necessary condition. Further, given that no one has, as a matter of empirical fact, consented to appropriation, consent theorists must maintain that such initial appropriation has not occurred, which, in turn, implies that all land remains unowned. Thus, consent theorists must deny that there are any existing property rights in land, with one anarchist thesis thereby entailing another.[9]

4.4 Land, Resources, and Artifacts

Note that the aforementioned conclusion only applies to *land-based* property rights. But what about property rights over objects and resources? Are such entitlements also ruled out by a consent theory of legitimacy? If not, then consent theorists are committed to a much less radical position than the anarchist contends, as there could still be ownership of any resources aside from land (setting aside the proviso-based argument of Section 3.1). However, there is reason for thinking that a lack of property rights in land entails that *all* resources and objects are similarly unowned. Specifically, it appears that all property rights over objects entail the power of territorial legitimacy. To see why, recall that *P* is territorially legitimate with respect to some territory if and only if *P* issuing the edict that *Q* must ϕ if she is within the territory entails that *Q* is obligated to ϕ if she is within the territory. But what counts as a territory? And what counts as being *within*

---

[9] The foregoing argument also puts dialectical pressure on many of those who reject the consent theory of legitimacy. Typically, those who reject the theory also want to deny the libertarian contention that persons have private property rights. However, if legitimacy is one of the powers conferred by property ownership, then critics of consent theory are actually endorsing the view that persons can unilaterally establish at least partial property ownership. Thus, if they want to avoid this conclusion, they must abandon their position vis-à-vis legitimacy and endorse the anarchist thesis that consent is a necessary condition of establishing this power.

4.4 Land, Resources, and Artifacts

that territory? The answers to these two questions, it will be argued, reveal that to use an owned object or resource is to be within its owner's territory.

With respect to the former question, territory might be thought of as a portion of physical space. However, this isn't quite right – at least, insofar as this portion of physical space is understood as being a fixed spatial region. Consider, for example, the territory claimed by the United States Federal Government: From a cosmic perspective, this territory is moving extremely rapidly in a corkscrew-like motion as the Earth simultaneously rotates and orbits the Sun, which is, itself, in motion. Thus, to make sense of territorial claims, territory must be understood as space defined in relation to some bit of mass such as a planet. Specifically, a territory is a portion of the surface of some massive object (it may also extend above and/or below the surface, but this is more controversial).

The answer to the question of what counts as being *within* a territory is more straightforward: To be within a territory is to be in contact with that territory. For example, when a person walks onto land claimed by the United States, she makes contact with the relevant surface region of the Earth, thereby qualifying her as being within that territory. One might also contend that those who tunnel under or fly above the surface are within the territory. However, the suggestion here is that to hold such a view is to presuppose the more controversial view (noted just prior) that the region below and above the surface is part of the territory as well. Thus, to remain neutral regarding whether one should hold this more expansive notion of territory, one might say that Q is within some territory T if – but not necessarily only if – she is in contact with the relevant surface region of the relevant massive object.

Given this account of being within a territory, P is territorially legitimate with respect to Q if, when P issues the edict that Q must ϕ if she is in contact with the surface of some massive object, Q is obligated to ϕ if she is making such contact.[10] Once territorial legitimacy has been recast in this way, the apparent distinction between property rights in land and property rights over objects collapses. To have property rights vis-à-vis some object is to be able to declare that Q must ϕ if she is in contact with the object and thereby make it obligatory that Q ϕ-s if she touches the object. Thus, the owner of that object is territorially legitimate with respect to all other persons.

---

[10] The account of territorial legitimacy drops its original necessary condition here to leave open the possibility that P might also be legitimate with respect to Q if Q is above or below the surface in addition to being in direct contact with the surface.

Put somewhat differently, the territorial legitimacy of the land owner (or head of state) entails that she is able to issue conditional exclusion orders barring others from making permissible noncompliant contact with some surface region of one of the very large objects that we call planets. Similarly, the object owner is able to issue conditional exclusion orders barring others from making permissible noncompliant contact with the surface region of the smaller objects that rest on what we call planets. Of course, there is a size difference between large objects (planets) and the smaller objects resting on those large objects, but, for these purposes, this difference does not seem morally salient. One might think of objects as microplanets that differ in size – but not in kind – from the macroplanets that we generally associate with territory.

Given the lack of a principled distinction between massive objects of different sizes, all property rights can be understood as belonging to a single kind (as opposed to there being distinct kinds of property rights over land vs. resources and objects). Specifically, a property right over any item includes a right to conditionally exclude others from coming into contact with some bit of mass – and, thus, bestows territorial legitimacy upon the rights-holder. Therefore, consent theorists cannot merely deny that there is any owned land; rather, they must also deny that there are any owned resources or artifacts. This conclusion represents a libertarian reason for rejecting external private property altogether.

4.5 Initial Appropriation and Obligation Imposition

There are a few different objections that libertarian defenders of private property might raise against this argument. First, they might appeal to a set of existing objections to the claim that initial appropriation requires consent. Specifically, a number of libertarian philosophers have raised objections to the popular argument that (a) initial appropriation imposes obligations on others and (b) one can impose obligations on others only if they consent to being so obliged. For example, Gerald Gaus and Loren Lomasky (1990), Simmons (2001), and Hugh Breakey (2009) have all objected to Contention (b) by arguing that there are many examples of nonconsensual obligation imposition; thus, there is nothing problematic about imposing obligations via initial appropriation. Gaus and Lomasky appeal to the case of the outstanding professor whose excellent performance unproblematically imposes an obligation upon the head of her department to sign off on a merit-based pay raise (1990, 492). Simmons cites (among others) the case of people who make use of a tennis court and

4.5 Initial Appropriation and Obligation Imposition

thereby nonconsensually – but unproblematically – oblige others to not use it (2001, 220). And Breakey presents a number of seemingly unproblematic cases of duty imposition, including the case of the person who tells another a secret and thereby obliges her not to tell anyone, as well as the case of the person who occupies some bit of physical space and thereby imposes obligations on others not to invade that space (2009, 622–3).

Alternatively, Bas van der Vossen (2015) has argued against Contention (a) by positing that no one *ever* imposes new obligations upon others, as acts like initial appropriation merely change the *practical requirements* of other people's *already existing* conditional obligations. To illustrate this point, van der Vossen suggests that, for any given agent Q, the following conditional statement would be obligatory (i.e., Q is obliged to make the conditional statement true): If some person P has hair, then Q does not touch P's hair without permission. Given the existence of this conditional obligation, it follows that P does not impose any new obligations on Q when she grows out her hair; rather, she merely changes the practical requirements of Q's preexisting conditional obligation, where these requirements follow from the conjunction of the obligation and empirical facts about the world (69–70). Similarly, van der Vossen contends that each person has a conditional obligation to treat other people as property owners if those people carry out acts of initial appropriation. Thus, when people engage in such acts, they do not problematically impose new obligations but, rather, change the practical requirements of that conditional obligation (74).

However, even if one concedes the objections to both Contentions (a) and (b), the argument of this chapter is still sound. Recall the previous contention that a (territorially) legitimate authority is not merely a person who has the power to impose obligations; rather, she is a person who has the power to *specify the content of people's obligations via the issuing of edicts*. Thus, those who affirm the prior claim that legitimacy – and, consequently, initial appropriation – requires consent need only maintain *that this particular method* of obligation imposition has consent as its necessary condition, without having to defend Contention (b)'s much broader claim that *all* obligation imposition requires consent. Given this limited commitment, one might fully concede that playing tennis or telling people secrets imposes obligations upon others without their consent while simultaneously maintaining that one cannot nonconsensually impose obligations on others via the issuing of edicts.[11] Indeed, while a person's choice

---

[11] This is not to say that one *must* concede these counterexamples. Consider, for example, Breakey's suggestion that telling someone a secret obliges her to not tell that secret to others. One might argue

to play tennis may oblige others to stay off of the court, it seems highly implausible that she can oblige them to stay off of the court simply by ordering them to do so – unless, of course, they agree to comply with her orders.

In other words, those who endorse a consent theory of legitimacy need not insist that the generation of obligations always has consent as its necessary condition. Rather, they need only affirm the more modest thesis that a certain sort of power to generate obligations has consent as its necessary condition, namely, the power to oblige others within a certain geographic space via the issuing of edicts. Thus, even if the arguments against Contention (b) succeed in showing that one can impose obligations without consent, that does not negate the claim that the more specific power of legitimacy – and, consequently, the possession of property rights – has consent as its necessary condition.

Further, note that if these arguments *did* succeed in showing that initial appropriation requires consent, this result would, in turn, entail the falsity of consent theories of legitimacy. As was argued in Section 4.3, to possess property rights is simply to be a (territorially) legitimate authority; thus, if one can obtain property rights without consent, then one can also become a legitimate authority without consent, which is to say that the consent theory of legitimacy is false. However, if this is the conclusion of Gaus et al.'s arguments, then they have seemingly proved too much, as those who criticize Contention (b) typically have other commitments that entail the consent theory of legitimacy. For example, practically all of these critics are libertarians who believe that anyone can acquire private property, where such ownership gives them both a permission to use their property as they like and an immunity from the nonconsensual loss of this

---

that this claim only seems plausible because people tacitly consent to not share others' secrets; absent such consent, it does not seem plausible that merely telling someone a secret obliges her to keep that secret. Suppose that a tax cheat tells another person that she is underreporting her income but then immediately says, "Oh, and, by the way, that's a secret, so you can't tell anyone about it!" Is the other party now obligated to refrain from passing along this information? Seemingly not, as she might reasonably respond, "Sorry, but I never agreed to that," with the naturalness of this response suggesting that persons are obliged to keep a secret only if they voluntarily receive it. By contrast, suppose that the tax cheat had first said "Hey, can I tell you a secret?" and the other party had responded in the affirmative. Only then does it seem plausible that the latter is obliged to keep the secret. Further, the apparent reason that there is an obligation in this case (but not the original version of the case) is that the offer to share a secret seemingly includes the tacit condition that the other party not tell the information to others – hence why the other party has to explicitly accept the offer. Thus, contra Breakey, consent appears to be a necessary condition of becoming obliged to keep a secret. Similar arguments can be made against many of the other posited counterexamples, though they will not be provided here.

permission. However, if a state is legitimate, it can enact laws that impose regulations on persons' property, thereby obliging them to only use their property in a certain way. Given that a legitimate state can strip people of their permissions in this way, the only way to preserve the claim that persons are immune from the nonconsensual loss of such permissions is to maintain that states are legitimate only if they have received everyone's consent. Thus, while libertarians might think that they are rescuing property rights by attacking Contention (b), they are actually opening the door to states having the power to nonconsensually regulate or even transfer away people's property claims.[12]

A similar reply can be made to van der Vossen's denial that initial appropriation imposes obligations on others. Suppose that one fully accepts his claim that an agent never imposes new obligations on others and, instead, merely realizes the antecedents of their already-existing conditional obligations.[13] Given this assumption, P can be understood to be territorially legitimate with respect to Q if and only if, for any given action ϕ, Q has the conditional obligation to ϕ if P issues the edict that Q must ϕ within her territory and Q is within said territory. Indeed, this is how territorial legitimacy was defined in Section 4.1. In other words, the consent theory of territorial legitimacy can be understood as insisting that Q's consent is a necessary condition of her having this particular set of conditional obligations. Further, the contention has been that the possession of property rights entails that this same set of conditional obligations obtains – and, thus, that initial appropriation has consent as its necessary condition.

This restatement of consent theory helps to clarify why van der Vossen's argument cannot function as an objection to this chapter's conclusion. Even if he is correct in claiming that initial appropriation does not impose any novel obligations, the claim being advanced by the chapter is that the conditional obligations entailed by initial appropriation obtain only if consent has been given. Thus, consent would still be a necessary condition of initial appropriation even if such appropriation imposes no new obligations.

4.6 The Propertarian Objection

There is a second possible objection that right-libertarians in particular might raise against the foregoing argument. According to this objection,

---

[12] Libertarians might reply that property rights function as a prior constraint on whether states qualify as legitimate. This proposal will be critically assessed in the subsequent section.
[13] For my more-detailed objection to van der Vossen's argument, see Spafford (2020a).

while property ownership entails territorial legitimacy, libertarians who think that state legitimacy requires consent need not concede that there is no private property. This is because their claim does not entail or presuppose the more general proposition that *anyone* must receive consent to be a territorially legitimate authority. Rather, only *states* must obtain consent because that is the only way for them to acquire the power of territorial legitimacy in a context of already-established property rights. The idea here is that, for any given region, private individuals arrived first, appropriated, and thereby became territorially legitimate with respect to – that is, owners of – certain holdings. Given their title to the land, later-arriving states are unable to establish ownership/legitimacy over individuals' already-claimed territory – unless, of course, the latter agree to transfer their claims to former, thereby ceding to states the power to conditionally exclude people from the relevant territories. Thus, despite the fact that both property owners and legitimate states possess an identical moral power, only states require consent to acquire said power, as they uniquely face the challenge of establishing rights over a territory that encompasses other people's already-claimed property. Call this the *propertarian* position.

There are four problems with this proposal. First, note that it makes the truth of the consent theory of state legitimacy a contingent matter, as the theory will be true only if certain empirical claims about the history of state formation and property formation are also true. Specifically, property claims over some territory must predate the formation of the state that claims that territory. While this temporal relation will certainly obtain in some instances, there are likely many regions that were uninhabited prior to a state claiming them, with people only establishing residence and state-sanctioned property claims (i.e., obtaining legal property rights rather than natural ones) in those regions later on.[14] Thus, the propertarian can, at most, claim that *certain* states are not legitimate with respect to *certain* unconsenting individuals. Indeed, there will be many people for whom the edicts of the state are morally binding even absent any form of consent having been given. Further, one cannot know whether a particular individual is obliged to comply with the edicts of a state without first conducting an elaborate empirical investigation of the history of that state and that individual's claimed property to see which territorial right was established first. Thus, the propertarian position represents a significant retreat from the claim favored by most libertarians, namely, that *any state* must acquire consent if it is to be legitimate.

[14] For a theory of how states might come to acquire property, see Cara Nine (2008a).

Second, propertarianism imposes an additional theoretical cost on libertarians because it entails that there could be nonvoluntary legitimate states in a world without previously acquired private property. Note that, in order to countenance the formation of private property without consent, the propertarian has to maintain that the *only* situation in which state territorial legitimacy has a person's consent as its necessary condition is when the territory in question overlaps with her already-established private property. Thus, in the absence of such property, the propertarian would have no theoretical resources to deny the legitimacy claims made by states. Perhaps some libertarians will bite the bullet and concede that some people might have the power to impose obligations on others via edict in such a world; however, most libertarians – particularly those attracted to a standard consent theory of legitimacy – will likely reject this conclusion.

A third and related point is that the propertarian position is dialectically weak. Note that the position's core claim is that there is an incompatibility between the existence of private property owners and a state being legitimate with respect to those owners. The propertarian then posits that there are such owners and rejects state legitimacy as part of a modus ponens argument. However, one might equally accept one of the many arguments for state legitimacy and employ the propertarian incompatibility premise as part of a modus tollens argument: Given that there are legitimate states and such states are incompatible with libertarian entitlements, it follows that there are not any such entitlements. Further, because the propertarian claim is that the *only* reason that states are illegitimate is because legitimacy is incompatible with private property, propertarians would have no independent grounds for denying the posited premise that there are legitimate states. Granted, they could appeal to their positive reasons for endorsing the existence of property rights. However, these reasons would then have to be weighed against the reasons for thinking that states are legitimate, with there being a nontrivial chance that the latter prove weightier, thereby negating the propertarian position.

Finally, note that propertarianism is incompatible with any consent theory of legitimacy grounded in considerations other than the conflict between state legitimacy and preexisting private property. As discussed just prior, the propertarian must concede that there is no problem with legitimacy obtaining without consent, as she insists that initial appropriation does not have consent as its necessary condition. On her view, consent is only needed when late-arriving states want to govern a territory, where some portion of that territory is already owned. However, this claim contradicts any position that holds that legitimacy requires consent irrespective of facts about property. For example, both Simmons' position as described in Section 4.2 as well as other influential arguments against nonconsensual legitimacy (e.g., those advanced by Huemer (2013) or van der Vossen (2019)) would contradict the propertarian claim that, in the absence of property, there can be legitimacy without consent. Given that such legitimacy allows for the establishment of arbitrary perfect, special obligations, Simmons would still insist that it has consent as its necessary condition. Similarly, van der Vossen (2019) observes that libertarians often reject nonconsensual legitimacy on the grounds that it amounts to an unacceptable form of moral subordination. Given this commitment, such libertarians would still seemingly reject nonconsensual legitimacy as an unacceptable form of subordination even when it does not conflict with preexisting private property rights. Thus, most libertarian consent theorists would not want to adopt propertarianism, as that would require rejecting their grounds for endorsing consent theory. Or, to put this point a different way, all of the arguments that they have developed for consent theory will bear against propertarianism, thereby calling its plausibility into question.

4.7 Commonsense Distinctions

Finally, property-sympathetic libertarians might object to the chapter's thesis by appealing to a family of existing arguments for the nonidentity of property ownership and state legitimacy. What these arguments all have in common is that they rest on various commonsense claims about the relationship between private property and state territory. However, it will be argued that these arguments are either flawed or unacceptable to those who endorse core libertarian theses, that is, the people at whom the foregoing argument is directed.

The first commonsense argument is one that has been put forward by Lea Brilmayer (1989, 15), Allen Buchanan (2003, 234), and Cara Nine (2008a, 149). It begins with the premise that, if person P buys a tract of land L within the borders of state S, P owns that land but S is still legitimate with respect to L, as S retains the right to regulate conduct within L, collect taxes on L, etc. If territorial legitimacy and ownership are identical powers as argued previously, then both P and S are owners of L. However, there cannot be multiple (non-joint) owners of L. Thus, ownership and territorial legitimacy are distinct relations. Specifically, on this view, legitimacy is a *jurisdictional* power to impose and enforce rules in L; by contrast, ownership exists within jurisdictions as a distinct power. Only if one accepts this distinction can one make sense of how all of the land within a territory belongs to the state (and, on a democratic view, those it represents) while certain tracts of that land are owned by private individuals (Buchanan 2003, 234).

The first problem with this argument is that it is not clear how the jurisdictional power is supposed to differ from property ownership, particularly given the foregoing argument that P's ownership entails the power to impose rule regulating conduct in L. While perhaps the above-mentioned philosophers might posit that ownership is in some sense subordinate to – and, thus, distinct from – legitimacy, that would seemingly just assert that which needs to be demonstrated. Second, note that libertarians cannot appeal to this argument because they reject its starting premise. On their view, ownership entails exclusive control of the owned thing by the owner. In other words, if P owns L, it cannot be the case that S retains the right to regulate and tax L. Admittedly, this understanding of property entails the counterintuitive result that the citizens of legitimate states cannot own property. However, libertarians would insist that this is the correct conclusion and that, while such citizens perhaps have *legal* property rights afforded to them by the state, such rights are not genuine *moral* ownership rights of the kind that they endorse. Indeed, the incompatibility of ownership and legitimacy is part of the reason that libertarians insist that legitimacy requires consent, as noted in the previous section.

A second quick argument also made by Buchanan holds that "property in land is conceptually and morally distinct from the right to territory ... because land is not the same as territory" (2003, 232). Specifically, he maintains that land is "a geographical concept" while territory "is a geographical jurisdiction," where a jurisdiction is domain in which an authority gets to make and enforce rules (232–3). However, while it is true that land is strictly a geographic notion, the *ownership* of land gives one the ability to make rules governing those within that region, as discussed previously. Thus, while the concept of territory might have normative implications that the concept of land lacks, it does not follow that the *ownership of land* is conceptually distinct from the possession of territorial legitimacy.

A third argument proposed by Nine (2008b) contends that ownership and legitimacy are distinct because they serve different functions. Nine argues that the rights associated with ownership protect people's ability to "pursue their own conception of the good" (961). By contrast, the rights established by legitimate states protect actions and relations of the kind that "makes possible the establishment of justice," for example, the enforcement of laws and the protection of the commons (961). This difference in function entails that ownership is not reducible to legitimacy (and vice versa).

However, libertarians who wish to defend the existence of property would have to reject this proposal for a number of reasons. First, most would deny that the proposed examples of justice-upholding actions are properly carried out by states rather than property owners. For example, anarcho-capitalists like Huemer (2013) contend that law enforcement should be carried out by private companies and purchased on the market. And David Schmidtz (1990) contends that private property rights are a way of protecting the commons from degradation and preserving resources for latecomers. Second, libertarians take the relations between people and their holdings to be relations of justice. Given that property rights protect the upholding of these relations, libertarians would deny that territorial rights are justice-promoting in a way that property rights are not. Finally, many libertarians would reject Nine's background assumption that rights "are social tools that we use to protect and encourage the realization of certain values" (2008b, 961). For most natural rights libertarians, rights express pre-social facts about the justice and permissibility of various actions. They would, thus, deny that property rights have a *function* (in the relevant sense), and, by extension, would deny that property rights have a function distinct from territorial rights.

The final argument to be considered is one independently advanced by both Margaret Moore (2004) and Buchanan (2003). Drawing from democratic theory, this argument contends that a state's territory differs from property in that the former *belongs* to the people of that state, where this belonging constrains state authority. For example, Buchanan argues that this belonging relation entails that exercises of state authority must be for the benefit of its citizens (2003, 234–5). Similarly, Moore argues that this relation precludes the state from transferring parts of its territory to other states, particularly if the inhabitants of those regions do not want such a transfer to occur (2004, 141–2). These restrictions set territorial legitimacy apart from ownership, which lacks any such constraints upon its associated rights of use, exclusion, and transfer.

Insofar as libertarians endorse a consent theory of legitimacy, they cannot employ this argument to fend off the preceding argument against private property. Specifically, such libertarians cannot consistently accept the proposed democratic restrictions on state legitimacy, as they would not see a legitimate state as subject to any restrictions beyond those imposed by the consenting parties. According to consent theory, if all parties agree to obey the laws of the state, then those parties would be obligated to obey territorial transfer laws mandating that they now obey the laws of a different state. Similarly, they would be obliged to obey laws that were not to their benefit. Of course, a state's subjects may have insisted on prohibitions on territorial transfer and/or non-beneficial legislation as a condition of their consent, thereby giving their state only partial legitimacy. However, the fact that it is possible for a state to have full legitimacy free of such constraints negates the claim that territorial legitimacy is limited in a way that ownership is not. Thus, libertarians sympathetic to consent theory could not appeal to this argument to reject the conclusion that property rights entail territorial legitimacy.

Even if one concedes that legitimacy is bounded in the sense described previously, the argument against property still goes through. Note that, in order to succeed, the argument does not have to demonstrate that legitimacy and the powers afforded by ownership are *identical*. Nor does it have to prove that property rights endow their possessors with a power identical to some alternative power that states possess (where it is Moore's and Buchanan's contention that this latter power is weaker than – and, thus, nonidentical to – property owners' territorial legitimacy). Rather, the argument merely needs to show that ownership entails territorial legitimacy, as one can then infer from the consent theory of territorial legitimacy that ownership has consent as its necessary condition (given that, if A implies B and B implies C, then one can validly infer that A implies C). In other words, even if Moore and Buchanan are correct that *states* are not territorially legitimate because their powers are constrained in various ways that territorial legitimacy is not, it would still follow that *property owners* are territorially legitimate. Thus, property ownership would still have consent as its necessary condition irrespective of whether or not states are territorially legitimate.

4.8 Consent Theory and Self-Ownership

While the foregoing objections do not succeed, the conclusion that property has consent as its necessary condition creates an apparent problem for the anarchist contention that persons are able to acquire ownership of their own bodies through appropriation. If the appropriation of any bit of matter grants the owners the power of territorial legitimacy, then self-owners possess territorial legitimacy, as the bodies they own are just bits of matter like any other resource. Thus, consent theory seemingly entails that self-appropriation has consent as its necessary condition – a result that precludes the kind of easily achievable self-appropriation that was posited in Chapter 3.

The quick response to this objection is to note that the anarchist position affirms ASO as opposed to the classical self-ownership thesis – that is, that self-owners have claims against only certain forms of contact, namely, contact that does not uniquely generate supplemental benefit. Because ASO's posited exclusion rights are much more limited than those posited by the classical self-ownership thesis, anarchist self-owners are correspondingly limited when it comes to their ability to issue edicts that conditionally oblige others. In the case of classical self-ownership, if self-owner P issues the edict that Q must ϕ if she is in contact with P's body, then Q is obligated to ϕ if she is making such contact (as P has the power to waive her right to exclude Q from her body on the condition that Q ϕ-s). By contrast, this is not true if P has only the exclusion rights posited by ASO. Given that P only has a right against Q using P's body in ways that do not uniquely generate supplemental benefit, she would have only the following power of *self-sovereignty*: If P issues the edict that Q must ϕ if she is in contact with P's body, then Q is obligated to ϕ if she is making such contact *and* such contact does not uniquely generate supplemental benefit. Given that this is a much weaker power than territorial legitimacy, it is not clear that the basis for positing a consent theory of territorial legitimacy will also support the claim that self-sovereignty has consent as its necessary condition. Anarchists might thereby avoid any contradiction between consent theory and the self-ownership thesis by denying that self-sovereignty requires consent in the way that territorial legitimacy does.

What if this quick reply does not succeed? Suppose it turns out that self-sovereignty is, in fact, relevantly similar to territorial legitimacy such that it has others' consent as its necessary condition as well. In this case, some anarchists may be tempted to simply abandon the self-ownership thesis and maintain that the permissible use of *all* resources – including bodies – is governed by distributive claims rather than property claims. This would not be an entirely intolerable outcome, as most of the anarchist position would remain intact: One would still end up with a rejection of private property and an endorsement of luck egalitarian distributive rights, both of which have been shown to follow from the moral tyranny constraint and other core libertarian theses such as the consent theory of legitimacy. However, as discussed in Sections 1.4 and 1.9, the self-ownership thesis has many attractive implications; thus, retaining the thesis would enhance the anarchist position's plausibility. Additionally, an anarchist position

4.8 Consent Theory and Self-Ownership

that included the thesis would better reflect the commitments of self-identified anarchists who typically prize bodily autonomy.

Fortunately, there are a number of possible ways to resolve the tension between consent theory and self-ownership, even supposing that one rejects the quick reply. Specifically, this section will critically discuss three additional ways to avoid the posited contradiction, beginning with the least promising proposal and concluding with the most promising. That said, each proposal has its own theoretical advantages and disadvantages, and reasonable people might disagree about which is best when it comes to resolving the contradiction between the two anarchist theses.

The first way to avoid a contradiction between self-ownership and consent theory is to weaken the latter such that consent becomes a necessary condition of a person *establishing* legitimacy rather than a necessary condition of legitimacy *tout court*. One would then need to reject the anarchist contention that self-ownership is acquired rather than native – that is, one would have to hold that people enter existence with self-ownership rights already in their possession (either at birth or when they first attain moral personhood). Together, these adjustments would allow one to maintain that persons possess self-ownership rights even absent others' consent due to the fact that these rights are given rather than established; by contrast, initial appropriation *would* require consent, as it bestows territorial legitimacy vis-à-vis some bit of matter on persons who did not previously possess this power. In this way, the anarchist could preserve the self-ownership thesis while still rejecting private property on consent theory grounds.

However, both of these proposed adjustments come at a cost. First, treating self-ownership as native rather than acquired gives rise to the theoretical problems discussed in Section 1.3 and Section 3.6. And, second, it is not clear why consent would be a necessary condition of establishing legitimacy but not a necessary condition of legitimacy itself. Perhaps one might hold that what is problematic is people having *discretionary control* over what powers they have. Thus, while consent is not needed to justify a person's territorial legitimacy, her *making* herself legitimate requires such justification. The problem with this suggestion is that it seems to be the power itself that requires consent, even when it is not subject to a person's control. Suppose, for example, that a monarch insisted that she has possessed territorial legitimacy over some region since birth. Few consent theorists would think that this makes her claimed power any less problematic than if it were acquired. This suggests that a distinction between established and native territorial legitimacy cannot support a more limited consent theory that only applies to the former; rather, such a weakening of the theory would be ad hoc and arbitrary.

A more promising way to resolve the tension between consent theory and acquired self-ownership is to further weaken the self-ownership thesis such that it not only assigns the more limited set of exclusion rights articulated by ASO but also does not assign self-owners the power to waive those rights conditional on certain future acts being performed. Without this power, self-owners cannot conditionally permit others to make contact with their bodies and, thus, cannot impose conditional obligations on others via the issuing of edicts. For example, standard ASO assigns self-owner P the power to waive her right against Q using P's body in a way that does not uniquely generate supplemental benefit on the condition that Q wears red, where such conditional waiving obliges Q to wear red if she touches P in a way that does not uniquely generate supplemental benefit. By contrast, the even-more-limited version of ASO would deny that P has this power. This, in turn, entails that Q is obliged to not make the specified use of P's body irrespective of what P says, thereby stripping P of her power of self-sovereignty. Given that the weakened version of ASO does not entail either self-sovereignty or territorial legitimacy, self-appropriation would be fully compatible with the conjunction of consent theory and the fact that no one has consented to anyone else's self-ownership.

There are three potential objections to this proposal, though replies can be made to each. The first objection is that the theoretical choice to exclude the power to conditionally waive from the bundle of self-ownership rights is both *ad hoc* and unmotivated. Why deny persons this power aside from the fact that it makes self-ownership compatible with consent theory? In response to this challenge, one might appeal to various objections that have been made to the conditional exchange of goods and services. For example, I have elsewhere argued that anarchists' opposition to limiting others' freedom leads them to assert that conditional exchange is morally objectionable (2020b). If this thesis is correct, it would represent a principled, anarchist-friendly reason for denying that persons have the power to waive their self-ownership rights conditional on others acting in some way.[15]

The second objection is that the proposal threatens to undermine this chapter's foregoing argument against the existence of private property, as

---

[15] See also Spafford (2019, 233–4) for an argument that socialists who care about community should oppose conditional exchange.

4.8 Consent Theory and Self-Ownership 145

the property proponent could make the same argumentative move and posit that property owners lack the power to conditionally waive their property rights. Given that property owners are territorially legitimate only if they can waive their claims to exclude, the acquisition of non-waivable exclusionary property rights would not require consent, thereby sidestepping the argument presented in Sections 4.1–4.4. Admittedly, this move would succeed in its aim of defusing this chapter's consent theory-based argument against private property. However, it will be unacceptable to the defenders of property who would seek to deny this argument. Additionally, Section 3.1's argument from the Lockean proviso would still be sound even if exclusionary property rights are not waivable. Thus, the anarchist could still maintain that no one owns any external natural resources (though she would have only one argument to support this claim rather than two).[16]

Finally, one might reject this proposal on the grounds that non-waivable exclusion rights are unattractive, as they do not give self-owners enough moral control over their bodies. Consider, for example, the person who wishes to spar in a boxing ring with a friend or be kissed by someone who made her laugh. Absent a power to waive her self-ownership rights, she could not give others moral permission to make such contact with her body. Such activities would thereby wrong her – and this would be true even if she held all of the attitudes and performed all of the actions associated with giving consent. Such a result would be highly implausible, thereby ruling out this strategy for rescuing self-ownership from consent theory.

In response to this objection, note that the proposed weakening of ASO does not deny self-owners the power to waive their rights. Nor does it deny them the power to waive their rights conditional on some already obtaining fact or even most future occurrences. Rather, it merely denies them the power to waive their exclusion rights conditional on the

---

[16] This reply requires qualification. Section 3.1 *did* appeal to the waivability of property rights as part of its argument for the claim that appropriation almost never satisfies the Lockean proviso. Specifically, it appealed to the interpretation of the proviso put forward in Section 1.2 wherein it was held that appropriation succeeds only if no subsequent waiving of the established claims could leave others worse off$_{FC}$. It then argued that practically all candidate appropriations would violate this necessary condition, as someone would almost always be left worse off$_{FC}$ if the appropriator's established exclusion rights were waived in the most disadvantageous way possible. However, if property rights do not include the specified power to waive, that limits the extent to which appropriators could realize cost$_{FC}$-imposing patterns of exclusionary claims via waiving. Thus, there will be more cases of appropriation that satisfy the Lockean proviso, potentially allowing for *some* ownership of external resources (though it would likely be quite limited given the scarcity of resources and the associated costs$_{FC}$ of (non-waivable) exclusion rights).

otherwise-excluded party performing some future action. Thus, in both the boxing and kissing cases presented just prior, the person would be able to waive her claims against bodily contact. Granted, there would still be some cases where this proposal would not allow for conditional waiving of the kind favored by libertarian-minded people. For example, sex work, hired surrogacy, and the purchase of kidneys or blood plasma would violate the self-ownership rights of the persons whose bodies are being used – and this would be true irrespective of whether they agreed to sell their bodies in this way. However, this is a relatively small theoretical cost to pay for rescuing the self-ownership from the consent theorist's argument against property ownership.[17]

The final proposed way to make ASO compatible with consent theory is to weaken the latter such that P can acquire the power of territorial legitimacy – or, more precisely, self-sovereignty – vis-à-vis Q if and only if (a) P acquires consent from Q *or* (b) she would not be responsible for leaving Q worse off$_{FC}$ regardless of how P exercised her acquired power. This added disjunct (b) would then be satisfied by self-appropriation for reasons similar to why self-appropriation satisfies the Lockean proviso (as discussed in Section 3.2). To see this, consider a case where Q's ϕ-ing would make contact with P's body and thereby generate x units of advantage for Q without uniquely generating any supplemental benefit. Further, suppose that P exercises her power of self-sovereignty and issues the edict that, if Q ϕ-s, she must also ψ, where ψ-ing imposes some cost of y on Q. Given that P's established claim is conditional, Q's choice to either ϕ or not ϕ will determine what her future full compliance involves, and, thus, what costs$_{FC}$ she incurs. In the full-compliance world where Q declines to ϕ, the cost$_{FC}$ she incurs is simply x, as she foregoes$_{FC}$ the advantage she would have had if she had made the specified contact with P's body. By contrast, the full-compliance world where Q ϕ-s is one where Q also ψ-s, with Q thereby avoiding the cost of x but incurring the cost of y.

Why, then, is P not responsible for leaving Q worse off$_{FC}$ when she issues her edict? Recall from Section 3.4 that P is responsible for imposing some cost$_{FC}$ on Q only if Q's incurred cost$_{FC}$ survives the nonexistence

---

[17] Interestingly, this result actually brings the position into greater alignment with the intuitions of many non-libertarians who believe that sex workers/plasma sellers/etc. are wronged despite explicitly agreeing to permit the use of their bodies in exchange for money. Thus, this implication of the proposed modification of ASO may actually be an *advantage* for the theory rather than a cost. That said, the argument of the book is primarily directed at libertarians who do not share these intuitions. For this reason, the fact that the proposal's implications run contrary to libertarian intuitions is presented as a theoretical weakness rather than a strength.

4.8 Consent Theory and Self-Ownership　　　　　　　　　　147

comparison – that is, Q would not suffer that cost in the closest possible full-compliance world where P does not exist. Further, note that the cost$_{FC}$ that Q would incur if P had never existed is equal to x, as P's nonexistence would preclude Q from obtaining the x units of advantage that she would otherwise acquire by using P's body. Thus, the costs$_{FC}$ of Q not ϕ-ing are equal to the costs$_{FC}$ she incurs in the world where P does not exist – that is, the former costs$_{FC}$ do not survive the nonexistence comparison. This, in turn, implies that P is not responsible for Q incurring a cost$_{FC}$ of x when she does not ϕ.

What if a fully compliant Q does ϕ? Given that her ϕ-ing entails that she will then ψ and incur a cost$_{FC}$ of y, there are two possibilities: either she ends up no worse off$_{FC}$ than if she did not ϕ (because $x \geq y$) or she ends up worse off$_{FC}$ (because $x < y$). If ϕ-ing leaves her no worse off$_{FC}$, then P is not responsible for leaving her worse off$_{FC}$, as she is no worse off$_{FC}$ in the world where she ϕ-s than the world where P does not exist. For, as noted in the previous paragraph, Q is no worse off$_{FC}$ in the world where she does not ϕ than she is in the nonexistence world; thus, if she is no worse off$_{FC}$ in the world where she ϕ-s than she is in the world where she does not ϕ, then, transitively, she is no worse off$_{FC}$ in the world where she ϕ-s than she is in the world where P does not exist.

Suppose, instead, that Q *is* worse off$_{FC}$ if she ϕ-s relative to the world where she does not due to x being less than y. In this case, Q may end up worse off$_{FC}$ than she would be in the world where P does not exist. However, recall from Section 3.4 that an additional necessary condition of P being responsible for leaving others worse off$_{FC}$ is P having *unilaterally* left them worse off$_{FC}$. In other words, any avoidable costs$_{FC}$ that Q incurs due to her subsequent choices do not count when assessing whether P is responsible for leaving her worse off$_{FC}$ (i.e., whether Condition (b) is satisfied). Given that Q could avoid the supplemental costs$_{FC}$ of ϕ-ing by not ϕ-ing, it follows that P is not responsible for these costs$_{FC}$. Thus, irrespective of which choice Q makes, P is not responsible for her incurred costs$_{FC}$, that is, P is not responsible for leaving Q worse off$_{FC}$. Further, given that P's edict was described generically, it follows that a self-sovereign P will *never* be responsible for leaving Q worse off$_{FC}$ by issuing an edict, with self-sovereignty thereby necessarily satisfying Condition (b) of the revised consent theory of self-sovereignty. Thus, self-sovereignty is compatible with the previously proposed revised consent theory.

There are two objections to this proposal that are worth addressing. The first worry is that the move to append Condition (b) to standard consent theory is ad hoc and, more problematically, in tension with the motivations for adopting consent theory in the first place. Here, one might reply by appealing to the claim in Chapter 2 about the relationship between consent theory and the moral tyranny constraint. Specifically, Section 2.4 suggested that the reason for endorsing consent theory is that legitimacy satisfies the moral tyranny constraint only if it has consent as its necessary condition. Because legitimate authorities are able to foreseeably and discretionarily leave others worse off$_{FC}$ via the issuing of edicts, they must be denied the ability to *unilaterally* do so; that is, consent must be a necessary condition of this power to oblige. However, Section 3.4 argued that the moral tyranny constraint should be generalized such that it condemns moral theories that allow people to leave others worse off$_{FC}$ *while being responsible* for leaving others worse off$_{FC}$ in this way. And it has now been shown that self-sovereign agents are never responsible for leaving others worse off$_{FC}$ in this way. Thus, there is no moral tyranny-related reason for insisting that consent is always a necessary condition of self-sovereignty and territorial legitimacy more generally. Rather, Condition (b) is an appropriate addition to standard consent theory, as, like Condition (a), it allows for (territorial) legitimacy so long as that power does not violate the moral tyranny constraint.

The second objection is that this amendment effectively reduces consent theory to the Lockean proviso. Once one makes non-worsening$_{FC}$ a disjunctive sufficient condition of legitimacy (and self-sovereignty) alongside consent, the resultant principle starts to closely resemble the proviso with its contention that an act of appropriation establishes (self-)ownership rights if and only if the established claims and the possible subsequent waiving of those claims would not leave others worse off$_{FC}$. After all, both consent theory (in its revised form) and the proviso are satisfied if the established rights of exclusion – when paired with the power to waive those rights – do not leave others worse off$_{FC}$. Thus, one might worry that this third compatibilist proposal renders the argument of this chapter redundant (even if it does allow for self-appropriation).

Two things can be said in response to this objection. First, one might reply that even if the Lockean proviso and the proposed revision of consent theory do not differ importantly in their content, this does not diminish the dialectical significance of the foregoing argument. Even if one ends up accepting a consent theory that is quite similar to the Lockean proviso, one does so because standard consent theory threatens to negate the existence of *all* private property including the modest self-ownership rights posited by ASO. In other words, the proposed revision represents the conclusion of an independent argument against private property that has the standard consent theory of legitimacy as its starting premise. This is of particular dialectical significance given that those who favor private property seemingly need to endorse a consent theory of legitimacy for the reasons discussed in Section 4.5: Absent such a theory, people are liable to have various permissions to use their owned property stripped from them by state regulation. Thus, one can understand the foregoing argument as a way of pressuring both consent theorists and property rights proponents into first giving up private property and then accepting a revised version of consent theory that approximates the Lockean proviso.

Second, note that there is an important difference between the compatibilist revision of consent theory and the Lockean proviso, namely, that the latter does not make consent a sufficient condition of appropriation. However, the foregoing discussion also suggests that this is something of an oversight and that the proviso should really take a disjunctive form with both consent and non-worsening$_{FC}$ serving as individually sufficient and disjunctively necessary conditions of appropriation. Thus, one might take the proposed compatibilist position to represent a synthesis of the proviso and standard consent theory. Specifically, each principle can be understood as an attempt to address initial appropriation's moral tyranny problem, with the proviso aiming to preclude culpable worsening$_{FC}$ while consent theory aims to preclude any sort of *unilateral* worsening$_{FC}$. Yet, when considered in sequence, each principle appears to be overly stringent. The proviso is too stringent because it precludes consensual appropriation that leaves the consenter worse off$_{FC}$ – an outcome that is unproblematic vis-à-vis the moral tyranny constraint. And standard consent theory is too stringent because it demands consent even when a successful appropriator would be unable to leave anyone worse off$_{FC}$ irrespective of how she exercised her established powers. By contrast, the posited compatibilist version of consent theory allows for appropriation given *either* consent or non-worsening$_{FC}$, thereby correcting for the respective overreaches of the proviso and standard consent theory. It is, thus, importantly distinct from the Lockean proviso (in addition to the fact that it is derived from standard consent theory).

4.9 Philosophical Anarchism and the Anarchist Conclusion

Before concluding, it is worth drawing attention to how the argument of this chapter – or, more precisely, the thesis that ownership entails territorial legitimacy – helps to contextualize what Section 1.6 called *the anarchist conclusion*. When it comes to discussions of state legitimacy, consent theorists are *philosophical anarchists* who insist that there are no existing legitimate states (while allowing that there *could* be a legitimate state under the appropriate conditions).[18] However, this position raises a natural objection, namely, that it seems to problematically imply that there is no obligation to comply with just laws. While much legislation is immoral, states also pass laws mandating that persons act in ways that morality seems to require, for example, laws that forbid murder. Thus, upon first encountering philosophical anarchism, many worry that it negates obligations to comply with these laws – that is, obligations to act in the way that morality requires – or to cooperate with state authorities who are enforcing these laws.

In reply to this worry, philosophical anarchists typically note that there are many independent grounds for obligations aside from the edicts of the legitimate state. For example, Simmons (1999) draws a distinction between justification and legitimacy. On this account, a *legitimate* state is one that has the exclusive right to impose novel obligations upon its subjects as a result of some sort of special relation that they stand in with respect to one another (746, 752).[19] By contrast, a *justified* state is one that a person has reason not to undermine (and perhaps even reason to support) in virtue of its moral quality (753). Additionally, Simmons introduces a notion that might be called *justified action*. The idea here is that the moral character of some *specific action* carried out by a state gives others reason to not interfere (and possibly assist) with that action. Thus, even if a state is neither legitimate nor justified, one might be morally required not to interfere with some moral action such as its deployment of police officers to prevent violence (770).

In other words, the philosophical anarchist reply to the aforementioned worry is that, even if a state is not legitimate, individuals might still have certain obligations with respect to that state and its actors. Similarly, the anarchist who rejects private property can apply this rejoinder to worries about what obligations people have vis-à-vis natural resources in a world without private property. Specifically, even if the anarchist position denies individuals the territorial legitimacy entailed by *property rights*, it can still assign them *distributive rights* that determine which uses of natural resources are permissible. Thus, the anarchist conclusion can be understood as an

---

[18] For a helpful discussion of philosophical anarchism, see Simmons (2001, 102–21).
[19] This statement of legitimacy is not quite identical to that introduced in Section 1.1, as the latter notion is not defined in terms of the *introduction* of *novel* obligations. However, that account of legitimacy is also based upon an account provided by Simmons, albeit a later one that appears to articulate his revised understanding of legitimacy.

application of Simmons' philosophical anarchism to the special case of property ownership: Given the absence of legitimate property owners, it appeals to other moral bases to posit a set of distributive obligations vis-à-vis the use of land and resources.

4.10 Conclusion

Thus concludes the anarchist argument against private property. The contention has been that two distinctively libertarian theses – namely, the Lockean proviso and the consent theory of legitimacy – independently entail that persons lack any sort of private property rights over natural resources. Social anarchism can, thus, be understood as an inversion of standard libertarianism: While it starts out with core libertarian premises, it arrives at the opposite conclusion regarding the existence of private property. However, this result does not establish that one ought to instead, accept the egalitarian anarchist conclusion introduced in Section 1.6. Defending this claim will be the task of Chapter 5.

CHAPTER 5

Entitlement Theory without Entitlements

> Likewise the land is indispensable to our existence, – consequently a common thing, consequently insusceptible of appropriation; but land is much scarcer than the other elements, therefore its use must be regulated, not for the profit of a few, but in the interest and for the security of all. In a word, equality of rights is proved by equality of needs. Now, equality of rights, in the case of a commodity which is limited in amount, can be realized only by equality of possession.
> Pierre-Joseph Proudhon, *What Is Property?*

Chapters 3 and 4 have argued that there are no existing property rights. Further, they argued that this conclusion follows independently from two principles that libertarians generally accept, namely, the Lockean proviso and the consent theory of legitimacy. The chapters, thus, articulated the distinctive anarchist thesis that private property ought to be rejected on libertarian grounds. However, this thesis underdetermines which permissions people have vis-à-vis the unowned resources that make up the natural world. One possibility is that, absent property rights, persons remain in the state of nature with respect to natural resources; that is, all persons have a permission to use any unowned resource and no one has a right against any other person using any resource. In this view, the only claims that persons can have vis-à-vis natural resources are the property rights that are generated by acts of initial appropriation. Thus, if practically all attempted appropriations fail because they violate the Lockean proviso or require consent that has not been given, it follows that there are simply no claims against others using any unowned object. Call this the *Hobbesian conclusion*. By contrast, the *anarchist conclusion* proposed in Section 1.6 maintains that people *do* possess certain claims against others using unowned resources. Specifically, these claims correspond to the prescriptions of a luck egalitarian principle of distributive justice such that each person has a set of claims against others interacting with unowned resources in a way that would generate an unjust distribution of holdings (where a distribution is just if and only if it is either equal or any inequality corresponds to some sanctionable choice on the part of the worse off).

Given that there are multiple conclusions that are compatible with the rejection of private property, why should one accept the anarchist conclusion rather than the Hobbesian conclusion? After all, there is a strong reason for favoring the latter over the former, namely, that the anarchist conclusion appears to be incompatible with the kind of entitlement theory of justice that is both a signature commitment of libertarian thought and seemingly presupposed by the endorsement of ASO in Chapter 1. Briefly, entitlement theories assert that justice is a function of the historical choices that persons have made. While there are many ways of formulating an entitlement theory, most variants approximate Nozick's paradigm account wherein the justice of some set of holdings depends on whether people are entitled to the holdings they possess (1974).[1] Specifically, Nozick's theory of entitlement posits that a person is entitled to some holding if and only if (a) it was unowned and she acquired it in accordance with the relevant principles of justice in acquisition or (b) it was owned by some person from whom she acquired it in accordance with the relevant principles of justice in transfer (1974, 151).[2] Justice in holdings, then, obtains if everyone is entitled to the holdings they possess (151).

In addition to positing this historical account of justice in holdings, Nozick also argues that entitlement theories are incompatible with any non-entitlement principle of distributive justice, where "non-entitlement theories" is inclusive of both "end-state" principles of justice (i.e., principles that make no reference to historical events) and "patterned" principles of justice (i.e., principles that make justice a matter of how much people have relative to some relevant property they possess, such as merit or their having contributed some quantity of labor to the social product) (1974, 153–60). Given that luck egalitarianism is a non-entitlement theory of justice, it follows that entitlement theories are incompatible with luck egalitarianism – and, thus, so are the set of distributive rights posited by the anarchist conclusion.[3]

---
[1] Some prominent proponents of entitlement theories of justice include Mack (1976), Rothbard (1978), Lomasky (1987), Steiner (1994), Narveson (1988), Feser (2005), and van der Vossen (2009).
[2] Nozick goes on to revise this account so as to incorporate a principle pertaining to the rectification of injustice. This principle holds that each person is entitled to the holdings they *would have had* absent all historical rights violations (Nozick 1974, 152–3). For a discussion of the shortcomings of both the original account and the revised version, see Lawrence Davis (1976, 838–40).
[3] The reason that "entitlement theories" is plural is because an entitlement theory is a *kind* of moral theory that posits that justice is a function of whether holdings were acquired in accordance with principles of just acquisition and just transfer. Given that there are various principles of just acquisition and just transfer that one might posit, there will be many different entitlement

If this is correct, this incompatibility would be a serious problem for the anarchist conclusion, as there are two reasons that the anarchist cannot simply reject entitlement theories of justice as false. First, note that one of the theoretical advantages of the anarchist position is that it puts dialectical pressure on libertarians to accept egalitarian conclusions. Because it embraces core libertarian principles as its starting premises, the anarchist argument is much harder for libertarians to dismiss than other egalitarian arguments. If, for example, one defends egalitarianism by arguing from some set of non-libertarian premises, libertarians can avoid the conclusion by, first noting that egalitarianism is incompatible with their preferred principles and, second, using that incompatibility to justify rejecting the most controversial non-libertarian premise. By contrast, the anarchist position is not so easily avoided, as it begins with libertarian premises – that is, premises that libertarians cannot easily reject. However, this dialectical advantage is compromised if the anarchist has to reject entitlement theories on the grounds that they are incompatible with the anarchist conclusion. For, in that case, libertarians might simply insist that the anarchist's *modus tollens* argument against entitlement theories is actually a *modus ponens* argument; that is, the anarchist conclusion must be rejected as its negation follows from the acceptance of an entitlement theory of justice.

Second, and more straightforwardly, the anarchist position presupposes an entitlement theory of justice, as it grants that people can establish property rights over things via proviso-satisfying acts of initial appropriation, thereby endorsing a central tenet of entitlement theories. Granted, the set of established self-ownership rights is weaker than those posited by entitlement theorists; however, given that these rights are acquired via actions that accord with a principle of just acquisition, the anarchist argument for ASO still presupposes an entitlement theory of justice. Thus, if the anarchist conclusion proves to be incompatible with entitlement theories of justice, the anarchist cannot simply reject such theories without potentially negating her thesis that people can appropriate their bodies. This suggests that anarchists might be forced to choose between self-ownership and egalitarianism, with those who favor the former having to give up the anarchist conclusion in favor of the Hobbesian conclusion.

This chapter will argue that this is a false dilemma, as the anarchist conclusion is, in fact, compatible with entitlement theories – at least, when

---

theories, where these theories are individuated based upon which combination of principles they endorse.

the latter are properly specified. First, though, it will argue that there *is* a serious cost to endorsing the anarchist's Hobbesian rival. Specifically, Section 5.1 will argue that the Hobbesian conclusion violates the moral tyranny constraint, and, for this reason, is unacceptable. Thus, those who accept the moral tyranny constraint (and the argument of the Chapters 3 and 4) ought to accept the anarchist conclusion rather than the Hobbesian one. Sections 5.2 through 5.6 will then argue that the anarchist conclusion is compatible with both entitlement theories of justice and the arguments for accepting such theories. Finally, Section 5.7 will defend the egalitarian component of the anarchist conclusion. Specifically, it will defend the conclusion's presumption that all persons start out with a claim to an equal share of advantage by arguing that it, too, follows from a core libertarian premise (albeit, not the moral tyranny constraint).

5.1 Hobbesian Moral Tyranny

The argument against the Hobbesian conclusion need not be terribly extensive, as even libertarians averse to the anarchist conclusion will likely find the implications of this alternative comparatively unattractive. For example, few libertarians would want to affirm the Hobbesian implication that a person who labors on some resource and improves its value has no claim against others coming and destroying that resource or taking it for themselves. However, it is worth briefly exploring *why* this result is a theoretical problem for the Hobbesian conclusion, as the answer to this question will help to further bolster the contention in Chapter 2 that the moral tyranny constraint entails a broad array of particular moral judgments and, thus, should be accepted as the conclusion of a process of reflective equilibrium.

A natural temptation is to reject the Hobbesian conclusion on the grounds that a world with neither private property rights (over external resources) nor distributive rights would be miserable and poor. According to this line of thinking, it would almost always be imprudent to improve resources in such a world, as others would be free to come and take whatever it is that one produced without having to bear any of the associated costs of production. Thus, all but the most altruistic persons would refrain from producing goods or carrying out even very basic economic activities like agriculture. This would make the Hobbesian world a world without industry – a world of hunters, gatherers, scavengers, and deep poverty. Given the unattractiveness of such a world, the Hobbesian conclusion must be rejected.

The problem with this argument is one that will be familiar from the discussion in Section 1.2. There, in the context of discussing the Lockean proviso, it was argued that moral changes are causally inert due to not being physical (or mental) events. When someone stakes a claim and declares herself to be the owner of some resource, people will behave in an identical fashion whether or not that attempted act of initial appropriation succeeds as a matter of moral fact. Thus, an act of initial appropriation will never leave others worse off. For this reason, it was posited that the real concern with initial appropriation was whether or not *counterfactual compliance* with the established rights would leave others worse off. Similarly, when considering what was wrong with strict egalitarian theories, it was noted that someone spitefully destroying her own advantage will not *actually* leave others worse off because their post-destruction holdings are a function of their society's contingent redistributive institutions, not any moral fact about whether their holdings are just. Rather, the problem with strict egalitarianism is that it enables the spiteful destroyer to leave others worse off *assuming* everyone were to fully comply with the prescriptions of that moral theory.

The posited objection to the Hobbesian conclusion seems to make the same kind of mistake. It presupposes that an absence of property claims and distributive claims will result in persons behaving differently than they would in the world where they have such claims. However, this presumption is incorrect for the reasons just discussed: People's behavior is a function of their beliefs and their social contexts, not the moral facts. Thus, any objection to the Hobbesian conclusion that appeals to its supposed undesirable outcomes cannot succeed. Even if the Hobbesian conclusion were true, people would not behave any differently than they would if it were false, which is to say they would have still set up systems of legally enshrined private property with all of the attendant economic and social consequences.

Rather, the unacceptability of the Hobbesian conclusion is better explained by appealing to the moral tyranny constraint. Note that if a person has a property claim or a distributive claim against others using some resource in an advantage-diminishing way, then they will owe her compensation if they infringe upon this claim. Given that this remedial duty would be discharged in the full-compliance world, she will end up no worse off$_{FC}$ as a result of their use of the resource, as the compensation would offset any costs$_{FC}$ she would have otherwise incurred due to their infringing action. By contrast, if the Hobbesian conclusion is correct, then persons lack any claims vis-à-vis natural resources. This, in turn, implies that they have no claim to any sort of compensation when others act on any given resource. For example, a scavenger could come and take everything that a farmer produces without owing the farmer anything in virtue of this action.[4] Thus, the scavenger would be able to unilaterally, discretionarily, and foreseeably leave the farmer worse off$_{FC}$, in violation of the moral tyranny constraint.

Given that the Hobbesian conclusion violates the moral tyranny constraint in this way, one can appeal to the constraint to explain the unacceptability of this conclusion. While the truth of the Hobbesian conclusion would not entail that people end up living up in a chaotic and impoverished state of nature, it *would* license people to foreseeably, discretionarily, and unilaterally leave others with less$_{FC}$. Thus, one can deny the Hobbesian conclusion on moral tyranny grounds. This result further bolsters the moral tyranny constraint's explanatory power, thereby strengthening the reflective equilibrium argument for the constraint presented in Section 2.3.

5.2 The Incompatibilist Argument

Given that the Hobbesian conclusion violates the moral tyranny constraint, one must posit some other thesis that *does* assign persons duties vis-à-vis natural resources. Further, given the arguments of Chapters 3 and 4, these duties cannot be property rights and must, instead, be distributive claims of some variety. Given these constraints, the anarchist conclusion seems like a promising candidate thesis to endorse to avoid the moral tyranny of both private property acquisition and the Hobbesian conclusion.[5] However, as noted earlier, this conclusion's incorporation of luck egalitarianism appears to render it incompatible with any entitlement theory of justice. Thus, one

---

[4] Granted, there are certain measures that the farmer could take to preclude this outcome. While she will not be able to protect her crops via coercive means when such coercion violates the rights of others, she might employ various noncoercive measures such as building a very secure wall around her farm. That said, barring a state of complete security where no person is able to seize any other person's products, the Hobbesian conclusion will still violate the moral tyranny constraint. Additionally, even if, as a matter of contingent fact, no person was able to seize someone else's holdings, one might think that both moral theories and meta-theories like the moral tyranny constraint are *necessarily* true; thus, the Hobbesian conclusion would still violate the moral tyranny constraint because it would allow people to leave others worse off$_{FC}$ in the possible worlds where people's holdings are not totally secured.

[5] Granted, the moral tyranny constraint would be satisfied by many theories of distributive claims so long as those theories are sensitive to responsibility in the sense discussed in Chapter 6. Thus, the foregoing argument does not show that one must accept the egalitarian aspect of the anarchist conclusion. Much more will be said about this point in Section 5.7.

might worry that accepting the anarchist conclusion requires rejecting entitlement theories with all of the attendant theoretical costs discussed in this chapter's introduction. The task of the subsequent four sections is to argue against this conclusion by demonstrating that the anarchist conclusion can be reconciled with entitlement theories of justice.

Why think that the anarchist conclusion is incompatible with an entitlement theory of justice? Begin by returning to luck egalitarianism's contention that an inequality is unjust if (and only if) it is due to luck – that is, if the worse-off party has not made some relevant sanctionable choice that justifies that inequality. By contrast, Nozick's articulation of entitlement theories holds that a distribution is just if each person is entitled to her respective holdings. Now consider a case where holdings are distributed contrary to the prescriptions of luck egalitarianism – that is, someone is worse off than another person despite not having chosen sanctionably – but, by hypothesis, all such holdings have been obtained via just appropriation and transfer. In such a case, luck egalitarianism would entail that the distribution is unjust while the entitlement theory would entail that it is just. Thus, one must reject one of the two theories to avoid contradiction.

Does this simple *incompatibilist argument* demonstrate that entitlement theories of justice are incompatible with the anarchist conclusion in addition to standard luck egalitarianism? Entitlement theorists might be tempted to answer this question affirmatively, as the anarchist conclusion assigns distributive claims in accordance with the prescriptions of a luck egalitarian principle of justice. As just noted, luck egalitarianism holds that a distribution is just if and only if any inequality reflects some sanctionable choice on the part of the worse off. The anarchist conclusion then incorporates this judgment by assigning to each person claims against others using unowned resources in a way that would leave her worse off than others (where a person forfeits some of these claims when she chooses sanctionably). Thus, entitlement theorists might reasonably infer that the anarchist conclusion is similarly incompatible with entitlement theories of justice.

Against this inference, one might contend that the anarchist conclusion does not presuppose or otherwise imply the luck egalitarian principle of justice. Rather, it simply employs this principle as a way of determining which claims people have, without affirming luck egalitarianism's assertion that any luck-based inequality is unjust. Thus, the anarchist conclusion sidesteps the incompatibilist argument, as it does not entail that distribution in the posited case is unjust. However, this move is a bit too quick, as there is arguably a conceptual relation between people's assigned claims and justice that allows for the incompatibilist argument to be applied to the anarchist conclusion. Specifically, one might think that, at least in most cases, if a person has a claim to some state of affairs obtaining, then it is just if that state of affairs obtains – that is, the state of affairs is just.[6] Or, more modestly, one might merely hold that a state of affairs is *unjust* if a person has a claim against the realization that state of affairs. (Perhaps she must hold this claim against all other persons.)

If this is right, then the anarchist conclusion's assignment of claims *does* entail that certain unequal distributions are unjust. Specifically, it will declare that a state of affairs is unjust if someone generated a luck-based inequality by acting on an unowned resource. Notably, this includes distributions where everyone is also entitled to their holdings – that is, distributions that are just according to an entitlement theory of justice. Thus, one cannot rescue the anarchist conclusion from the incompatibilist argument by denying that it declares distributions unjust.

5.3 The Left-Libertarian Solution

One strategy for avoiding the incompatibilist argument is to constrain entitlement theories in a way that precludes the possibility of the posited case obtaining (i.e., someone suffering luck-based disadvantage when everyone is entitled to their holdings). This approach is popular among left-libertarians, who maintain that the appropriation of resources is constrained by an egalitarian proviso. For example, Otsuka (2003), in defending a luck egalitarian principle of equal opportunity for welfare, argues that there can be no case where this principle is violated but all holdings have been acquired through either just transfer or just appropriation.

---

[6] The reason for the qualifier is that there are some potential counterexamples to the unqualified version of this claim. For example, David Miller (2017, §1.2) suggests that emergency situations might give rise to duties – and more specifically *enforceable* duties – that exceed what is required by justice. Similarly, Buchanan (1987, 562–3) argues that people might have enforceable duties that are not duties of justice, for example, duties to solve collective action problems. However, as Miller notes, these exceptions are rare. More importantly, when it comes to the foregoing dialectic, the incompatibilist argument will extend to the anarchist conclusion so long as its posited case is one where duties to refrain from realizing some state of affairs imply injustice. In other words, the anarchist conclusion will be incompatible with entitlement theories if there is *at least one case* where (a) a luck-based inequality obtains, (b) everyone has justly acquired their holdings according to the relevant entitlement theory, and (c) duties to refrain from realizing a state of affairs *in this case* imply that the state of affairs is unjust.

Specifically, he argues that an egalitarian proviso obtains such that one can appropriate some natural resource only if everyone else is left an equally good share of unowned natural resources – where two shares are equally good if and only if the holders of those shares have an equal opportunity to obtain welfare via the use and/or exchange of their holdings. Given that luck-based inequality can obtain between two people only if they did not have equal opportunities to obtain welfare, it follows that any luck-based inequality implies a violation of Otsuka's egalitarian proviso. Thus, the existence of luck-based inequality implies that the better-off did not justly acquire their property. This, in turn, implies that the case posited by the incompatibilist argument is impossible: There cannot be a situation where a luck-based inequality obtains but each person is entitled to her respective holdings.

While this strategy may succeed, it is vulnerable to various objections. For example, Mathias Risse notes that anti-egalitarian libertarians might simply reject Otsuka's egalitarian proviso on the grounds that they reject the fairness considerations that ground it (2004, 354–5). Notably, Otsuka defends his proviso by suggesting that it would be *unfair* if the first person to encounter a natural resource were able to acquire it and thereby preclude later arrivals from reaching the level of welfare that they would have achieved had they arrived first and appropriated that resource (1998, 78). However, in response to this complaint, an anti-egalitarian libertarian might simply deny that fairness is a genuine moral concern, or, more modestly, contend that it does not bear upon whether a holding is just. Thus, she would deny the egalitarian proviso, thereby readmitting the possibility of cases where the anarchist conclusion and entitlement theories entail incompatible claims about justice.

More importantly, note that the posited egalitarian proviso is incompatible with the Lockean proviso introduced in Chapter 1 and defended in Chapters 2 and 3. Because the latter allows for appropriations that deny others an equal opportunity to obtain welfare (so long as no one is left worse off$_{FC}$), there will be cases where the two provisos will yield contradictory judgments. Thus, the anarchist cannot employ the kind of egalitarian proviso favored by left-libertarians while sustaining her commitment to the Lockean proviso. Of course, she could abandon that part of her position, but doing so would undermine the argument of Chapter 3, which, in turn, would leave her endorsement of ASO without its foundational supporting argument. Given the high theoretical costs of abandoning the Lockean proviso, some other strategy is needed for making the anarchist conclusion compatible with entitlement theories of justice.

5.4 Just Holdings vs. Just Distributions

Fortunately for the anarchist, there is an alternative compatibilist strategy available to her. This approach revises entitlement theories but does so without any appeal to fairness or egalitarian notions that entitlement theorists might be happy to reject. Rather, it contends that there is an internal problem with the foregoing account of entitlement theories that should motivate any entitlement theorist to revise her theory in the way suggested subsequently. Recall that entitlement theories have so far been defined using Nozick's formulation: A distribution is just if all persons are entitled to their respective holdings. However, suppose that someone's holdings include some unowned thing that she has never bothered to appropriate but nonetheless possesses.[7] Given such possession, Nozick's posited sufficient condition of justice would not obtain, as it would not be the case that each person is entitled to her respective holdings. While this does not imply that the distribution is *unjust* (as it might be neither just nor unjust), it does mean that, even if everyone else is entitled to their holdings, this is insufficient for establishing the justice of the overall distribution *and everything that justice entails*. For example, one implication of a distribution being just is that one cannot permissibly redistribute or destroy anyone's holdings without her consent. Indeed, the reason that Nozick seemingly posits an entitlement theory of justice is to explain the purported wrongness of such nonconsensual redistribution/destruction. Thus, if a single person's possession of an unowned object is sufficient for negating the justice of the entire distribution – where this implies that it might be permissible to redistribute or destroy *any* holding – then the posited account of entitlement theories seems inadequate.

To resolve this problem, the entitlement theorist should maintain that what justice predicates is not the distribution as a whole but, rather, any given holding or set of holdings. In other words, Nozick's suggestion that a distribution is just if each person is entitled to her holdings should be rejected in favor of the following *revised entitlement theory*: Some holding is

---

[7] An anonymous reviewer suggests that proposed case is impossible, as Nozick might take the possession of any unowned thing to entail its appropriation so long as such appropriation satisfies the Lockean proviso. It is not fully clear whether Nozick would endorse this view, but even if one grants that he would, the posited case can simply be adjusted by stipulating that the possessed object cannot be appropriated because such appropriation would violate the Lockean proviso. Or, alternatively, one might even take the object to be stolen. For the argument to succeed, one must merely grant that there is at least *some* case where a person possesses a thing without owning it.

just if its possessor is entitled to it.[8] This theory would allow the entitlement theorist to maintain that it is impermissible to nonconsensually redistribute or destroy those holdings to which people are entitled (as those holdings are just), even if that person or some other person possesses an unowned thing. At the same time, it would allow that one might permissibly redistribute unowned holdings. Such a result seems to best capture what entitlement theorists like Nozick have in mind when advancing their theories.

However, if one accepts this restatement of the relationship between entitlements and justice, then one must reject the argument that entitlement theories are incompatible with the anarchist conclusion. Recall that this argument posits a case where everyone is entitled to their holdings but someone uses an unowned resource in a way that generates a luck-based inequality between two persons. The anarchist conclusion entails that the worse-off party had a claim against this use of resources, which, in turn, implies that the resulting distribution is unjust. By contrast, the entitlement theory *as originally stated* entails that the resulting distribution is just, as everyone is entitled to their holdings. Thus, a contradiction was reached. However, the revised entitlement theory does not affirm that the distribution is just; rather, it merely maintains that the owned holdings are just – a result that is entirely compatible with the anarchist conclusion's implication that the entire distribution is unjust. One is therefore free to endorse the anarchist conclusion without having to give up the entitlement theory presupposed by the social anarchist position (at least, once this entitlement theory is appropriately specified in the way just described).

5.5 Is Entitlement Necessary for Justice?

Proponents of the incompatibilist argument might object to this conclusion by disputing the way in which entitlement theories of justice have been characterized. Note that the foregoing discussion of the incompatibilist argument follows Nozick in positing that a distribution is just if every person is entitled to her holdings. However, the incompatibilist might argue that entitlement is not merely a *sufficient* condition of justice but also a *necessary* one. In other words, a proper interpretation of Nozick's theory would assert that justice obtains if *and only if* each person is entitled to her

---

[8] Or, more precisely, if its possessor is entitled to it *and* does not owe anyone compensation for past wrongdoing.

5.5 Is Entitlement Necessary for Justice?

respective holdings.[9] Similarly, the revised entitlement theory should maintain that a holding is just if *and only if* its possessor is entitled to it (as opposed to how it is stated previously, where entitlement is a sufficient – but not necessary – condition of a holding being just).

If entitlement is a necessary condition of some holding being just, that would allow for a revitalization of the incompatibilist argument. Specifically, consider the case where P is not entitled to a particular resource R but it is in her possession. Additionally, suppose that P would be left worse off than Q if Q were to interact with R in any way. Finally, assume that the comparative disadvantage that P would suffer if Q were to interact with R would not reflect any sanctionable choice on P's part (in the sense proposed in Chapter 6). In this case, the anarchist conclusion would entail that Q has a duty to refrain from interacting with R. This, in turn, implies that the state of affairs where Q refrains from interacting with R is just (given the conditional relationship between duties and justice posited earlier). However, if entitlement is a necessary condition of justice, an entitlement theory would hold that Q's exclusion from R is not just, as P is not entitled to her holding. Thus, entitlement theories of justice still contradict the anarchist conclusion.

But why think that entitlement is a necessary condition of justice? There are two reasons for denying this proposition and, by extension, the revitalized incompatibilist argument. First, if one grants that a holding is just only if its possessor is entitled to that holding, that seemingly entails that borrowed holdings are not just, as a borrowed item is, by definition, an item that one possesses but does not own. Further, given that the return of a borrowed holding would meet the sufficient condition of justice (as the possessor of the item would now be the person who is entitled to that item), it seems that borrowers have a duty of justice to return the item to its owner even though they had full permission to be in possession of the item in question. Given that practically any entitlement theorist would reject this result as unacceptable, one ought to reject the proposal that entitlement is a necessary condition of a holding being just.

There are various replies that could be made to this objection. Mack, for example, suggests that this counterexample might be avoided by positing that a person with a borrowed holding is entitled to said holding (2018, private communication). However, endorsing this suggestion would require making significant modifications to other parts of a Nozick-inspired

---

[9] Vallentyne endorses such an interpretation, arguing that Nozick's failure to posit such a necessary condition was an oversight on his part (2011, 151).

entitlement theory. For example, while Nozick says little about his principle of justice in transfer, presumably it holds that a transaction is just if the holding in question is voluntarily given and received. Thus, if a borrower is entitled to the borrowed item – and, she then gives that item to a third party – it would follow that the third party is now entitled to the item per Nozick's account. However, entitlement theorists would reject this conclusion. More generally, it seems that Nozick understands entitlement as something very close to full ownership of the holdings (with the caveat that certain exclusion and transfer rights are limited by his posited version of the Lockean proviso). However, borrowers have fairly limited rights over borrowed items, as they lack a right to destroy, transfer, or exclude others from said items. Thus, borrowers cannot be said to be entitled to borrowed items, at least as Nozick uses the term.

The second objection to making entitlement a necessary condition of justice is that this amendment does not follow from the considerations that motivate libertarians to endorse entitlement theories of justice in the first place. Absent such a logical connection to the premises that ground an entitlement theory of justice, making entitlement a necessary condition of justice seems ad hoc and, thus, an implausible way of demonstrating that entitlement theories are incompatible with the anarchist conclusion. Most notably, the primary motivation for positing an entitlement theory is seemingly to negate the permissibility of redistributing those things that persons have justly appropriated or received via just transfer. However, this result is achieved by simply positing that entitlement is a sufficient condition of justice – at least, if one accepts the plausible supplemental premise that it is impermissible to transform a just holding into one that is not just via redistribution. Given that the original statement (and restatement) of entitlement theory satisfies this core theoretical *desideratum*, the proposed amendment to make entitlement a necessary condition of justice seems unmotivated.

5.6 Wilt Chamberlain and the Anarchist Conclusion

It is worth considering a final reason for thinking that entitlement theories of justice are incompatible with the anarchist conclusion. This third incompatibilist argument would concede that there is no contradiction between the implications of the two positions. However, it would maintain that the arguments for rejecting non-entitlement theories in favor of entitlement theories apply equally to the anarchist conclusion. Thus, even if entitlement theories are not technically incompatible with the anarchist conclusion, any entitlement theorist would still reject the anarchist

5.6 Wilt Chamberlain and the Anarchist Conclusion

conclusion on the grounds that it is negated by the arguments that led her to accept an entitlement theory in the first place. The anarchist conclusion would thereby lose its dialectical significance for the reasons discussed in the introduction to this chapter.

The problem with this proposal is that the anarchist conclusion sidesteps the primary arguments for favoring entitlement theories of justice over non-entitlement theories. Consider, for example, Nozick's (1974) influential Wilt Chamberlain argument. In this thought experiment, holdings are distributed in accordance with the prescriptions of one's preferred non-entitlement principle. However, each person then voluntarily pays Wilt Chamberlain a small amount of money to watch him play basketball, with the result being the emergence of a new distribution that is (by hypothesis) unjust according to the non-entitlement principle.

While Nozick is not fully explicit regarding the structure of his argument, he is best understood as making two distinct *reductio* arguments against non-entitlement principles of justice.[10] The first begins with the observation that, if the post-transfer distribution of resources is unjust according to the non-entitlement principle, then one would act permissibly if one enforced the original distribution and thereby prevented the unjust distribution from arising. However, Nozick argues that such enforcement must take the form of either (a) unacceptably interfering with freedom by blocking free exchanges between consenting adults, or (b) allowing such acts but then redistributing the fruit of Chamberlain's labor – an act that is unacceptable because it is tantamount to slavery (1974; 163, 169–72). In other words, a non-entitlement theory declares the enforcement of the original distribution permissible when such enforcement is, in fact, impermissible. Thus, any non-entitlement theory must be rejected to avoid contradiction.

The second *reductio* posits that if one has a just share according to a non-entitlement principle of justice, then one has the right to dispose of that share as one wishes, with any resultant state of affairs thereby qualifying as just (1974, 161). Thus, given that the starting state in the Wilt Chamberlain case is just, it follows that the state of affairs after people choose to give some of their holdings to Chamberlain is also just.

---

[10] Different interpreters of Nozick tend to focus on only one of these *reductios* at the expense of the other (e.g., with Onora O'Neill (1981, 308) primarily addressing the first and Cohen (2011, 127) and Mack (2002, 81–4) focusing on the second). However, for these purposes, it will be granted that Nozick is making both arguments.

However, the resultant distribution is also unjust according to the posited non-entitlement principle because it does not align with its prescribed pattern/end-state. To avoid this contradiction, one must reject the assumed non-entitlement principle of justice.

When considering these *reductios*, one question to ask is whether Nozick assumes that all persons in the Wilt Chamberlain case are entitled to their holdings. Seemingly, the answer to this question must be "yes" given Nozick's own understanding of the moral status of unowned holdings. Nozick must maintain that there is nothing morally problematic about interfering with unowned holdings, as the person who possesses a resource but does not own it has no claim against others coming and using it without permission. Similarly, the possessor would have no claim against them taking that thing and redistributing it to someone else (assuming the absence of any distributive claims). And she would lack any power to give a person a claim to exclude others from that resource. These Hohfeldian no-claims and disabilities follow from non-ownership as a matter of definition. However, there would then be nothing wrong with blocking transfers made by someone who is not entitled to a thing (e.g., someone attempting to bequeath an unowned thing to someone else). Given that Nozick's first *reductio* rests on the premise that such blocking is wrong, he must be presupposing that the people in the Wilt Chamberlain case are entitled to their holdings. Similar remarks apply to the second *reductio*'s contention that the people have a right to dispose of their share as they see fit – a claim that would be true only if they were entitled to their shares. Thus, by his own lights, Nozick's Wilt Chamberlain *reductios* are sound only if it is assumed that the people in the scenario are entitled to their holdings.

There are two things to note about this conclusion. First, as a more general point, it reveals a dialectical weakness in Nozick's argument, as those who endorse some non-entitlement theory of justice can avoid his posited *reductios* by simply denying the possibility of people being entitled to their holdings. Specifically, a non-entitlement theorist can deny that persons are able to acquire the power to transfer claims to others; this, in turn, would allow her to insist that there is nothing problematic about blocking transfers between consenting adults. To preclude this reply, Nozick would have to maintain that the power to transfer follows directly from a person's holdings conforming to the non-entitlement theory in question. If such conformance entailed the power to transfer, then the non-entitlement theorist would be vulnerable to Nozick's *reductios*. However, it is unclear why the non-entitlement theorist should affirm this conditional and give up her denial that anyone has the power to transfer

5.6 Wilt Chamberlain and the Anarchist Conclusion

claims to resources. Additionally, the foregoing discussion reveals that Nozick cannot consistently assert this conditional, as it conflicts with his own distinction between entitlement and non-ownership. Nozick's contention is that the power to transfer is a distinctive feature of entitlement – that is, it has entitlement as its necessary condition. Thus, he cannot consistently maintain that a particular distribution of holdings obtaining is a sufficient condition of the power to transfer holdings. This leaves him with no way to object to the non-entitlement theorist who denies both the proposed entailment relation (i.e., that a just distribution entails that each person has the power to transfer her holdings) and the more general premise that persons can possess the power to transfer holdings.

That said, the anarchist cannot avail herself of this argument because she *does* grant that persons can possess the power to transfer. She is thereby precluded from denying the premise that the people in the Wilt Chamberlain case have the power to transfer their holdings. Rather, like Nozick, she must affirm that persons have this power if and only if they are entitled to their holdings. Granted, she denies that persons could, in practice, acquire such entitlements via appropriation for the reasons discussed in Chapters 3 and 4. However, she must concede that, at least in theory, a scenario could arise where a group of people *do* acquire property either via everyone's consent or because a total absence of scarcity entails that the Lockean proviso is satisfied vis-à-vis natural resources. Thus, unlike the pure non-entitlement theorist, she must allow that there is a possible Wilt Chamberlain scenario where persons are entitled to their initial holdings (in addition to those holdings conforming to the prescriptions of her favored non-entitlement theory).

Fortunately for the anarchist, she can reject a different premise of Nozick's *reductios* to avoid having to reject the anarchist conclusion. Specifically, both *reductios* contend that the post-transfer distribution is unjust according to the non-entitlement theory in question. However, while this implication does follow from standard non-entitlement distributive principles, it does not follow from the anarchist conclusion. This is because the anarchist conclusion only assigns persons luck egalitarian distributive claims vis-à-vis *unowned* resources. Given that Nozick must affirm that all of the holdings in his Wilt Chamberlain case are owned, it follows that there would be no distributive claims restricting the permissible use of these holdings. Rather, the permissible use of these holdings would be strictly governed by people's property claims over those holdings. Thus, the anarchist conclusion does not entail that Wilt Chamberlain has any duty to redistribute his post-transfer holdings; rather, it concedes that he has property claims against such redistribution. This, in turn, implies that the post-transfer distribution is just according to the anarchist conclusion – a result that does not contradict Nozick's contention that the post-transfer distribution is just. The anarchist conclusion thereby sidesteps both of Nozick's Wilt Chamberlain *reductios*.

The anarchist conclusion similarly avoids a third argument against non-entitlement theories that Mack (2002, 82–3) attributes to Nozick. This argument holds that, if some state is unjust, one must be able to explain how it came to be unjust via appeal to some historical occurrence – that is, one must be able to identify the particular event responsible for the emergence of the injustice. However, given that the post-transfer state in the Wilt Chamberlain case is reached via just steps from a just pre-transfer state, there is no such apparent explanation. Thus, the post-transfer state cannot be unjust, contra what a non-entitlement theory implies – and one must, therefore, reject such a non-entitlement theory. However, again, this argument is only valid because non-entitlement theories declare the post-transfer state unjust. By contrast, the anarchist conclusion affirms the justice of the distribution, as there are no luck-based inequalities *that have resulted from the use of unowned resources*. It thereby sidesteps this interpretation of Nozick's Wilt Chamberlain argument in addition to the ones presented previously.

Unfortunately, it is not possible to consider whether the anarchist conclusion avoids every objection to non-entitlement theories of justice. However, the fact that it is able to sidestep all three interpretations of Nozick's Wilt Chamberlain argument is at least suggestive that it will similarly survive whatever other arguments entitlement theorists might develop in the defense of their theory. The general reason for thinking that the anarchist conclusion will avoid such arguments is the fact that it concedes to the entitlement theorist that a holding is just if its possessor is entitled to it. By granting people ownership rights over whatever resources they justly acquire, the anarchist conclusion effectively incorporates an entitlement theory into its broader account of how to assess the justice of holdings. This incorporation means that it will be difficult for entitlement theorists to object to the position.

5.7 Libertarian Egalitarianism

The previous sections have defended the thesis that the anarchist conclusion is the appropriate philosophical response to the fact that no one has acquired ownership over natural resources outside of their bodies (as argued in Chapters 3 and 4). Specifically, Section 5.1 argued that one cannot simply concede that people have no claims vis-à-vis natural resources, as such a conclusion would violate the moral tyranny constraint.

5.7 Libertarian Egalitarianism

Thus, one must posit that people have *some* such claims, for example, those posited by the anarchist conclusion. Sections 5.2–5.6 then argued that there is no tension between the anarchist conclusion's posited distributive claims and the anarchist position's incorporation of an entitlement theory of justice. Thus, one might be an orthodox libertarian – that is, one who endorses an entitlement theory of justice – while still accepting the anarchist conclusion.

However, there is a gap in this argument when it comes to defending the particular distributive claims posited by the anarchist conclusion. Note that one can avoid the moral tyranny of the Hobbesian conclusion by positing *any* set of distributive claims so long as full compliance with those claims would sustain a particular pattern of advantage (and the theory holds people responsible for sanctionable choices). Recall that the Hobbesian conclusion allowed for moral tyranny because it did not posit any distributive claims. Absent such claims, a person can act on unowned resources in a way that leaves others worse off$_{FC}$, as she will not owe any compensation to others for costs imposed by her usage. Thus, future full compliance would do nothing to offset those costs, with others ending up worse off$_{FC}$ as a result. By contrast, the anarchist conclusion's assignment of luck egalitarian distributive claims precludes persons from leaving others worse off$_{FC}$. While person P might still impose costs upon another person Q and/or infringe upon Q's claims, Q would still be entitled to the same quantity of advantage according to the anarchist conclusion. Thus, if P were to act in the posited way(s), the anarchist conclusion would reassign distributive claims such that full compliance with those claims would leave Q with just as much advantage as she would have had if everyone had complied with the original set of distributive claims (i.e., the claims assigned prior to P's action). Given this reassignment, full compliance will leave Q with the same amount of advantage irrespective of P's action, with P being thereby precluded from leaving Q worse off$_{FC}$.

However, one can avoid the moral tyranny of the Hobbesian conclusion without assigning persons *luck egalitarian* distributive claims – that is, the set of distributive claims such that full compliance would eliminate all inequalities except those that reflect sanctionable choice. Rather, one merely needs to posit a set of distributive rights where full compliance would yield *some* fixed pattern of advantage.[11] For example, consider a

---

[11] As noted in parentheses in the previous paragraph, this pattern must be sensitive to responsibility for the reasons discussed in Section 2.4. There it was suggested that one must reject strict egalitarianism in favor of luck egalitarianism, as the former was inadequately sensitive to

theory that assigns each person a set of distributive claims such that full compliance would leave one person with 100 units of advantage and everyone else with 5 units. So long as this theory reassigns claims in light of persons' actions such that full compliance would generate these same outcomes, it will equally satisfy the moral tyranny constraint, as people will be unable to leave anyone worse off$_{FC}$ than she would have otherwise been. Thus, one cannot appeal to the constraint to justify the anarchist's assignment of *egalitarian* distributive claims – which is to say that the argument of Chapters 2, 3, and 4 does not quite deliver the anarchist conclusion as promised. Rather, it demonstrates that the moral tyranny constraint entails both (a) the absence of external private property and (b) that there is *some* (responsibility-sensitive) advantage$_{FC}$-preserving set of distributive rights. Further argument is therefore required to demonstrate that one ought to accept the anarchist conclusion over rival theories of distributive rights.

There are two approaches one might take to filling in this argumentative gap. First, one might appeal to existing defenses of luck egalitarian principles of distributive justice to ground the anarchist conclusion's egalitarian distributive claims. While these defenses do not typically put things in terms of distributive claims, they do affirm that justice requires that each person receive an equal share of advantage (absent sanctionable choice). Given that the anarchist conclusion insists that each person has a claim to an equal share of advantage, it seems that any proposed argument for luck egalitarianism will also provide support for the anarchist conclusion's egalitarian presumption.

The disadvantage of this approach is that the overarching argument of the book loses some of its dialectical force. As noted previously at various points, the argument is intended to be a libertarian defense of egalitarian conclusions that puts dialectical pressure on libertarians to give up private property rights and, instead, endorse a variety of luck egalitarianism. For this reason, the foregoing chapters have granted as many libertarian premises as possible when arguing for the anarchist position. Similarly, this chapter has attempted to preserve this dialectical pressure by demonstrating that the anarchist conclusion is compatible with libertarian entitlement

---

responsibility – and, thus, would allow some people to unilaterally, discretionarily, and foreseeably leave others with less$_{FC}$. However, similar remarks would apply to the comparison between any responsibility-insensitive distributive principle and its responsibility-sensitive counterpart. Thus, any share-assigning theory must be structured in such a way that an agent forfeits some claim to advantage if she makes a sanctionable choice – that is, a choice where full compliance conditional on that choice would leave others worse off than full compliance conditional on a rival choice (much more on this in Chapter 6).

5.7 Libertarian Egalitarianism

theories of justice. However, if the anarchist conclusion follows from both libertarian premises *and* non-libertarian egalitarian premises – that is, those posited by the luck egalitarian defenses mentioned in the previous paragraph – then libertarians could, at low theoretical cost, deny the anarchist conclusion by rejecting the egalitarian premises. Granted, it is not clear what alternative pattern of advantage the libertarian would endorse instead (for she must endorse *some* pattern to avoid the moral tyranny of the Hobbesian conclusion). Nonetheless, one can imagine certain anti-egalitarian libertarians insisting that there is no positive reason to favor egalitarian distributive claims, with any arbitrary set of advantage$_{FC}$-preserving distributive claims being an equally acceptable theoretical alternative to the anarchist conclusion.

Fortunately, there is a second approach available to the anarchist that restores the dialectical pressure of the anarchist argument. Specifically, the anarchist might observe that practically all libertarians *already* accept an egalitarian approach to the assignment of claims. This point is made by many libertarians themselves, as they argue that their rejection of distributive egalitarianism is grounded in a more fundamental kind of egalitarianism. Specifically, these libertarians contend that their view uniquely recognizes human moral equality by initially assigning all persons *equal rights* – which is to say either identical or symmetrical rights.[12] For example, if one person starts out with the Hohfeldian power to appropriate some object, then all persons start out with an identical power to appropriate that object. Similarly, if one person initially has the right to exclude others from her body, then all persons initially have the symmetrical right to exclude her from their bodies. Of course, some people might end up with fewer rights than others in virtue of having either waived or forfeited their rights; however, there remains a presumption of initial moral equality that insulates libertarianism from charges of moral arbitrariness.

Given this commitment to assigning persons equal rights, it follows that libertarians should assign persons equal distributive rights as well. Granted, libertarians have not heretofore recognized that people have distributive

---

[12] Some notable examples include Locke (2005, §§ 4–7), Herbert Spencer (1851, 77–8), Anthony Fressola (1981, 316–7), Lomasky (1987, 122–3), Wendy McElroy (1991, 3), Rothbard (1998, 42–3), Narveson (1988, 98), Long (2005, 18–9), and Flanigan (2019b). Critics of libertarianism have similarly recognized libertarianism as egalitarian in this respect including Amartya Sen (1992, 13, 21–3), Cohen (1995, 213), Carl Knight (2009, 340), and Matthew Braham and Martin van Hees (2014, 427, 431). The claim that treating like people alike entails assigning individuals equal rights is also endorsed by Steiner (1974, 223). However, he contends that people should be understood as having equal rights vis-à-vis natural resources, thereby staking out a left-libertarian view that is much closer to the anarchist conclusion proposed here.

rights. However, if the foregoing argument is correct and there are such rights, then they should be assigned in the same egalitarian fashion that libertarians assign other rights. There is admittedly some ambiguity here regarding what qualifies as an assignment of equal rights. As just noted, one might take two persons to have equal rights if both have *the same right*, for example, P and Q each have a claim that R not ϕ. More commonly, libertarians propose that persons have symmetrical rights, where P and Q have a symmetrical right if and only if P and Q *would have* an *identical* right if every reference to P in P's right is replaced by a reference to Q and every reference to Q is replaced by a reference to P. For example, if P has a claim that Q not touch P's body and Q has a claim that P not touch Q's body, then the two have symmetrical rights, as changing P's right in the way just discussed yields a right that is identical to Q's. However, there is no apparent reason why equal assignments of rights might not also include cases where P and Q are assigned distributive claims that entitle each of them to an equal share of advantage. After all, such an assignment seems to equally avoid the accusation of moral arbitrariness that motivates libertarians to assign persons identical or symmetrical rights.

Additionally, seemingly any rights schema that assigns persons strictly identical and/or symmetrical distributive claims would not generate a fixed pattern of advantage under conditions of full compliance. This, in turn, implies that all such schemas violate the moral tyranny constraint. To see this, note that the Hobbesian conclusion represents just such a schema, as it assigns to each person a set of claims that are either identical or symmetrical to those possessed by each other person. Specifically, each person has a symmetrical right against others making ASO-infringing contact with her body and all persons have an identical permission to use any given unowned resource. However, because they lack advantage$_{FC}$-preserving distributive claims over unowned objects, the Hobbesian conclusion violates the moral tyranny constraint (as discussed in Section 5.1). Similarly, assigning persons additional identical/symmetrical claims will fail to resolve this problem unless those claims somehow offset imposed costs$_{FC}$ in the way discussed at the start of this section. Thus, there does not appear to be a way to assign persons claims in an advantage$_{FC}$-preserving fashion while also assigning each person a claim if and only if each other person is assigned an identical/symmetrical claim. Given this result, libertarians should concede that the proposed schema of luck egalitarian distributive claims instantiates an equal assignment of rights (lest their insistence on moral equality be rendered incompatible with the moral tyranny constraint). They would then be able to affirm human moral equality while avoiding moral tyranny by endorsing the anarchist conclusion.

5.8 Conclusion

The bulk of the argument for anarchism is now complete. The foregoing chapters have attempted to show that a single plausible theoretical *desideratum* entails a number of conclusions typically embraced by anarchists. Specifically, these chapters argued that the moral tyranny constraint entails the Lockean proviso and the consent theory of legitimacy, each of which further entails the absence of external private property (despite it still being the case that people can easily acquire ownership over their own bodies). This chapter has argued that the moral tyranny constraint also implies that the non-ownership of external resources cannot entail an absence of all claims vis-à-vis those resources. Rather, each person must be assigned some set of advantage$_{FC}$-preserving distributive claims that preclude other agents from discretionarily leaving her worse off$_{FC}$. Additionally, this chapter argued that such distributive claims are fully compatible with an (appropriately interpreted) entitlement theory of justice – a result that sustains social anarchism's claim to being a thoroughly libertarian position. Finally, the chapter argued that libertarians should endorse the luck egalitarian distributive claims posited by the anarchist conclusion, as such rights best reflect libertarians' egalitarian approach to assigning rights to persons.

In short, libertarians who are sympathetic to the moral tyranny constraint should reject private property in external resources and endorse the anarchist conclusion. However, this conclusion is still in need of a bit of further precisification. Notably, the distributive claims posited by the anarchist conclusion are not simply egalitarian in character but, rather, *luck* egalitarian in character; that is, compliance with those claims would leave everyone equally well off *excluding those who have chosen sanctionably*. This italicized qualifier is included for the reasons described in Section 2.4: An egalitarian theory that does not hold people responsible for sanctionable choices (e.g., the choice to spitefully destroy all of one's holdings) will still run afoul of the moral tyranny constraint. But which choices count as sanctionable? This question has so far been left unanswered. It is the task of Chapter 6 to provide a theory of sanctionable choice that brings luck egalitarianism – and, by extension, the anarchist conclusion – into full compliance with the moral tyranny constraint.

CHAPTER 6

Luck Egalitarianism without Moral Tyranny

> We want to put everything in common, starting from the principle that everybody should do some work and all should live as well as possible. It's not possible to live in this world without working, so if one person doesn't do anything he has to live at the expense of others, which is unfair and harmful. Obviously when I say that everybody should work I mean all those that are able to, and do the amount suited to them. The [disabled], the weak and the aged should be supported by society, because it is the duty of humanity that no one should suffer.
>
> Errico Malatesta, *Between Peasants*

Chapters 3, 4, and 5 have attempted to provide a libertarian argument for luck egalitarianism.[1] Chapters 3 and 4 each took a prominent libertarian thesis and argued that it entails that there are no existing private property rights. Chapter 5 then argued that, in the absence of property, libertarians ought to embrace the anarchist conclusion, which assigns persons luck egalitarian distributive claims over unowned natural resources. More precisely, this conclusion posits that each person has a claim against others interacting with unowned resources in a way that (a) would leave her worse off than someone else where (b) this comparative disadvantage does not appropriately correspond to previous sanctionable choices on her part. The obvious – and so far unanswered – question is: What choices count as sanctionable and which inequalities can be said to appropriately correspond to those choices? This chapter seeks to answer both parts of this question by appealing to the moral tyranny constraint.

Recall from Section 2.4 that luck egalitarianism avoids the moral tyranny of strict egalitarianism by holding people responsible for making sanctionable

---

[1] This chapter is an adapted version of a paper originally published in *Philosophical Studies* (Spafford 2022). While the animating idea is the same in both versions, some of the technical details of the paper have been adjusted here to improve the proposed theory (particularly in Sections 3–5).

choices. The problem with strict egalitarianism is that it allows a spiteful destroyer to preserve her claim to an equal share of advantage even as she destroys any advantage in her possession. Because the destroyer preserves this claim, full compliance would require that others make costly equalizing transfers to her. She is thereby able to discretionarily, foreseeably, and unilaterally leave those others worse off$_{FC}$ when she destroys her holdings. By contrast, luck egalitarianism declares that the destruction of her holdings is a sanctionable choice, which, in turn, implies that she forfeits a claim to some portion of advantage (where this forfeiture negates her claim to any transfer). The theory thereby holds her responsible for her sanctionable choice and, in this way, satisfies the moral tyranny constraint.

However, as was noted in Section 1.6, there are two respects in which this general idea of holding people responsible needs to be specified if the anarchist conclusion is to have determinate content. First: Which choices qualify as sanctionable? Some general theory is needed here that can be applied to cases like the spiteful destroyer or Cohen's parable of the ant and the grasshopper. Second: To what quantity of advantage does a person lose her claim when she makes a sanctionable choice? Most luck egalitarians answer these questions by either explicitly or tacitly assuming what might be called *prudential contextualism*: A person chooses sanctionably if and only if she is responsible for leaving herself worse off than she could have been otherwise.[2] She then forfeits a claim to however much additional advantage she would have had if she had chosen differently. For example, if the norm in a given society is that people who park on a certain street have their car towed, then the person who parks there and has her car towed forfeits her claim to the extra advantage she would have possessed had her car not been towed.

Unfortunately, this interpretation of luck egalitarianism has left the position vulnerable to three serious objections – each of which would equally apply to the anarchist conclusion. Most notably, one of these objections holds that this interpretation puts both luck egalitarianism

---

[2] The term "prudential contextualism" is a slight modification of Olsaretti's term "contextualism," which she uses to describe this dominant interpretation of luck egalitarianism (2009, 180). The chapter will not take a stand on the exact sense in which an agent must be *responsible* for leaving herself worse off – at least, beyond a few claims about the necessary conditions of such responsibility discussed subsequently. It should be noted that not all luck egalitarians are prudential contextualists with some explicitly rejecting the position (e.g., Olsaretti (2009), Stemplowska (2009), and Thaysen and Albertsen (2017)). These alternative views will also be discussed. It should also be noted that there is some dispute over whether certain influential luck egalitarians were contextualists. For a critical discussion, see Stemplowska (2013).

and the associated anarchist conclusion in violation of the moral tyranny constraint. The task of this chapter is to present an alternative account of sanctionable choice that avoids these objections. Specifically, it will propose that an agent chooses sanctionably if and only if the choice, under conditions of full compliance, can reasonably be expected to produce less appropriately distributed advantage than some alternative choice that could have been made. The remainder of the chapter will explain what is meant by each of these terms and how the proposed account resolves the three objections. First, though, these objections need to be introduced, with particular attention paid to the moral tyranny objection.

6.1 Three Objections to Prudential Contextualism

The first objection to contextualist luck egalitarianism has been forcefully raised by Richard Arneson, who argues that luck egalitarianism delivers incorrect results in cases of charitable action. For example, a Mother Teresa figure who impoverishes herself assisting the poor would, on the prudential contextualist view, have made a sanctionable choice, as she leaves herself worse off in a way that could have been avoided. Thus, the luck egalitarian (or social anarchist) who endorses prudential contextualism would seemingly be committed to saying that she is not entitled to any sort of compensatory redistribution; however, Arneson contends that this is the wrong result, with luck egalitarianism then being rejected as part of a *modus tollens* argument (Arneson 2011a, 244; 2011b, 33–4).[3]

Second, there is what Susan Hurley has called luck egalitarianism's "boring problem." This objection aims to call into question the core luck egalitarian contention that sanctionable choice can justify inequality. Hurley argues that this contention is plausible only if sanctionable choosers are responsible for the inequality in question. However, on the prudential contextualist view, a person chooses sanctionably if and only if she is responsible for *her particular level of advantage*. Given that someone can be responsible for her level of advantage but not the associated inequality – as the inequality is partly a function of the advantage levels of others for which *they* are responsible – it follows that sanctionable choice cannot justify inequality in the way that luck egalitarians contend (Hurley

---

[3] For an alternative version of this argument, see Larry Temkin's case of a good Samaritan who rescues a drowning child from a pond but injures himself in the process (2011, 63). Here, again, it is maintained that her failure to act prudently means she is held responsible for this personal cost via the denial of any compensation.

6.1 Three Objections to Prudential Contextualism

2003, 160–1).[4] Similarly, insofar as the anarchist is motivated by egalitarian concerns, she will want to posit that, while there is something prima facie unjust about inequality, there is nothing unjust about inequality corresponding to sanctionable choice. Thus, her position will similarly be vulnerable to the objection that sanctionable choice fails to defeat the prima facie injustice of inequality.

Finally – and most importantly for the purposes of this chapter – there is Serena Olsaretti's objection (though she does not use this language) that contextualist luck egalitarianism violates the moral tyranny constraint. Specifically, she begins with the observation that most luck egalitarians tacitly assume a contextualist theory of sanctionable choice where a person forfeits a claim to however much advantage she foregoes due to contingent social circumstances and the choices that others make (2009, 180). However, given such a prudential contextualist view, a person's claim to advantage will often – and problematically – depend on the capricious choices of others (176). To illustrate this point, Olsaretti introduces Marc Fleurbaey's (1995) case of a reckless motorcyclist who crashes and is injured as a result of driving too fast and not wearing a helmet. She notes that, on the contextualist theory, the quantity of advantage to which the motorcyclist forfeits a claim will be a function of whether a passerby provides assistance, leaves her unaided, or confiscates her motorcycle – a result that makes contextualist luck egalitarianism seem unacceptable (2009, 175–6).

While Olsaretti does not provide a general theory of why this is a problem for contextualism, one can provide such an explanation by appealing to the moral tyranny constraint. Specifically, contextualism allows the passerby to unilaterally, foreseeably, and discretionarily reduce the quantity of advantage to which the motorcyclist has a claim which, in turn, would reduce how much advantage she would have in the world of full compliance. If the passerby declines to assist the motorcyclist, the latter will be left with less$_{FC}$ advantage than if she would possess if she were assisted. And she would be left with less$_{FC}$ still if the passerby were to confiscate her motorcycle. Contextualist luck egalitarianism thereby violates the moral tyranny constraint, as it enables the passerby to unilaterally, discretionarily, and foreseeably leave the motorcyclist worse off$_{FC}$. This result explains why prudential contextualism is an unacceptable theory of

---

[4] For a recent paper that attempts to extend the boring problem into a more general objection to theories that declare luck-based inequality unjust, see Matthew T. Jeffers (2020). For an alternative reply to the boring problem, see Spafford (2023).

which choices count as sanctionable (particularly given the fact that satisfying the constraint was the motivating reason for adopting luck egalitarianism in the first place). Thus, the anarchist conclusion must employ some alternative account of sanctionable choice – ideally, one that also resolves the other two objections to luck egalitarianism discussed just prior.

6.2 Moralized Contextualism

What is needed is an alternative account of sanctionable choice that satisfies the moral tyranny constraint. The task of the remainder of the chapter is to provide such an account. First, though, it is worth briefly considering an alternative account that might seem like a simple solution to contextualism's moral tyranny problem. This account posits that a person chooses sanctionably if and only if (a) she leaves herself worse off than she would have been otherwise and (b) *she does not end up worse off as a result of someone infringing upon her rights*. She then forfeits a claim to the surplus advantage that she would have possessed had she chosen differently.[5]

This *moralized contextualism* seems to rule out some of the more intuitively problematic forms of moral tyranny endorsed by standard contextualist accounts. For example, in the motorcycle case, one might think that Condition (b) is not met, as the passerby who confiscates the motorcycle infringes upon the rights of the motorcyclist to continue to use her motorcycle. Thus, the motorcyclist does not choose sanctionably, which, in turn, implies that she does not forfeit a claim to the advantage that would result from her continued use of the motorcycle. Further, given that she still has a claim to this advantage, full compliance with her claims would ensure that she retains possession of this advantage (e.g., because the passerby would immediately return the motorcycle), thereby preventing the passerby from leaving the motorcyclist with less$_{FC}$. This result suggests that moralized contextualism satisfies the moral tyranny constraint.

---

[5] This seems to be what Olsaretti is suggesting when she says that "the notion of responsibility a theory of justice employs is necessarily moralized, in that it must presuppose a view of what individuals owe to one another in order to determine the legitimate consequences of choices" (2009, 186). A more formal articulation of moralized contextualism is proposed by Zofia Stemplowska (2009), though she significantly qualifies the view. Unfortunately, working through the interesting details of her view would take things too far afield.

However, there are two problems with this suggestion. First, even if moralization *limits* the extent to which a person is able to leave others with less$_{FC}$, it does not *eliminate* her ability to leave them with less$_{FC}$. For example, while the motorcyclist may have a right to her motorcycle, she does not obviously have a right to assistance after the accident (at least, if assisting would be reasonably costly to the passerby). Given the absence of such a right, moralized contextualism delivers the same result as standard contextualism in the case where the passerby chooses not to assist the motorcyclist: The motorcyclist forfeits a claim to however much advantage she fails to secure as a result of the passerby's choice. Thus, full compliance under moralized contextualism would still allow the passerby to (unilaterally, foreseeably, and discretionarily) leave the motorcyclist with less$_{FC}$. The fact that moralized contextualism grants the passerby this ability entails that the theory still violates the moral tyranny constraint.

The second problem with the moralized contextualist approach is that it would render the anarchist conclusion circular. Note that the anarchist conclusion is supposed to answer the question of which rights people have over objects and resources. Indeed, this is the very point at issue in debates over taxes and transfers, with anarchists contending that natural resources should be distributed in a responsibility-sensitive egalitarian fashion. However, one cannot then assume that there is a given set of rights over objects for the anarchist to use as an input for her theory. For example, it cannot be maintained that the passerby infringes upon the motorcyclist's right to use her motorcycle, as it is an open question whether the motorcyclist does, in fact, have a right to use that motorcycle (particularly given her choice to ride without a helmet). Thus, an anarchist position that assigns claims in accordance with moralized contextualist luck egalitarianism not only fails to satisfy the moral tyranny constraint, but also appears to be unacceptably circular.

6.3 A Theory of Sanctionable Choice

Given the unacceptability of (moralized) contextualism, anarchists need a theory of sanctionable choice that satisfies the moral tyranny constraint. This section proposes the following account: An agent chooses sanctionably if and only if she fails to maximize *warranted expected distributed advantage assuming full compliance*. The task of this section is to explicate each of these italicized concepts and explain why the theory defines sanctionable choice in this way.

To begin, recall that a theory satisfies the moral tyranny constraint if and only if it does not enable any person to unilaterally, foreseeably, and discretionarily leave others with less$_{FC}$. Further, recall that there are two ways that a theory might enable a person in this way. First, it might grant her the power to directly strip others of their claims to advantage (or impose advantage-diminishing obligations on them), thereby changing how much advantage they would possess under conditions of full compliance. Second – and more importantly for these purposes – it might fail to adequately sanction those who diminish the total quantity of advantage that would be available if all persons were to fully comply with the demands of morality. To put this point a bit more precisely, such a failure occurs when a person reduces$_{FC}$ the total quantity of advantage by some quantity x but the theory in question holds that her just share is diminished by a quantity that is less than x. Indeed, this is what a strict egalitarian theory asserts in the case of the spiteful destroyer: Even as the destroyer reduces$_{FC}$ the total amount of available advantage by x, the theory holds that she only forfeits a claim to a quantity of x/n, where n is the number of people in the scenario. As a result, if others were to respect her adjusted claim to advantage, at least some persons would end up with less advantage than they would have had otherwise.

To avoid moral tyranny, then, a theory must hold that those who reduce$_{FC}$ the total quantity of advantage forfeit a claim to a sufficient quantity of advantage such that compliance with their claims would not leave others worse off. In other words, when people reduce$_{FC}$ the total quantity of advantage, the theory must declare that they choose sanctionably and hold them responsible by reducing the quantity of advantage to which they are entitled, thereby making them internalize the costs$_{FC}$ of their actions. This is the core idea of the theory of sanctionable choice presented here. However, some additional groundwork and a few refinements are needed to both make the theory acceptably egalitarian and ensure that the correct people are held responsible.

To further explicate the theory, it will be helpful to stake out a position regarding the *equilisandum* of the anarchist conclusion (i.e., the thing to which persons have equal distributive claims). Specifically, it will be assumed that what is to be equalized is *lifetime* levels of advantage, as opposed to the advantage persons possess at a particular time or over some specified period. Thus, there is no injustice in an arrangement where one person labors for the first half of her life while another relaxes, so long as the two switch roles for the second halves of their respective lives. Early on,

6.3 A Theory of Sanctionable Choice

the two people will have very different quantities of advantage; however, injustice only obtains if things are not adequately evened out in the future.[6] Given this assumption, any future use of terms like "the distribution of advantage" should be understood as referring to how lifetime advantage is distributed.

With this simplifying assumption in place, it becomes possible to determine the quantity of destroyed$_{FC}$ advantage that an agent must internalize. A natural temptation is to simply calculate the total quantity of advantage destroyed$_{FC}$ by her choice by taking the total advantage$_{FC}$ that obtains given her choice and comparing it to the maximum quantity that would have obtained had she chosen differently (assuming full compliance in both cases). However, this approach is unacceptable for two reasons. First, it would still violate the moral tyranny constraint. Note that a consequence of using this method is that later choices by other parties will sometimes determine how much destroyed$_{FC}$ advantage an agent has to internalize. Thus, a theory that calculates lost advantage in this way grants later choosers the power to unilaterally, discretionarily, and foreseeably render an agent's earlier choice sanctionable, thereby leaving her with less$_{FC}$. Second, this approach would make sanctionable choice a function of luck, as a choice might reduce$_{FC}$ the quantity of total advantage more than a rival choice due to an unforeseeable future event. Assuming that sanctionable choice requires that the agent be responsible for the state of affairs that grounds the forfeiture of her claim to advantage – and given the fact that agents are not responsible for the unforeseeable consequences of their actions – it follows that the sanctionability of a choice cannot be a function of whether or not it reduces$_{FC}$ the total quantity of advantage relative to a counterfactual choice.[7]

---

[6] This assumption helps to simplify things in the following way. Later, there will be much talk of how advantage is distributed. If the *equilisandum* of the luck egalitarian principle is lifetime advantage, then there is only one distribution to be assessed, namely, the lifetime levels of advantage everyone ends up with. By contrast, alternative approaches entail that there are many distributions that obtain across time, each of which would have to be assessed. That said, there are objections to taking entire lives as the basic unit of egalitarianism. See, for example, McKerlie (1989) and Temkin (1993).

[7] This assumption is posited because forfeiture seems unacceptably arbitrary if it is not grounded in some kind of responsible choice. Absent responsibility as a necessary condition, it seems one might equally forfeit claims to advantage in virtue of others' choices. Granted, such a condition does allow persons to act in ways that leave others with less$_{FC}$, as it allows them to sustain their claim to having as much advantage as everyone else despite diminishing the total quantity of available$_{FC}$ advantage. However, it does not allow them to *foreseeably* leave others with less$_{FC}$, thereby avoiding any contradiction with the moral tyranny constraint.

The observation that responsibility requires foreseeability suggests an alternative approach to quantifying how much destroyed$_{FC}$ advantage an agent must internalize: Instead of determining whether her choice reduces$_{FC}$ the total quantity of available advantage, one must determine whether that choice is *expected* to reduce$_{FC}$ the total quantity of advantage. Note that, at any point in time, there is a set of possible ultimate distributions of advantage that could still arise given all of the preceding events (where distributions extend across lifetimes as described earlier). Further, for any given choice that an agent might make, each of those distributions will have a particular probability of obtaining conditional on that choice being made and future full compliance. These conditional probabilities make it possible to calculate the *expected advantage* of that choice (assuming full compliance) by taking the total quantity of advantage of each distribution, multiplying it by the aforementioned conditional probability, and summing the results. This value can then be compared to the expected advantage value of other rival choices that could have been made. When a person makes a choice that has a lower expected advantage value than a rival choice that she could have made, she can be preliminarily understood as having chosen sanctionably, as her action is expected to diminish$_{FC}$ the total quantity of advantage.[8]

This account of sanctionable choice is merely preliminary because a significant revision must be made vis-à-vis calculations of expected value. To calculate the expected value of a choice, one must assign an *advantage value* to each of the possible distributions and then multiply that value by the probability of that distribution obtaining conditional on the choice being made and future full compliance. So far, this advantage value has been set equal to the total quantity of advantage that obtains in that distribution (as bringing about a distribution with less total advantage leaves others with less$_{FC}$, *ceteris paribus*). However, using total advantage obscures how advantage is *distributed* across persons. This is a problem because the moral tyranny constraint requires that agents must not be able to leave *any person* with less$_{FC}$ than she would have had otherwise, not *people on average*. But agents *will* be able to leave particular persons with less if sanctionable choices are specified to be all and only those choices that do not maximize expected value.

---

[8] This use of expected value has been embraced by a number of luck egalitarians including Arneson (1989), Knight (2013), and Vallentyne (2002; 2008).

6.3 A Theory of Sanctionable Choice

To see this, consider the case where agent P can either ϕ or ψ. If she ψ-s, she will realize a distribution where she, Q, and R each end up with 10 units of advantage. Alternatively, if she ϕ-s, she will realize a state of affairs where R has 20 units of nontransferrable advantage and she and Q have 16 units to split between the two of them (at P's discretion). In this scenario, there are two possibilities: either P's ϕ-ing is sanctionable or it is not. If P's ϕ-ing does not count as sanctionable, then P would retain her claim to an equal share of the available distributable advantage (8 units).[9] Thus, in the world of full compliance, she keeps 8 units for herself and similarly leaves Q with 8 units of advantage – that is, P is able to leave Q worse off$_{FC}$ by ϕ-ing relative to the world where P had chosen to ψ instead. By contrast, if P's choice to ϕ is sanctionable, then she loses her claim to a full 8 units of advantage, thereby allowing a portion of that advantage to be reassigned to Q such that Q would receive 10 units of advantage under conditions of full compliance. Given this result, it follows that P's choice to ϕ must be declared sanctionable if the proposed theory is to satisfy the moral tyranny constraint. However, note that P ϕ-ing also maximizes the expected total quantity of advantage (by producing 36 units of advantage rather than the 30 produced by ψ-ing). Thus, an acceptable theory cannot hold that a person chooses sanctionably if and only if she fails to maximize$_{FC}$ expected total advantage.[10]

---

[9] It is assumed here that P and Q have an equal claim to the quantity of *distributable* advantage; i.e., they each have a claim to 8 units of the 16 that can be split between them. Alternatively, one might maintain that P and Q have a claim to an equal share of the *total* advantage, which is to say they each have a claim to 12 units of advantage. However, the former approach is endorsed here because it simplifies some of the subsequent discussion and also avoids any incompossibility of rights (i.e., cases where two rights cannot be simultaneously respected). Either way, the following point remains true about this case: P is able to leave Q with less$_{FC}$ by ϕ-ing relative to ψ-ing if her choice to ϕ is non-sanctionable.

[10] It is worth noting that P ψ-ing will also leave R with less$_{FC}$ than R would have had if P had ϕ-ed. Thus, one might worry that moral tyranny is inevitable in cases where advantage is nontransferrable. However, this concern can be sidestepped by qualifying the moral tyranny constraint such that moral tyranny does not obtain if the person who is left with less$_{FC}$ (a) ends up with a just share of advantage and (b) is only left worse off relative to a counterfactual where full compliance would have delivered her a quantity of advantage that exceeded her just share (due to agents' limited ability to transfer). Indeed, there is seemingly nothing problematic about a theory that enables agents to deny full compliers advantage exceeding that to which they have a claim. For the sake of parsimony, though, the rest of the chapter will gloss over this qualification.

Alternatively, one might hold that while both ϕ-ing and ψ-ing leave someone with less$_{FC}$, P does not *discretionarily* leave R with less when she ψ-s because ψ-ing is the only way to respect Q's claim to receiving an equal share of advantage (in addition to everyone else). Given that ϕ-ing does not respect Q's claim in this way, P is obliged to ψ. Thus, it is only ϕ-ing that is problematic vis-à-vis the

This observation demands that the theory be refined as follows: A sanctionable choice does not merely fail to maximize the expected total advantage under conditions of full compliance but, rather, fails to maximize the total quantity of *appropriately distributed advantage* under conditions of full compliance. The idea here is as follows. At any given point in time, a luck egalitarian theory of justice – and, by extension, the anarchist assignment of distributive claims – will dictate what quantities of possessed advantage are just: Each person is entitled to as much advantage as everyone else minus however much advantage she has forfeited due to previous sanctionable choices. When each person possesses her just share, advantage can be said to be appropriately distributed, with full compliance entailing that people do everything permissible to realize this state of affairs. The problem is that certain choices preclude the possibility of fully compliant persons bringing about an appropriate distribution of advantage, with some persons thereby ending up with less$_{FC}$ than they could have had otherwise (and less than the amount of advantage to which they have a claim). To avoid this form of moral tyranny, the theory must treat such choices as sanctionable *in addition to* choices that leave others with less$_{FC}$ by failing to maximize$_{FC}$ the total quantity of transferrable advantage.

To deliver the result that such choices are sanctionable, one can modify the advantage values used to calculate the expected advantage of a choice. Specifically, any distribution where advantage is appropriately distributed receives an advantage value equal to the total quantity of advantage (i.e., the sum of each person's lifetime advantage). By contrast, for any distribution U where advantage is inappropriately distributed, U's advantage value is calculated via the following procedure. First, of those distributions that have a nonzero probability conditional on all past events obtaining, identify the distribution E that has the greatest total appropriately distributed advantage. Second, identify all those persons in U who have less advantage than they would have had in E. Third, sum the differences between how much advantage each such person has in E and how much she has in U. Fourth, calculate the advantage value of U by subtracting this sum from the total value of E (as this reduction reflects how much less$_{FC}$ advantage people end up with in U relative to the counterfactual E where

> moral tyranny constraint, as the worsening$_{FC}$ due to ψ-ing is nondiscretionary given that ψ-ing is obligatory. This means that a theory of sanctionable choice should only treat P's ϕ-ing and the associated loss$_{FC}$ of advantage as sanctionable. This is the aim of the theoretical refinement proposed in the next paragraph. Additionally, Section 6.6 will say more about the relationship between obligatory actions and the proposed theory of sanctionable choice.

6.3 A Theory of Sanctionable Choice

their just shares are maximized). Fifth, weight the advantage value of each distribution by multiplying it by the probability that the distribution obtains conditional on the choice in question being made and all persons complying with the demands of justice going forward.[11] Finally, calculate the *expected distributed advantage value* of the choice by summing those weighted advantage values.

Once the expected distributed advantage value of each possible choice has been calculated, it becomes possible to compare the value of the actual choice to those of rival choices that could have been made. When the former is less than one of latter values, the agent is responsible for leaving everyone with less$_{FC}$, where this difference quantifies the total advantage lost$_{FC}$ due to her choice. More precisely, everyone's combined loss$_{FC}$ of advantage is equal to the absolute value of the difference between the expected distributed advantage value of her choice and the value of the choice with the maximal expected distributed advantage value.

Note that the proposed theory of sanctionable choice does not need to prevent an agent from leaving *everyone* with less$_{FC}$. Rather, to satisfy the moral tyranny constraint, it must merely preclude her from leaving *others* with less$_{FC}$. Thus, the relevant question is what portion of the expected total loss$_{FC}$ of distributed advantage would be imposed upon others if the agent were not held responsible for her choice. Fortunately, calculating this value is fairly straightforward. Because the anarchist conclusion is egalitarian in character, it holds that, in the absence of sanctionable choice, any diminution in the total stock of advantage is distributed equally across persons. Thus, if the total quantity of lost$_{FC}$ advantage is equal to x and there are n persons in the world, each person will absorb $1/n$ of that lost$_{FC}$ advantage, that is, $\frac{1}{n} \times x$.[12] Given that the total number of people who are not the agent – that is, all those upon whom the cost$_{FC}$ would be

---

[11] Note that to avoid circularity, the theory must maintain that, when determining what fully compliant people will do given some choice, it must be assumed that they will treat the choice as non-sanctionable. Otherwise the theory will problematically maintain that the sanctionability of a choice depends on what fully compliant people will do in response to that choice, which, in turn, depends on whether the choice is sanctionable. This stipulation is perhaps a bit ad hoc, but this slight theoretical vice does not seem like a significant problem given the account's many significant theoretical virtues.

[12] This is a slight oversimplification, as it ignores cases where some people receive a quantity of nontransferrable advantage that is either equal to or exceeds their just share. In such cases, they will not absorb any of the cost imposed by the agent (because none of their advantage can be transferred away). Thus, rather than standing for the total number of people, "n" should really stand for the total number of people minus those whose nontransferrable advantage insulates them from the effects$_{FC}$ of any choice-responsive adjustment of claims.

imposed – is equal to $n - 1$, the sum of all of their incurred costs$_{FC}$ would then be equal to $\frac{n-1}{n} \times x$. This value represents the costs$_{FC}$ that the agent would impose upon others absent any forfeiture. The theory of sanctionable choice then holds the agent responsible by asserting that she forfeits a claim to this same quantity of advantage – that is, this forfeited quantity is subtracted from the quantity of advantage to which she would have been entitled absent forfeiture. Additionally, everyone else acquires a claim to a share of the total quantity of forfeited advantage such that they are not left worse off$_{FC}$ by the agent's choice.[13] Together, this forfeiture and accompanying claim acquisition forces the agent to internalize$_{FC}$ any foreseeable losses$_{FC}$ of advantage attributable to her action (by effectively transferring her claim to this advantage to those who would otherwise be left worse off$_{FC}$). Thus, the proposed theory of sanctionable choice precludes the agent from foreseeably leaving others with less$_{FC}$ and thereby satisfies the moral tyranny constraint.

One final bit of elaboration is needed to complete the formal account of sanctionable choice. So far, sanctionable choice has been defined in terms of expected distributed advantage, where this value is a function of distributions' distributed advantage values and the conditional probabilities of those distributions obtaining. However, note that the term "probability" is ambiguous. On the one hand, it might refer to *objective* probabilities, which, in this case, represent how likely it is in some metaphysical sense that a distribution will arise. Alternatively, it might refer to *subjective* probabilities representing the agent's beliefs about how probable it is that a distribution will arise. To eliminate this ambiguity, one can adopt Carl Knight's suggestion that the proper account of probability to incorporate into luck egalitarian (and, in this context, anarchist) calculations of expected value is *warranted subjective probability adjusted for non-culpable incapacity* (2013, 1067). Briefly, Knight contends that the relevant probability is that which the agent *should* have assigned given the evidence available to her – at least, in those cases where she is capable of assessing that evidence (1067). The advantage of this evidentialist view is that it does not differentially hold people responsible for their unchosen epistemic states. By contrast, on the objective probabilities approach, people might be unaware of relevant objective probabilities "through no

---

[13] For the sake of concision, the chapter will only talk of the sanctionable party forfeiting a claim going forward. However, this should always be taken as shorthand for the assertion that the sanctionable party forfeits a claim *and* the relevant non-sanctionable parties acquire claims in the way just described.

fault or choice of their own," and this makes it unfair to hold them responsible for non-maximizing choices (1066). Similarly, using subjective probabilities is unfair because those who are, as a matter of luck, overly confident that their choices are optimal will be found less culpable than those who lack that confidence (1066).

For the purposes of this argument, it is helpful to restate Knight's argument in terms of responsibility. An agent cannot seemingly be responsible for that which she could not have known given the evidence available to her. Further, even if she could know certain things, she may not be responsible for failing to form the proper beliefs given certain extenuating circumstances.[14] Given that responsibility is a necessary condition of sanctionable choice, it follows that an account of sanctionable choice that incorporates calculations of expected value should adopt Knight's notion of probability.[15] Thus, sanctionable choice should be understood as a failure to maximize *warranted* expected distributed advantage (WEDA) under conditions of full compliance.[16]

6.4 Applying the Theory

This abstract description of the theory can be illustrated by applying it to a highly simplified version of Fleurbaey's (1995) reckless motorcyclist case. Specifically, it will help to provide some invented numbers to demonstrate how the relevant calculations are carried out, beginning with the WEDA value of the motorcyclist choosing to wear a helmet:

---

[14] For more on this point, see Vallentyne (2002, 536).
[15] One might slightly amend Knight's account in the following way. Knight suggests that, in cases where an agent is not culpable for her failure to assess the evidence, she should be treated as having not made a choice at all, and, thus, not acted sanctionably (2013, 1068). However, one might alternatively think that, in cases where an agent is not responsible for her incorrect beliefs about how likely various distributions are to obtain, she might still be responsible for making a suboptimal choice *given* those beliefs. Thus, one might calculate expected distributed value using subjective probabilities in such cases.
[16] One consequence of incorporating Knight's suggestion is that the proposed theory of sanctionable choice does not countenance *option luck*. Briefly, option luck is generally understood to be the outcome that results from a deliberate and avoidable gamble, with many luck egalitarian theories taking persons to have chosen sanctionably if (a) they choose to make such a gamble and (b) they lose out on advantage as a result (see, e.g., Dworkin (1981, 293)). In other words, if a person gambles and loses, this is judged to be bad option luck for which the person is held responsible (i.e., the fact that she ends up worse off than others is held to be just by the theory). By contrast, the proposed theory does not hold people responsible for losing a gamble; rather, it holds them responsible for making any gamble that does not maximize WEDA, irrespective of how that gamble turns out. It is, thus, a variety of what Shlomi Segall has called "all-luck egalitarianism" (2010, 46).

Table 6.1 *Calculating the WEDA Value of Motorcycling with a Helmet*

	Distribution 1	Distribution 2	Distribution 3	Distribution 4
		Wears a Helmet		
	Does Not Crash	Crashes		
	No Transfer	Assist (No Transfer)	Assist (Transfer)	Failure to Assist
Distributed Advantage	M = 500, P = 500	M = 480, P = 500	M = 490, P = 490	M = 360, P = 500
Advantage Value	1000	980	980	860
P(Distribution | Helmet)	0.7	0	0.1	0.2
Expected Advantage	700	0	98	172
WEDA		970		

Each column of Table 6.1 represents a distribution, where that distribution is defined in terms of the unique set of events compatible with the ultimate quantity of advantage possessed by all persons (in this case, the motorcyclist and the passerby). In Distribution 1, the motorcyclist wears her helmet, does not crash, and no subsequent transfers of advantage (or additional events) occur. In Distribution 2, the motorcyclist wears a helmet, crashes, and is then assisted by a passerby. Distribution 3 is defined by the same series of events as Distribution 2 except the passerby also makes an equalizing transfer to the motorcyclist. And, finally, in Distribution 4, the passerby simply drives past the injured motorcyclist and does not assist her. (For simplicity, assume that the passerby cannot help the motorcyclist.)[17]

The first row of Table 6.1 represents how much advantage each person is stipulated to possess in each distribution. In Distribution 1, where the motorcyclist does not crash, she and the passerby each end up with 500 units of advantage. In Distribution 2, the passerby is able to costlessly treat the motorcyclist's injuries from the crash and, thus, is left with the same quantity of advantage that she would have had if no crash had occurred (500 units). The motorcyclist, however, is a bit bruised and battered, so she ends up with only 480 units of advantage. In Distribution 3, the passerby's supplemental transfer increases the motorcyclist's advantage

---

[17] Additionally, it will be assumed that the passerby is unable to make any transfer to the motorcyclist in this scenario, perhaps because she continues traveling to a distant location where her spatiotemporal position makes it impossible to relocate the motorcyclist and transfer advantage to her.

to 490, but that comes at the expense of the passerby, who also ends up with 490 units of advantage. Finally, if no assistance is given, the passerby maintains her original 500 units of advantage while the motorcyclist's untreated injuries reduce her advantage to 360 units.

The second row of Table 6.1 represents the advantage value of each of the four distributions, where this value is a function of the values listed in the first row. As noted earlier, the first step of calculating the advantage value of a distribution is to identify the distribution with the greatest total quantity of advantage that is appropriately distributed and that has a nonzero probability of obtaining conditional on the choice under consideration being made under conditions of full compliance. Assuming no prior sanctionable choice on the part of either party, Distribution 1 satisfies these conditions, and, thus, receives an advantage value equal to the total advantage possessed by all persons (1000 units). The next step is to calculate the advantage value of each additional distribution by identifying every person in that distribution who ends up worse off than she would have been in the comparison distribution. In Distributions 2 and 4, only the motorcyclist ends up worse off, while in Distribution 3, both the motorcyclist and the passerby end up worse off. Each difference in advantage is then subtracted from the advantage value of the comparison distribution. So, for Distribution 3, one would subtract 10 (the difference between how much advantage the motorcyclist has in Distribution 1 and how much she has in Distribution 3) and another 10 (the difference between how much advantage the passerby has in Distribution 1 and how much she has in Distribution 3) from 1000 to get an advantage value of 980.

The third row of Table 6.1 represents the warranted probability of each distribution obtaining conditional upon the motorcyclist not wearing a helmet under conditions of full compliance. For the purposes of this example, it is stipulated that the motorcyclist's evidence suggests there is a probability of 0.7 that Distribution 1 obtains, a probability of 0 that Distribution 2 obtains, a probability of 0.1 that Distribution 3 obtains, and a probability of 0.2 that Distribution 4 obtains. Distribution 2 has a probability of 0 because the theory is only concerned with the probability of a distribution obtaining under conditions of full compliance. Given that fully compliant people would equalize holdings (as neither party has chosen sanctionably prior to the motorcyclist's choice), it is assumed that the passerby transfers 10 units of advantage to the assisted motorcyclist, as this is what the latter is owed as a matter of justice. Thus, Distribution 2 is assigned a probability of 0, and whatever probability it would have been assigned assuming actual compliance (say, 0.1) is added to the probability of Distribution 3 obtaining assuming

190   Luck Egalitarianism without Moral Tyranny

actual compliance (again, 0.1) to yield the probability of Distribution 3 obtaining under conditions of *full* compliance (0.2).

The fourth row lists the probability-adjusted distributed advantage value of each distribution. The values in this row are determined by multiplying the advantage value of each distribution by its conditional probability. For example, Distribution 3 has an advantage value of 980, which is then multiplied by the conditional probability of .1 to get an expected distributed advantage value of 98. The WEDA value for the choice not to wear a helmet is then the sum of the distributed advantage values of all possible distributions, which, in this case, equals 970.

The WEDA value of not wearing a helmet can be similarly represented by the following table:

Table 6.2 *Calculating the WEDA Value of Motorcycling without Wearing a Helmet*

	Distribution 5	Distribution 6	Distribution 7	Distribution 8
	Does Not Wear a Helmet			
	Does Not Crash	Crashes		
	Transfer	Assist (No Transfer)	Assist (Transfer)	Failure to Assist
Distributed Advantage	M = 510, P = 510	M = 460, P = 500	M = 480, P = 480	M = 100, P = 500
Advantage Value	1020	960	960	600
P(Distribution | No Helmet)	0.7	0	0.1	0.2
Expected Advantage	714	0	96	120
WEDA	930			

As with Table 6.1, the distributions represented in Table 6.2 are defined in terms of the sets of events that generate a particular distribution of advantage. However, Table 6.2 describes the possible distributions that might arise from the motorcyclist choosing *not* to wear a helmet. Thus, the numbers in the distributed advantage row have been adjusted to model the distributional consequences of this choice. For example, the motorcyclist is assigned more advantage in Distribution 5 than she is in Distribution 1, as it is assumed that she derives greater enjoyment from riding without a helmet. Additionally, because WEDA calculations are made under the assumption of full compliance, it is assumed that the motorcyclist transfers half of this surplus advantage

6.4 Applying the Theory

to the passerby, thereby leaving each party with 10 more units of advantage than she possesses in Distribution 1. Similarly, it is assumed that an accident without a helmet is much more severe than an accident with a helmet. Thus, the motorcyclist is assigned less advantage in Distributions 6, 7, and 8 than in counterpart Distributions 2, 3, and 4. Finally, because the fully compliant passerby makes an equalizing transfer in Distribution 7, she ends up with less advantage than she is assigned in counterpart Distribution 3.

Using the procedure described earlier, these inputs yield a WEDA value of 930 for the choice to not wear a helmet. Given that this value is 40 units less than the WEDA value of wearing a helmet, the proposed theory maintains that the motorcyclist chooses sanctionably when she declines to wear a helmet. She then forfeits a claim to a quantity of advantage that is equal to the quantity of advantage that all others would be expected to forego$_{FC}$ absent such forfeiture. Recall that this value is calculated by dividing the total expected loss$_{FC}$ of advantage by the total number of people and then multiplying that by the total number of people minus 1. So, in this simplified two-person world, one would divide 40 by 2 and then multiply by 1 to get 20 units of forfeited advantage. Additionally, the passerby would acquire a supplemental claim to this same quantity of advantage.

Finally, one can use these values to calculate the quantity of advantage to which each person is entitled. Specifically, one would subtract 20 units from the quantity of advantage to which the motorcyclist *would have had a claim* were her choice not sanctionable. For example, suppose that the motorcyclist crashes but is assisted by the passerby. According to Table 6.2, this pair of events leaves everyone with a total of 960 units of available advantage that can be distributed between the two parties. Were the motorcyclist's choice non-sanctionable, then a luck egalitarian principle of justice would assign her a claim to an equal quantity of advantage – that is, 480 units – as no one has made any past sanctionable choice that would justify inequality. However, because her choice *is* sanctionable, one must subtract the forfeited 20 units of advantage to arrive at a just share of 460 units. Additionally, one would add 20 units to the passerby's counterfactual share to yield a just share of 500 units. Thus, a just distribution is realized without any supplemental transfer from the passerby to the motorcyclist. The anarchist conclusion would then assign both the motorcyclist and the passerby a claim against anyone (i.e., the other party) using unowned resources in a way that would diminish – or, in the case of the motorcyclist, further diminish – her respective share. In other words, the passerby sustains all of her prior claims against the motorcyclist using various resources despite the fact that respecting those claims will now leave the motorcyclist comparatively worse off.

6.5 Anarchism without Moral Tyranny

Sections 6.3 and 6.4 have explained how the proposed theory of sanctionable choice holds people responsible for destroying$_{FC}$ advantage such that they cannot leave others with less$_{FC}$. In other words, these sections have demonstrated that the theory satisfies the moral tyranny constraint in a way that standard prudential contextualism does not. However, note that this demonstration does not show that the theory *fully* satisfies the moral tyranny constraint. To fully satisfy the constraint, a theory must not only preclude sanctionable choosers like the motorcyclist from leaving others with less$_{FC}$ but also preclude those others (e.g., the passerby) from leaving sanctionable choosers with less$_{FC}$. Only then will the proposed account have a theoretical advantage over contextualism.

Fortunately, the demonstration of this point is fairly straightforward. Note that contextualism's moral tyranny problem follows from (a) its claim that the sanctionability of a choice is a function of the actual advantage the chooser foregoes as a result of that choice and (b) the fact that other agents are able to determine the quantity she forgoes *after* her choice has been made. Together, these two propositions entail that other people have the power to unilaterally render a person's choice sanctionable, thereby stripping her of a claim to advantage, which, in turn, leaves her with less$_{FC}$. By contrast, the theory proposed here makes sanctionable choice strictly a function of the agent's choice and the evidence already available to her (namely, the evidence about the consequences of various choices under conditions of full compliance). As a result, the agent is able to avoid choosing sanctionably, meaning that others lack the ability to *unilaterally* leave her with less$_{FC}$. Given that such unilaterality is a necessary condition of moral tyranny, it follows that the proposed theory fully satisfies the moral tyranny constraint in a way that contextualism does not.

Suppose, for example, that, after the motorcyclist crashes without a helmet, the passerby refuses to assist her. According to the proposed theory, this choice would also be sanctionable, as the WEDA value of not assisting (600) is lower than the WEDA value of providing assistance without transfer (960).[18] Thus, according to the proposed theory, the passerby would forfeit a claim to 180 units, as this value is equal to the

---

[18] It is assumed that the probability of each distribution obtaining is 1 conditional on the choice to not assist and assist, respectively. Thus, the WEDA value of each choice is equal to the distributed advantage value of the distribution it will bring about.

total lost$_{FC}$ advantage (360) multiplied by $\frac{2-1}{2}$. This value must then be subtracted from what would have been the passerby's just share, were her choice not sanctionable. In this case, this counterfactual just share is equal to 320. Note that there are 600 total units of advantage available to distribute, with an equal distribution assigning 300 units to each party.[19] However, given the motorcyclist's past sanctionable choice to not wear a helmet, her share has to be adjusted downward to 280 units to reflect the 20 units of advantage she forfeited in virtue of that choice. These units are then reassigned to the passerby such that her counterfactual just share is 320 rather than 300 units. One then subtracts the forfeited quantity of 180 units from this amount to yield a just share of 140 units of advantage. Finally, one reassigns these 180 units to the motorcyclist, who ends up having a just share of 460 units (with the anarchist conclusion assigning her the appropriate corresponding set of distributive claims). Crucially, this is the same quantity of advantage to which she would have been entitled had the passerby assisted her; thus, assuming future full compliance, the motorcyclist will end up with just as much advantage without assistance as she would with assistance. In other words, the passerby is unable to leave the motorcyclist with less$_{FC}$ – a result that demonstrates that the WEDA-based anarchist conclusion satisfies the moral tyranny constraint in a way that a contextualist version of the position does not.

6.6 Amending the Theory

Before completing the argument, a quick amendment must be made to the theory to avoid an objection that might otherwise undermine its plausibility. In its present form, the proposed theory makes sanctionable choice a function of the failure to maximize WEDA *assuming full compliance*. However, in many cases, people will not actually comply with others' claims. As a result, there will be cases where the choice that maximizes full-

---

[19] When calculating the WEDA value of the motorcyclist's choice, it was assumed for simplicity that there was no opportunity for further advantage transfer conditional on the passerby declining to assist the motorcyclist. This assumption has now been relaxed so as to illustrate how advantage is to be distributed in virtue of the passerby's choice. If one were being very precise, all of the possible distributions of advantage conditional on non-assistance should have been included in the two tables and each assigned a probability. However, given that this would have added hundreds of columns to the tables without changing the result of the WEDA calculations, these distributions were excluded from the foregoing discussion.

compliance WEDA runs contrary to the demands of justice. Consider, for example, David Estlund's Slice and Patch case:

> **Slice and Patch Go Golfing**
> Suppose that unless a patient is cut and stitched he will worsen and die (though not painfully). Surgery and stitching would save his life. If there is surgery without stitching, the death will be agonizing. Ought Slice to do the surgery? This depends, of course, on whether Patch (or someone) will be stitching up the wound. Slice and Patch are each going golfing whether the other attends to the patient or not. Does anyone act wrongly? (2020, 33)

In this case, Slice choosing to operate would maximize WEDA under conditions of full compliance, as a fully compliant Patch would stitch up the wound, thereby leaving everyone with maximal equal advantage. However, given that actual Patch *will not* stitch up the wound, it seems plausible to think that justice demands that Slice refrain from operating. (For these purposes, this can simply be stipulated.) Given these premises, the posited theory entails a seemingly unacceptable result: Slice declining to operate is both a just choice and a sanctionable choice in virtue of which she forfeits a claim to advantage.

To avoid this problem, the theory can be amended as follows. Rather than define sanctionable choice strictly in terms of a failure to maximize WEDA under conditions of full compliance, a second necessary condition of sanctionable choice can be added to the theory: A person chooses sanctionably if and only if she fails to maximize WEDA under conditions of full compliance *and* fails to maximize the chances that advantage is appropriately distributed assuming actual compliance. Thus, when Slice chooses not to operate on the patient, she does not choose sanctionably, as the added necessary condition is not met.

Further, the amended theory still satisfies the moral tyranny constraint. Admittedly, when Slice declines to operate, she leaves the patient with less$_{FC}$ advantage than if she chose to operate. However, recall from Chapter 2 that the moral tyranny constraint is only violated when a theory enables a person to *discretionarily* leave others with less$_{FC}$, where a discretionary action is one that is not obligatory according to the theory in question. Given that it is obligatory that Slice not operate, the fact that this choice leaves the patient with less$_{FC}$ advantage under the proposed theory does not entail that the theory permits moral tyranny. The amended theory thereby avoids declaring just actions sanctionable while also satisfying the moral tyranny constraint.

6.7 Additional Advantages of the Theory

In addition to resolving the moral tyranny objection, the proposed theory of sanctionable choice also allows the anarchist conclusion to avoid the other problems with luck egalitarianism presented in Section 6.1. Recall, first, Arneson's objection that luck egalitarianism delivers incorrect results in cases of costly rescue, for example, by declaring Mother Teresa to have chosen sanctionably when she gives her money to the poor (Arneson 2011a, 244; 2011b, 33–4). While this objection seems like a genuine problem for prudential contextualist luck egalitarianism, there are two reasons that the proposed theory would not entail that Mother Teresa chooses sanctionably.

First, there are certain ways of filling in the details of the case such that Mother Teresa maximizes WEDA under conditions of full compliance and, thus, does not choose sanctionably. For example, if the poor are in their position due to bad luck and Mother Teresa has a comparative advantage in transferring advantage, then her actions would be expected to leave others with more$_{FC}$ than if she focused on generating advantage. Second, even if her actions do not maximize WEDA assuming full compliance, the poor would have distributive claims that others only use natural resources in ways that increase their advantage, thereby making her transfers obligatory. Given such a duty to transfer, Mother Teresa's choice to aid the poor does not meet the second necessary condition of sanctionable choice introduced in Section 6.6. Thus, the anarchist conclusion avoids delivering an incorrect result in this case because it does not entail that she forfeits any distributive claims.

Section 6.1 also introduced Hurley's "boring problem." Recall that this problem emerges from (a) luck egalitarianism's claim that inequality is justified if and only if those with less have chosen sanctionably and (b) the standard contextualist view that sanctionable choice is a function of whether or not a person has imprudently failed to maximize her possessed advantage. When taken together, these two claims entail that a comparative relation between levels of advantage can be justified by appealing to a responsibility relation that obtains between a person and her individual holdings. However, Hurley argues that the latter relation does not appear to justify the former: The fact that a person is responsible for having a particular quantity of advantage would not seem to justify others having *more* advantage, as the person is not responsible for this *difference*. Thus, Hurley worries that luck egalitarianism is internally incoherent (2003, 160–1).

What is now apparent is that this objection is specific to contextualist versions of luck egalitarianism, as only contextualism maintains that a person's imprudent choices – that is, those that leave her with some diminished quantity of advantage – justify a comparative inequality in advantage. By contrast, the proposed theory holds a person responsible for failing to position herself and others in a way that would allow everyone to bring about justice via compliance without anyone needlessly foregoing advantage. This seems like a much more apt *justificans* for comparative inequality than a person being responsible for her own level of advantage.[20] Alternatively, the comparative relation might be justified by the fact that this relation obtaining is a necessary condition of avoiding moral tyranny. Regardless of the exact justification offered, the proposed theory solves Hurley's boring problem by explicating why an individual's sanctionable choice justifies inequality despite that individual not being responsible for the inequality in question. Thus, the anarchist who takes inequality to require justification (for the reasons discussed in Section 5.7) can avoid Hurley's worry that sanctionable choice is not a suitable *justificans*.

---

[20] Gerald Lang (2015; 2021) has suggested that the boring problem might be solved by modifying the *justificandum* of sanctionable choice: Rather than have such choice justify a comparative inequality between two persons – that is, the gap between their respective levels of advantage – it would, instead, justify a gap between an agent's level of advantage and some egalitarian baseline. On this proposal, each person is assigned some baseline share of advantage. If she then ends up with either more or less advantage than her assigned baseline share, that deviation would be just if and only if the difference between her share and the baseline is attributable to her choices rather than luck (2015, 706). The thought here is that, while a person is not responsible for the fact that she has less advantage *than someone else*, she *is* responsible for the fact that she ends up with less *than her baseline share*. Thus, there is no longer a justificatory gap of the kind identified by the boring problem, as the agent's sanctionable choices make her responsible for the state of affairs that those choices are supposed to justify.

However, there are three problems with this proposal. First, as Lang notes, it is unclear how to determine each person's appropriate baseline share (714). Second, the proposal seems to fail on its own terms. Lang's suggestion is that, while all *interpersonal inequalities* qualify as luck because they depend on the choices of the better-off party in addition the choices of the worse off, deviations from the baseline depend solely on the choices of the agent and, thus, are controlled in a way that renders these deviations non-luck (and therefore justifiable). However, deviations from the baseline would equally qualify as luck (so construed), as such deviations almost always depend on the uncontrolled choices of others. For example, the person who drops below the baseline due to losing at roulette ends up in this state only because of how forcefully the casino employee spun the wheel – a fact over which she had no control. Finally, note that Lang's proposal still assumes a prudential contextualist theory of sanctionable choice where a choice justifies a deviation from the baseline if and only if it leaves the agent worse off than she might otherwise have been. Given this assumption, Lang's baseline account is still vulnerable to the moral tyranny objection, making the proposed WEDA account a superior solution to the boring problem.

6.8 The Disadvantage Creation Account

The proposed theory of sanctionable choice is similar in certain respects to a revised version of luck egalitarianism proposed by Jens Damgaard Thaysen and Andreas Albertsen (2017). Thus, it is worth explicating their theory in some detail so as to clarify the similarities and differences between the two theories. Specifically, this section will suggest that their theory is best understood as asserting that sanctionable choice is a function of how agents' choices affect the total quantity of advantage. It will then argue that the proposed WEDA-based theory of sanctionable choice has three advantages over this interpretation of Thaysen and Albertsen's account.

Like the proposed account, Thaysen and Albertsen attempt to solve the problem of costly rescues – that is, the problem illustrated by Arneson's Mother Teresa case – by revising which choices count as sanctionable. Specifically, they posit that a choice is sanctionable if and only if it *creates* disadvantage that would not have otherwise been possessed by anyone. For example, if a villain drops a brick off of a building and it strikes someone, she creates disadvantage because she leaves someone worse off while no one would have been worse off had she chosen differently (95). By contrast, the hero who pushes someone out of the way of a falling brick and gets struck herself *distributes* disadvantage, as she merely changes who possesses disadvantage that would have obtained irrespective of her choice (96). In this way, Thaysen and Albertsen's theory avoids the implication that Mother Teresa makes a sanctionable choice when she aids the poor, as she is merely distributing disadvantage to herself rather than creating disadvantage.

To fully explicate Thaysen and Albertsen's proposal, a more precise account of disadvantage creation must be provided. Their formal statement is that an "agent is responsible for creating a (dis)advantage if, and only if, she is responsible for behaving in such a way that *somebody* was (dis)advantaged" (94). If taken literally, this statement is misleading, as it suggests that an action ϕ creates disadvantage if and only if there is a person who is left worse off in the world where ϕ occurs relative to the counterfactual world where it does not.[21] However, this is clearly not how Thaysen and Albertsen intend their analysis to be interpreted, as such an account would entail that the hero creates disadvantage due to the fact that there is a person who is left worse off by her action (namely, herself).

---

[21] This is also the natural way of precisifying Thaysen and Albertsen's later restatement of duty creation wherein they assert that such creation obtains when "nobody would be worse off if not for [the agent's] exercise of responsibility" (95).

To clarify Thaysen and Andersen's analysis of disadvantage creation, it will be helpful to consider their analysis of disadvantage *distribution*, as the former is supposed to contrast with the latter. Specifically, they posit that disadvantage distribution occurs if and only if "X, rather than Y, was (dis)advantaged" by the agent's action. However, there is some potential ambiguity in this statement that calls for additional precisification. One way of interpreting this analysis is as follows: An agent distributes disadvantage by ϕ-ing if and only if X is worse off in the world where the agent ϕ-s than in the world where she does not ϕ and Y is worse off in the latter world than she is in the former. Notably, this restatement delivers the correct results in the hero case, as the hero is worse off in the world where she pushes the beneficiary than she is in the world where she does not push, while the beneficiary is worse off in the latter than she is in the former. One could then define disadvantage creation as cases where (a) the agent's action leaves someone worse off relative to inaction and (b) the action is not an instance of disadvantage distribution.

The problem with this proposal is that the restated analysis of disadvantage distribution seems to deliver incorrect results. Consider, for example, a modified case where a villain has a small quantity of fun dropping a brick on her victim. In this case, the victim is worse off in the world where the brick is dropped than she is in the world where it is not dropped; at the same time the villain is worse off in the latter world than she is in the former (because she has less fun). Thus, the restated account would entail that the villain distributes disadvantage rather than creates it. Given that this is seemingly a paradigmatic case of disadvantage creation, this result is a *reductio* of the proposed restatement.

So what is a better statement? The apparent solution is to put things in terms of the total quantity of disadvantage resulting from an action: An agent distributes disadvantage by ϕ-ing if and only if (a) some person has either more or less advantage in the world where the agent ϕ-s than the counterfactual world where the agent does not ϕ and (b) there is the same total quantity of disadvantage in the former world as there is in the latter. This account seems to deliver the correct results in the paradigmatic cases. For example, when the hero saves the beneficiary from the falling brick, the resulting world contains the same quantity of disadvantage as the world where no rescue occurred; the only difference is that the beneficiary has more advantage in the rescue world while the hero has less. Thus, the hero merely distributes disadvantage in that case. By contrast, the villain who derives enjoyment from dropping a brick off of a building does not distribute disadvantage, as there is more disadvantage in the world where

6.8 The Disadvantage Creation Account

she drops the brick than there is in the world where she does not act in this way.

One final adjustment is needed. The fact that Thaysen and Albertsen use the term "(dis)advantage" when articulating their distribution/creation distinction suggests that they actually take there to be four distinct phenomena: advantage distribution, disadvantage distribution, advantage creation, and disadvantage creation. This fourfold division is incompatible with the just-posited restatement, as this restatement would only allow for disadvantage creation/distribution with there being no apparent acts of advantage creation/distribution. To fix this problem, the analysis can be amended as follows. An agent distributes *disadvantage* by ϕ-ing if and only if (a) there is the same total quantity of disadvantage in the world where she ϕ-s as there is in the counterfactual world where she does not ϕ and (b) there is less total advantage after she ϕ-s than there was just prior to her ϕ-ing. This joint counterfactual and trans-temporal comparison seems to capture the idea that people are worse off – that is, there was *dis*advantage generated – but the agent merely distributes that worsening without contributing to it. The account of *advantage* distribution would then be identical to the just-proposed analysis except that Condition (b) asserts that there is *more* total advantage after the agent ϕ-s.

The restatement of (dis)advantage creation is a bit more straightforward, as one can capture the idea of leaving everyone (worse off) better off without having to make any trans-temporal comparisons. Specifically, an agent creates disadvantage by ϕ-ing if and only if there is less total advantage in the world where she ϕ-s than there is in the counterfactual world where she does not ϕ. And she creates advantage by ϕ-ing if and only if there is more total advantage in the world where she ϕ-s than in the counterfactual world where she does not ϕ.

This explication helps to reveal the similarities and differences between Thaysen and Albertsen's theory of sanctionable choice and the one posited by this chapter. The primary similarity is that both theories reject contextualist theories of sanctionable choice and, instead, make sanctionable choice a function – at least in part – of what effect the agent's choice has on the total quantity of advantage (more on the qualifier later). This allows both theories to sidestep Arneson's objection that luck egalitarianism unacceptably entails that costly rescues are sanctionable. Given that such rescues do not paradigmatically affect the total quantity of advantage, they would not count as sanctionable choices under either theory.

However, there are three important differences that give the posited WEDA-based account a theoretical advantage over Thaysen and Albertsen's proposal. First, their theory makes sanctionable choice strictly a function of created disadvantage rather than the *expected advantage value* of choices. As a result, their theory entails that a person chooses sanctionably when she makes a choice that maximizes expected advantage but ultimately creates disadvantage due to bad luck. For example, suppose that a person reasonably believes that there is a probability of .9 that she will create 100 units of advantage if she ϕ-s and a probability of .1 that she will create 10 units of disadvantage (i.e., −10 units of advantage). By contrast, if she does not ϕ, she will create 5 units of disadvantage with a probability of 1. Given that the expected value of ϕ-ing is 89 while the expected value of not ϕ-ing is −5, the agent chooses to ϕ; however, she gets unlucky and generates 10 units of disadvantage. Given that there is more total advantage in the world where the agent ϕ-s than the counterfactual world where she does not, the posited restatement of Thaysen and Albertsen's proposal entails that she has created disadvantage and can thereby be held responsible – a seemingly unacceptable result.[22] By contrast, the WEDA account avoids this implication by making sanctionable choice a function of expected total advantage rather than counterfactual advantage comparisons.

A second important difference is that Thaysen and Albertsen's account seemingly declares inequality to be just both when someone chooses sanctionably – that is, creates disadvantage – and *also* when someone makes a choice that creates advantage. For example, they hold that the miner who happens to strike a vein of gold that no one else would have found creates advantage and is, thus, entitled to keep some of the profits even if that results in inequality (98).[23] However, it seems inappropriate for a luck egalitarian theory to declare such a luck-based inequality just. After all, the fact that the miner was lucky enough to be uniquely positioned to extract the gold does not seem to justify her ending up better off than everyone else. By contrast, the WEDA theory incorporated into the anarchist conclusion does not posit such a category of *rewardable choice*; rather, anything short of maximizing WEDA is sanctionable while only the maximizing choice entitles a person to an equal share of advantage

---

[22] Thaysen and Albertsen do specify that a choice is sanctionable only if it was *foreseeable* that it would create disadvantage (100). However, they do not consider cases where the disadvantage creation was foreseeable but not the reasonably expected outcome.

[23] Note the caveat that the miner is only entitled to *some* of the profits. This is because, according to Thaysen and Albertsen, she is only responsible for generating part of the created advantage, as some of that advantage is attributable merely to the resources rather than anything the miner did (98). Unfortunately, they do not provide an account explicating how one determines the portion of created advantage for which a person is responsible.

relative to the shares of other successful maximizers. Thus, the proposed theory would not license the inequality in question.

Finally, while Thaysen and Albertsen make sanctionable choice a function of counterfactual differences in total advantage, the posited account makes sanctionable choice a function of both the quantity *and* distribution of advantage in the relevant counterfactual worlds. This allows the posited WEDA account to avoid seemingly counterintuitive implications of Thaysen and Albertsen's proposal. Consider, for example, a case where P has a choice between realizing world E where she and Q each have 10 units of advantage or world U where she has 5 units of advantage and Q has 20 (assume, for simplicity, that the warranted probability of each outcome is 1). On Thaysen and Albertsen's account – at least, as it has been interpreted here – P would create disadvantage if she realizes E, as it has less total advantage than U. In other words, if P were to realize the egalitarian distribution, she would thereby make a sanctionable choice for which she could be held responsible. However, this result is seemingly a *reductio* of any posited theory of luck egalitarianism. By contrast, the theory proposed in this chapter would assign a higher WEDA value to E, thereby making P's choice to realize an egalitarian distribution non-sanctionable.

In sum, Thaysen and Albertsen make the right kind of theoretical move by rejecting contextualism in favor of an account that makes sanctionable choice a function of total advantage. However, their failure to build expected value into their theory, their endorsement of rewardable choice, and their neglect of distributive considerations all compromise the extensional adequacy of their account. Thus, luck egalitarians troubled by Arneson's objection ought to adopt the proposed WEDA-based theory rather than Thaysen and Albertsen's proposal.

6.9 Conclusion

This concludes the argument for the anarchist position. It began with a fairly simple and plausible constraint on which theories of duties are acceptable. It then argued that a number of influential libertarian and egalitarian principles follow from this constraint, namely the consent theory of legitimacy, the Lockean proviso, and luck egalitarianism's incorporation of responsibility. These principles, in turn, were shown to entail other components of the anarchist position: Both the Lockean proviso and the consent theory of legitimacy independently entail the absence of external private property, while the former entails that persons can easily appropriate their bodies, thereby allowing for (near) universal self-ownership of the kind articulated by ASO. Finally, it was argued that, in the absence of private property, both egalitarians and libertarians have reason to accept the anarchist conclusion – that is, the contention that each person has a claim against others using unowned resources in a way that (a) would leave her comparatively worse off where (b) that inequality did not correspond to any sanctionable choice on her part. This conclusion, it was argued, is both compatible with libertarian entitlement theories of justice and follows from libertarians' egalitarian approach to assigning persons rights and powers.

The purpose of this chapter was to render the anarchist conclusion fully determinate by specifying which choices qualify as sanctionable – and, more specifically, to do so in a way that brings the position into full compliance with the moral tyranny constraint. This chapter posited that a choice is sanctionable if and only if it fails to maximize warranted expected distributed advantage under conditions of full compliance (and fails to maximize the chances that advantage is appropriately distributed assuming actual compliance). Such an account ensures that no person is able to unilaterally, discretionarily, and foreseeably leave others with less$_{FC}$, thereby satisfying the moral tyranny constraint. Additionally, this theory of sanctionable choice allows the anarchist conclusion to avoid some of the major objections that plague standard luck egalitarian theories of distributive justice while still delivering equally egalitarian prescriptions vis-à-vis the use of natural resources.

In this way, the foregoing chapters have aimed to defend a heterodox philosophical position that synthesizes both libertarian moral principles and an egalitarian principle typically associated with the socialist left. Of course, the suggestion that these principles might be combined in this way will be intuitive to social anarchists, as their movement is composed of people who endorse (or would, upon reflection, endorse) just such a set of principles. However, they might still have been surprised to discover that this position can be largely derived from a single, simple theoretical *desideratum* and, thus, has the kind of coherence discussed in Section I.2. Similarly, libertarians may have been surprised to find that some of their core principles commit them to rejecting private property in favor of egalitarianism. And, for those who were not already sympathetic to either libertarianism or the anarchist position, the foregoing argument has hopefully demonstrated that there is at least a plausible and coherent variety of anarchism that deserves serious consideration when assessing what duties we have vis-à-vis resources and the state.

CHAPTER 7

A State-Tolerant Anarchism

Given that this book is about anarchism, it may seem odd that so little has been said about the state. Section 1.1 did introduce the consent theory of legitimacy and the associated conclusion that no one is obligated to comply with the laws of the state (as practically no one has actually consented to the state's governance). However, this *philosophical anarchism* is a much weaker claim than the *political anarchism* typically espoused by self-identified anarchists. For the philosophical anarchist, the state merely lacks a certain kind of moral power, where this does not necessarily entail that one has any obligation to dismantle the state. Indeed, the philosophical anarchist may even allow that persons are obliged to *support* the state and the activities of its agents if doing so aligns with demands of justice. By contrast, the political anarchist contends that states are *unjust*, where this, in turn, implies that persons have a duty to abolish existing states (or, more modestly, that each state has a duty to abolish itself). More strongly, the political anarchist holds that similar duties would obtain vis-à-vis all – or at least most – possible states.[1] Thus, the fact that the proposed social anarchist position does not declare states unjust in this sense may come as a disappointment to those interested in a more radical sort of political anarchism.[2]

---

[1] As noted in Footnote 17 of Chapter 2, Simmons persuasively argues that there is no reason to deny the legitimacy of a state if everyone has consented to comply with its laws; thus, one should reject Wolff's (1970) contention that there are *necessarily* no legitimate states and, instead, take philosophical anarchism to assert that there are no *existing* legitimate states (1987, 269fn2). Further, there is no obvious reason for thinking that the existence of a state is unjust if it is legitimate or all persons otherwise endorse its existence. Thus, a charitable interpretation of political anarchism would not assert that states are *necessarily* unjust. Rather, it would allow that consensual states are just but no others. Or, perhaps some other possible states would be excepted, so long as it is still the case that the vast majority of possible states are declared unjust.

[2] An anonymous commenter has suggested that the proposed position might be redescribed as "socialist minarchism," as it holds that a state is just if and only if it takes the minimal form required to promote luck egalitarian redistribution while respecting self-ownership rights. Any regulatory action of the state beyond advancing this end would be unjust – and, thus, persons would have reason to strip the state of the power to carry out such activities.

This chapter will argue that political anarchism is misguided. This is not because there are pragmatic disadvantages to eliminating the state in favor of some non-state political arrangement. Rather, the chapter will argue that there is a conceptual problem with political anarchism that undermines its plausibility. Specifically, it will note that the political anarchist must provide an analysis of statehood such that one can determine what must be changed if existing states are to be abolished. Further, if political anarchism is to be plausible, the posited analysis must satisfy two *desiderata* (introduced in the subsequent section). However, it will be argued that none of the most plausible analyses of statehood satisfy both of these *desiderata*. Thus, political anarchism is implausible and should not be incorporated into the social anarchist position.

7.1 Two *Desiderata* of Political Anarchism

As was just noted, the political anarchist must provide an account of the necessary and sufficient conditions of some group qualifying as a state. Further, if political anarchism is to be plausible, these conditions must satisfy two *desiderata*. First, the analysis must support the political anarchist's contention that the mere existence of a state constitutes an injustice, where that injustice is negated by the elimination of the state. Thus, the political anarchist must endorse the following *grounding desideratum*: Any acceptable analysis of statehood must entail that (a) any given state is unjust and (b) the elimination of that state would eliminate the injustice.[3] One can test whether Proposition (a) is true by considering whether there is any case where some group meets the posited sufficient condition of statehood but no injustice obtains. If, for example, the posited analysis held that some group constitutes a state if and only if it has more than 1,000 card-carrying members, then Proposition (a) would be false, as there are many possible worlds where some group exceeds that size but no injustice obtains. This is a way of testing the adequacy of the sufficient condition(s) of the proposed analysis. Additionally, if injustice obtains when the sufficient condition of statehood is met, one must ensure that

---

[3] Proposition (a) needs to be qualified in light of the discussion that appears in Footnote 1. If the state has obtained universal consent to carry out the activities that render it a state, then the political anarchist will presumably have to concede that there is nothing unjust about the state. However, this is a special case, and the political anarchist might reasonably maintain that all states that lack this consent are unjust. Thus, the grounding *desideratum* should be understood to be satisfied by an analysis if and only if that analysis entails that Proposition (a) is true for all states *except* those that have obtained universal consent.

Proposition (b) is true by considering whether, for each posited necessary condition of statehood, that same degree of injustice would still obtain in the closest possible world where that necessary condition of statehood is not met. If the injustice persists, then Proposition (b) is false and the grounding *desideratum* goes unsatisfied. This test assesses the adequacy of the analysis' posited necessary conditions of statehood.

Second, the political anarchist needs an analysis of statehood that delivers the result that there are actually existing states, where these states at least roughly correspond to the groups that are pre-theoretically understood to be states. For example, the proposed analysis should not deliver the result that the United States Federal Government is not actually a state. Such a result would conflict with the intuition that motivates the political anarchist in the first place, namely, that the existing institutions that we call states are unjust. Call this constraint on analyses of statehood the *actuality desideratum*.

The political anarchist is committed to endorsing both of these *desiderata*, as they are presupposed by her claim that arrangements like the United States Federal Government are morally defective and should be abolished. However, the subsequent section will argue that none of the most plausible analyses of statehood satisfy both *desiderata*. Thus, political anarchism does not meet its own presupposed criteria of plausibility and should be rejected in favor of the more modest philosophical anarchism posited by the social anarchist position. Finally, the chapter will conclude by considering a recent argument that philosophical anarchism collapses into either political anarchism or statism.

7.2 Twelve Analyses of Statehood

So what is a state? As just discussed, the political anarchist must provide an answer to this question that satisfies both of the posited *desiderata*. To this end, she might draw upon Max Weber's influential claim that a state is "a human community that (successfully) claims the *monopoly of the legitimate use of physical force* within a given territory" (1991, 78).[4] This proposal suggests a number of potential analyses of statehood, beginning with one that makes use of Weber's appeal to legitimacy. Previously, the term "legitimacy" has been used to refer to the Hohfeldian power to oblige others via the issuing of edicts. However, political anarchists cannot posit that some group is a state if and only if it is legitimate in this sense, as they

---

[4] Emphasis in the original text.

are also philosophical anarchists who deny that those entities popularly assumed to be states – and more generally, any existing candidates for statehood – are legitimate.[5] Thus, if legitimacy in the just-specified sense is a necessary condition of statehood, then there will also be no existing states, where this result entails that the proposed analysis does not satisfy the actuality *desideratum*.

Alternatively, one might construe Weber's claim that states monopolize "the legitimate use of physical force" as an assertion that some group is a state if and only if it possesses *political authority*, that is, a special moral permission to use violence/coercion that ordinary people lack (e.g., a permission to coercively regulate behavior or violently enforce rights). However, this second proposed analysis of statehood runs into the same problem as the first, as political anarchists also deny that states possess political authority in this sense. Given this commitment, the second analysis of statehood would imply that there are no existing states, thereby failing to satisfy the actuality *desideratum*.

Given the failure of an analysis that makes reference to the actual moral status of candidates for statehood, one might employ the notion of "legitimacy" as Weber interprets it, that is, to express a claim about what people *believe* about the moral status of these candidates for statehood. According to this third analysis, a group is legitimate if and only if its purported subjects believe that they are obliged to obey the edicts issued by some members of the group (but not edicts issued by nonmembers). Or alternatively, the group is legitimate if and only if its purported subjects believe that the group possesses political authority – that is, that coercion/violence deployed by some members of the group is permissible while identical acts of violence by nonmembers is impermissible. In either case, this proposed analysis makes statehood a function of the beliefs that the purported subjects have about the candidate's Hohfeldian incidents rather than the actual Hohfeldian incidents that it possesses.

This revised analysis aims to satisfy the actuality *desideratum*, as one can concede that all existing candidates for statehood are not legitimate and lack political authority while also observing that most people mistakenly believe that entities like the United States Federal Government, the Government of the United Mexican States, etc., are legitimate and possess political authority. However, note that *not all* of the purported subjects of

---

[5] Technically, one could be a political anarchist without being a philosophical anarchist. In other words, one might think that states both have the power to oblige their citizens and are unjust and ought to be abolished. However, in practice, no one seems to hold this conjunction of views.

7.2 Twelve Analyses of Statehood 207

these entities hold these beliefs. As a contingent matter, every society contains at least a few philosophical anarchists who explicitly deny that the purported state of that society possesses legitimacy or political authority. Thus, strictly speaking, the actuality *desideratum* is not satisfied by this third analysis of statehood.

If one wanted the proposed analysis to satisfy the actuality *desideratum*, one would need to posit a fourth analysis of statehood such that a group is held to be a state if and only if *some suitable portion* of its purported subjects believe that it has special powers to oblige and/or special permissions to enact violence. However, it is not clear how one would specify the required portion without rendering the analysis of statehood arbitrary and *ad hoc*. Additionally, the proposed analysis would fail to satisfy Proposition (b) of the grounding *desideratum*. Suppose that everyone in the United States were to endorse philosophical anarchism. On the posited account, the United States Federal Government would not, in this world, qualify as a state. However, presumably the political anarchist would not judge the United States Federal Government to be just in this world. Thus, the *desideratum* is not satisfied, and the revised legitimacy-based account of statehood must also be rejected.

Perhaps these problems can be avoided by embracing Weber's proposal that a state *claims* the monopoly on legitimate violence. On this line of thinking, what matters is not whether a group has special moral status or is believed to have special moral status but, rather, whether *it contends* that it has a special moral status (i.e., that it possesses either political authority or the power to oblige and that its subjects lack the associated permissions and powers). This fifth analysis of statehood would maintain that a group qualifies as a state if and only if it publicly affirms that, unlike its subjects, it is legitimate and/or possesses political authority. However, as Nozick notes, this analysis proposes an implausible sufficient condition of statehood, as it is implausible that any single person can transform herself into a state by making a public moral claim (1974, 23).[6] Or, to slightly restate this point, the analysis does not satisfy the grounding *desideratum* because it allows that there are many possible just states (since, presumably, there is no injustice when an arbitrary person insists to her friends that she has the power to impose obligations on them via the issuance of edicts). Additionally, suppose that the United States Federal Government formally endorsed the philosophical anarchist position while sustaining all of its

---

[6] It is not fully clear whether this is Nozick's observation or if he is recapitulating a point made in an unpublished paper by Marshall Cohen.

current activities. Such a resolution would render it no longer a state on the proposed analysis. However, given that this endorsement does nothing to eliminate the injustice posited by the political anarchist, Proposition (b) of the grounding *desideratum* goes unsatisfied.

Fabian Wendt (2015, 329) revises this proposal by suggesting that the defining feature of a state is that it both denies that persons have a permission to privately enforce their rights – that is, it asserts that it alone has political authority – *and* it legally enshrines that assertion by denying them the legal right to carry out acts of private enforcement. The problem with this sixth suggested analysis is that, from the perspective of the philosophical anarchist, there is no moral difference between a group that refuses to grant persons some legal right and a group that publicly asserts that they lack this right. In her view, laws do not have any normative implications; thus, the issuance of a law can seemingly do more than command people to act in certain ways and inform them that there might be consequences for noncompliance. Granted, laws are typically enacted via a complicated social process, where the exact nature of this procedure will depend upon one's substantive view of the necessary conditions of lawmaking. However, irrespective of how one fills in those details, it is unclear how that process could render the issuance of a law against private enforcement more unjust than a mere public declaration that only the state has political authority. Thus, the proposed legal analysis of statehood would fail to satisfy the grounding *desideratum* for the same reason that the previous analysis failed to satisfy it: There would be no improvement vis-à-vis justice if the United States Federal Government were to eliminate its laws against private enforcement (while still continuing to carry out all of its current coercive operations to preclude such enforcement). And, similarly, a private individual might – without committing any injustice – develop her own legislative process and declare others' rightful actions illegal according to her set of laws (so long as she does not coercively enforce those laws). In this way, the proposed analysis fails to make statehood adequately track injustice in the way that the grounding *desideratum* requires.

The foregoing discussion has demonstrated that, for the political anarchist's purpose, statehood cannot be a function of the special moral properties of some candidate for statehood, the beliefs that people have about its moral properties, or the assertions it makes about its moral properties (where the passing of laws is one such mode of assertion). Rather, there must be some other property of groups, the possession of which is a necessary and sufficient condition of statehood. Here one might

7.2 Twelve Analyses of Statehood

appeal to the final component of Weber's account of statehood and contend that some group is a state if and only if it has an actual monopoly on violence; that is, it successfully uses its power to preclude its subjects and/or those within its claimed territory from employing unauthorized violence or coercion. However, this seventh analysis also fails to satisfy the actuality *desideratum*. As Marshall Cohen has noted in an unpublished paper, for any given purported state, some of the subjects in its territory continue to use violence and coercion that is not authorized by the state (e.g., various gangs).[7] Given that no group successfully monopolizes violence, this proposed analysis would unacceptably entail that there are no existing states.

This result suggests an alternative analysis of statehood that drops the requirement that states must *successfully* monopolize coercion/violence in the way just described. Specifically, one might, instead, endorse Nozick's proposal that, although states need not actually monopolize the use of violence or coercion, "a necessary condition for the existence of a state is that it... announce that, to the best of its ability (taking into account costs of doing so, the feasibility, the more important alternative things it should be doing, and so forth), it will punish everyone whom it discovers to have used force without its express permission" (1974, 24). However, while Nozick puts things simply in terms of what the group announces, it seems better to analyze the notion of statehood in terms of what the state actually attempts. Otherwise, the proposed analysis will fail to satisfy the grounding *desideratum* for the same reason that the fifth proposed analysis of statehood failed to satisfy it: If mere assertion is a sufficient condition of statehood, then a person would become a state simply by making the relevant assertion, despite there not being any attendant injustice. Thus, to avoid this problem, the eighth proposed analysis of statehood posits that some group qualifies as a state if and only if it attempts to preclude its subjects and/or those within its claimed territory from employing unauthorized violence or coercion whenever doing so is both feasible and within the bounds of prudence.[8]

---

[7] This paper is not available but its details are discussed by Nozick (1974, 23).

[8] This seems to be what Vallentyne proposes when he contends that "to be a state, an organization need neither have, nor claim to have, a de jure (i.e., rightful) monopoly on the use of force. It just has to prohibit the use of force without its permission (i.e., it has to claim a de facto monopoly)" (2007, 189n5). As Wendt notes, it seems odd to think that the defining feature of a state is that it *asserts* that it has a *de facto* monopoly on the use of force, as opposed to actually having such a monopoly (2015, 321). However, one might make sense of this claim if one interprets Vallentyne's assertions that states "prohibit the use of force" and "claim a de facto monopoly" to mean that states *attempt* to regulate all use of force by their respective subjects and/or those within their respective territories.

Unfortunately for the political anarchist, this analysis has problems of its own. First, consider the case of a large armed group that attempts to preclude all other persons from using unauthorized violence – that is, a group that qualifies as a state according to the proposed analysis. However, that group also authorizes each person to carry out all and only those acts of violence/coercion that the political anarchist deems morally permissible (acts of proportionate self-defense, coercive acts required to preserve the just distribution of resources, etc.). Further, the group's agents act in only those ways that the anarchist judges permissible. Would such a state be just? It is unclear on what basis the political anarchist could deny that it is. From her point of view, the actions of its agents are all morally impeccable. And the only actions it attempts to prevent are those that she believes ought to be prevented. Thus, there is no apparent basis for her maintaining that the state is unjust, with the proposed analysis thereby failing to satisfy the grounding *desideratum*.

Alternatively, consider the single anarchist who attempts to directly realize justice via her actions. Presumably, she will also attempt to preclude unauthorized acts of violence – at least, when doing so seems feasible and reasonably prudent. For example, she will intervene to break up fights or threaten people to deter them from violating the rights of others. Further, there is no obvious limit to her ambitions: If she could prevent all rights-violating coercion and violence, she would. The only reason she does not attempt to intervene is because she knows that she will either not succeed or incur great costs for doing so. However, this makes her efforts of a kind with those of the hypothetical state discussed in the previous paragraph, as it, too, presumably tolerates a certain degree of unauthorized violence simply because it lacks the ability to prevent that violence from occurring. While there is a difference in the degree to which these two entities are able to regulate others' use of violence, they are both still states as far as the eighth analysis of statehood is concerned. And, because their respective efforts are seemingly just, these cases entail that the proposed analysis fails to satisfy the grounding *desideratum*.

Does the mere act of authorization render the state posited two paragraphs prior unjust (despite the fact that it authorizes all and only morally permissible acts)? Wendt argues that it does, as he contends that imposing "an authorization process on others is a violation of their moral immunity protecting their moral power to enforce their rights" (2015, 325). However, there are a few problems with this suggestion. First, it seems to problematically imply that individual anarchists act unjustly when they allow some acts of violence while trying to prevent others.

The only way to avoid this implication is to contend that a state's authorization process goes beyond that of the individual in a way that is morally significant. But what is the morally salient difference? The political anarchist cannot claim that, unlike individual anarchists, the state changes the moral status of actions when it authorizes or refuses to authorize them, as this would presuppose that states are legitimate – a premise that she rejects. In her view, state authorization can be no more than the declaration of an intention to prevent certain acts of violence. Given that such a declaration might be equally issued by any street gang or individual anarchist, it is unclear on what basis she might maintain that the individual anarchist's authorization process is just while the morally impeccable state's authorization process is not.

Second, even if one sets aside this problem, Wendt's proposal seems to be making a pair of category mistakes. He contends that state authorization – or, really, the state's refusal to authorize – violates a moral immunity protecting the power to enforce one's rights. However, first, people have *permissions* to enforce their rights, not powers. Powers give people the ability to alter what Hohfeldian incidents they or others possess while enforcement is a physical activity that is either permitted or not. Second, while rights might be violated, immunities cannot be. Assuming that one working within the Hohfeldian analytical system, an immunity is the correlative incident of the absence of a power. In other words, to say that a person is immune from the loss of her permission to enforce her rights is just to say that no other person has a power to negate her permission (i.e., oblige her to not enforce her rights). Thus, when the state refuses to authorize some person's act of enforcement, the immunity implies that this refusal does not strip her of her permission to enforce. But no violation occurs that would ground the proposition that the state has acted unjustly.

Of course, if some group like the United States Federal Government goes out and actually prevents people from enforcing their rights, it will violate their claims against interference and thereby act unjustly. One, might, thus, suggest that *this* is the necessary and sufficient condition of statehood, as such an analysis will ensure that the grounding *desideratum* is satisfied. However, this ninth proposed analysis of statehood also runs into problems. First, if statehood is defined in terms of unjust actions such as violating claims against interference, then it follows that a group could cease to be a state simply by refraining from carrying out such actions – a result that will likely run contrary to the intuitions of most political anarchists, who may not want to concede that the United States Federal Government would no longer be a state if it refrained from violating persons' claims against interference. More significantly, this result trivializes political anarchism: If the only difference between a state and its counterfactual non-state counterpart is that the former carries out some unjust action(s) that the latter does not, then clearly justice requires that the latter entity be realized rather than the former. If this is all that political anarchism demands, then there would be no disagreement between the position and the one advanced by this book (as well as by other philosophical anarchists who are typically taken to reject political anarchism).

Additionally, this analysis of statehood would counterintuitively imply a proliferation of states, as private individuals will often try to prevent others from enforcing their rights. Further, there is no apparent basis for insisting that an agent is a state if and only if she violates one kind of right – namely, a person's claim against interference when enforcing her own rights – while also holding that she is not a state if she violates other kinds of rights. Thus, a consistent political anarchist would seemingly have to maintain that states are abolished if and only if no one violates others' rights. However, this contention would both further proliferate the number of states and also further trivialize political anarchism.

Perhaps the idea of the state having a monopoly on violence can be salvaged by appealing to another popular account of statehood put forward by exponents of anarchism (e.g., David Miller (1984, 5–8) and Michael Huemer (2013, 232–3)). In this view, the defining feature of a state is its nonvoluntary character and the absence of choice when it comes to state affiliation. For example, an analysis focusing on the absence of choice would posit that some group is a state if and only if (a) there are other people who receive services from the group conditional on deferring to its regulations and (b) there is an insufficient number of alternative groups that those persons could choose to receive services from instead. Such an account would help support the anarcho-capitalist's claim that she is endorsing the abolition of the state when she proposes that the police and military should be replaced with competing private security firms that people hire in an open market. Additionally, it might appeal to social anarchists who envision security and welfare provision being administered by small, decentralized, and voluntarist private societies. However, this tenth proposed analysis would also seemingly violate the actuality *desideratum*, as the fact that there are multiple existing governed regions that allow immigration entails that persons are able to choose to receive security (and welfare) services from a variety of groups.

Granted, the conditions that persons must meet to change security services in the status quo are a bit more onerous than what anarcho-capitalists envisage when they propose their security markets. For example, for a Canadian to receive (indefinite) protection from the United States Federal Government, she must move locations, go through a difficult bureaucratic process, and be subjected to a novel regulatory regime. However, it is not clear that these barriers are different in kind from what she might encounter in a private security market. It seems entirely likely that the anarcho-capitalist's private security firms would limit the areas in which they operate such that a person must move to a particular location if she wishes to be protected. Similarly, one might expect that these firms would run background checks on prospective clients and require them to go through an onboarding process that is not substantially dissimilar from that which the United Sates Federal Government imposes on people who apply for American citizenship. And such firms would similarly make regulatory compliance a condition of service provision. (They will protect some person only if she refrains from theft, does not start fights with others, refrains from the use of amphetamines, etc.) Thus, there is not an obvious basis for maintaining that the status quo does not offer people genuine choice of security provider of the kind provided by private security markets. This, in turn, makes it difficult for the political anarchist to contend that the actuality *desideratum* is satisfied by the tenth proposed analysis of statehood.

In response to this worry, Huemer argues that competition between security firms would keep the costs of choosing a different security firm low – much lower than choosing a different state via emigration (2013, 232–3). Thus, he might maintain that a group is a state if and only if it provides persons with security *and* the cost of their receiving services from a rival provider exceeds some threshold. This eleventh analysis would then satisfy the actuality *desideratum* if and only if the posited cost threshold is set to be lower than the current costs of emigration (but higher than the costs of switching security providers in a free security market, as this is needed to prevent Huemer's security firms from qualifying as states). However, the analysis would not seemingly satisfy the grounding *desideratum*, as the difference in cost between emigrating and switching security firms does not appear to ground a difference in justice between the current system of security provision and its replacement with a private security market. The difference in cost might ground a difference in justice if the cost of emigrating were prohibitively high such that persons did not have a genuine exit option. In this case, there would be a difference in kind between the cost of emigrating and the cost of switching firms, where such a difference could explain why the current system of security provision is unjust in a way that a security market is not. But if the difference in cost is merely a matter of degree – as appears to be the case – then it does not seem that one can posit a nonarbitrary threshold such that security provision arrangements with exit costs above the threshold are unjust while those with exit costs below the threshold are just. This, in turn, implies that the posited analysis of statehood would not satisfy the grounding *desideratum*, as a state dropping below the threshold would cease to be a state without any concomitant improvement vis-à-vis justice.

In response to this objection, Huemer might reply there is a unique injustice that arises when some group artificially drives up exit costs by preventing competition in a way that violates the rights of competitors. Such a proposal would seemingly articulate the difference between the current state system and the private security market, as the former is characterized by groups like the United States Federal Government violently preventing certain varieties of security provision. However, Huemer would not need to appeal to increased exit costs to establish that the group in question is unjust; rather, he would merely need to cite the fact that it violates the rights of its competitors when it suppresses competition. But this reveals that this posited reply trivializes political anarchism as it has been previously described: If a state is just a group that acts unjustly, then justice trivially demands the abolition of the state, thereby rendering political anarchism an uninteresting thesis.

Given these difficulties, a final posited analysis of statehood might suggest that it is not the absence of choice *between* security providers that renders them states. Rather, it is the absence of a choice about whether to affiliate with a security provider *at all* that makes those security providers states; that is, it is the nonvoluntary character of state regulation and security provision that is the defining feature of statehood. Stated explicitly, this twelfth analysis of statehood holds that some group is a state if and only if it either provides others with benefits or regulates their behavior without their consent. However, this analysis also fails to satisfy the grounding *desideratum*. Consider, again, the individual anarchist who acts in a morally impeccable fashion. Sometimes she will provide people with benefits even when those benefits are not requested (e.g., when those benefits are necessary and sufficient for ensuring that the recipient acquires her just share of advantage). Similarly, the anarchist will sometimes coercively regulate others' behavior without their consent, for example, by preventing them from violating others' rights. Thus, the proposed analysis of statehood entails that such anarchists are states despite the fact that they act in a just fashion. This result implies that the grounding *desideratum* is not satisfied by the proposed analysis.

It is not possible to provide an exhaustive list of potential analyses of statehood. However, this section has attempted to present the most plausible analyses that the political anarchist might incorporate into her position. And, in each case, it has argued that the proposed analysis fails to satisfy one of the political anarchist's crucial *desiderata*. Thus, there does not appear to be a plausible, nontrivial version of political anarchism – and, for this reason, the proposed social anarchist position rejects political anarchism in favor of a more modest philosophical anarchism.[9] Granted, there may be some overlooked analysis that satisfies both the grounding and actuality *desiderata*, in which case political anarchism might be shown to be a viable position. However, Section 7.3 will argue that there is a general reason for thinking that no such analysis can be provided.

7.3 A State-Tolerant Anarchism

The similarity of many of the previous objections to proposed analyses of statehood suggests that there is a more general problem with political anarchism. Specifically, it appears that political anarchists face a general dilemma that precludes them from providing a satisfactory analysis of statehood. Note that, when analyzing statehood, one must hold that the defining feature of a state is either (a) some action that the state carries out (e.g., preventing private rights enforcement) or (b) some structural

---

[9] Wendt (private communication, 2022) wonders whether the difficulties of analyzing statehood also create problems for the philosophical anarchist position defended here. After all, philosophical anarchism is typically characterized as the position that there are no existing legitimate states. But how can one assess this claim if no satisfactory analysis of statehood can be provided? In response to this question, it should be noted, first, that the foregoing argument merely maintains that there is no analysis of statehood *that is compatible with the political anarchist's own prior commitments*. Thus, one cannot infer that there is no analysis of statehood suitable for the philosophical anarchist's purposes. More directly, the philosophical anarchist can contend that her thesis does not have to be stated in terms of there being no existing legitimate states. Rather, she merely contends that the entities that *we pretheoretically think of as* states are illegitimate. Note that the position defended here grounds the philosophical anarchist thesis in the consent theory of legitimacy: If consent theory is correct, then the United States Federal Government and other such entities are illegitimate because they have not obtained the consent of those whom they claim to govern. However, note that this conclusion does not presuppose that these entities have anything in common, and the premise that the United States Federal Government is a state does not play any role in the proposed argument. Given this proposed argumentative structure, no analysis of statehood needs to be provided to support the proposed philosophical anarchist conclusion. By contrast, political anarchists are committed to the view that the United States Federal Government is unjust *in virtue of the fact that it is a state*. Thus, it seems that they *do* have to provide an account of statehood to support this contention – and, more specifically, an account that satisfies both the grounding and actuality *desiderata* introduced earlier.

property that does not entail that the state carries out any set of actions. If one opts for the latter variety of analysis, then one is faced with the problem of the possible state that meets the sufficient condition in question while acting in a morally impeccable fashion. The possibility of such a state – and there should always be such a possibility given that the sufficient condition of statehood implies nothing about the candidate for statehood's actions – entails that the grounding *desideratum* goes unsatisfied, as there is seemingly nothing unjust about the state that acts impeccably. That means that the political anarchist must adopt an analysis that declares some group a state if and only if it acts in some unjust way. But such an analysis will trivialize political anarchism for the reasons discussed previously. Thus, political anarchism ends up being either implausible or trivial.

Given this dilemma, the suggestion here is that political anarchists should abandon their view in favor of a position that tolerates groups like the United States Federal Government conditional on their acting justly. When these groups discharge their duties, there is no reason for an anarchist to resist their activities. By contrast, when these groups violate others' rights, then the anarchist does have reason to resist the rights-violating activities in question. In this way, the proposed social anarchist position puts states on a moral par with private individuals: In both cases, one is concerned strictly with the deontic status of the agent's actions rather than some other property possessed by the agent. Further, this approach seems to follow from the denial of state legitimacy (which political anarchists endorse). Once one rejects that states have any special moral status, one should treat them as one would any individual or group agent. Given that anarchists typically respond to bad behavior by individuals and groups by positing that others have permissions and obligations to resist the unjust actions – as opposed to insisting that the rights-violating individuals or groups should be *abolished* – it seems that anarchists should adopt a similar attitude toward states.

That said, there is a contingent, empirical argument for political anarchism that is compatible with the posited social anarchist position and the arguments advanced previously. This argument begins with the plausible starting premises that (1) persons sometimes have obligations to prevent other agents from violating rights and (2) if one is obliged to ϕ and ψ-ing is a necessary condition of ϕ-ing, then one is obliged to ψ.[10] The argument

---

[10] Some libertarians and anarchists might reject (1) because they might insist that persons have only negative duties to refrain from actions without any positive duties to act in particular ways. The argument of the book has tried to remain neutral on the question of whether persons have positive duties, so it should be noted that the proposed argument for political anarchism does presuppose

would then propose that (3) there are certain properties of individuals or groups that are both (a) a necessary and sufficient condition of statehood and (b) a necessary and sufficient condition of some rights violation of the kind that all persons are obliged to prevent. Together, these three premises entail that persons have an obligation to prevent states from existing because they are obliged to negate the necessary conditions of statehood (as negating the necessary conditions of statehood is, itself, a necessary condition of preventing rights violations, which is obligatory).[11] For example, suppose that some group is a state if and only if it has a certain amount of power to realize its desired states of affairs. Further, suppose that simply having this degree of power will, as a matter of contingent empirical fact, lead any given group to violate the rights of others. In this case, other agents would be obliged to preclude any group from acquiring or possessing the quantity of power in question – that is, to abolish any existing state.

This argument is valid and may turn out to be sound. However, its soundness will depend upon whether empirical Proposition (3) is true, where the truth of this proposition seems quite difficult to establish. Thus, the political anarchist faces a demanding burden of proof that cannot be obviously met, even if the posited argument cannot be rejected *a priori*. If it were to be met, however, then one might amend the posited social anarchist position to include a political anarchist thesis in addition to its philosophical anarchist component.

7.4 In Defense of Philosophical Anarchism

Before concluding, this section will briefly address Wendt's (2020) recent argument against philosophical anarchism, as it seems to threaten the posited endorsement of the position presented just prior. Specifically, Wendt suggests that the position is unstable and ultimately collapses into either political anarchism or a form of statism. Given that the social anarchist position advanced by the book includes a philosophical anarchist

---

the existence of such duties. That said, the political anarchist might avoid this commitment by restating the argument strictly in terms of the negative duties possessed by the state and/or the agents who compose it. Specifically, she would posit that these agents have negative obligations to refrain from carrying out actions that are a sufficient condition of the properties that are themselves a sufficient condition of both statehood and future rights violations.

[11] One might, alternatively, construct a probabilistic version of this argument, where this variant would contend that individuals are obliged to eliminate social structures that make rights violations *more likely* (with states being instances of such social structures).

component – and that this chapter has been a critique of political anarchism – it is worth discussing and replying to Wendt's argument.

Wendt takes philosophical anarchists to be committed to three propositions. First, philosophical anarchists deny that the state has political authority, where Wendt stipulates that political authority entails both the power to impose obligations on others and permissions to coercively enforce laws (2020, 528). Second, because philosophical anarchists deny that states possess political authority, they also deny that the state has *legitimacy*, where Wendt defines this notion as referring to "the moral rights that allow the institution to function as the institution that it is" where "these moral rights are the rights that constitute political authority" (529). This definition is a bit odd because it seems to identify political authority and legitimacy, thereby rendering the second philosophical anarchist thesis trivial. For this reason, it seems better to revise Wendt's definition of "legitimacy" such that the referent of the term is limited to the permission to enact and enforce certain kinds of laws.[12] Additionally, to avoid trivializing the second proposition, it seems better to redefine "political authority" such that it merely refers to the power to oblige, as opposed to the conjunction of the power to oblige and the permission to coercively enforce laws, which is to say, the power to oblige and legitimacy (otherwise, states would, as a matter of mere definition, lack legitimacy in virtue of lacking political authority). Thus, the first thesis would merely assert that states lack the power to oblige while the second would assert that, in virtue of this lack of authority, states also lack a permission to enforce certain kinds of laws – that is, they have a duty to not enforce certain kinds of laws. Finally, philosophical anarchists hold that states can be either justified or act justly, where the former notion entails that persons have content-dependent reasons to comply with laws or otherwise support states (e.g., because noncompliance would bring about a morally bad state of affairs) and the latter notion entails that states act permissibly when they enforce certain laws due to the content of those laws (e.g., laws against murder) (529).

---

[12] To avoid confusion, it is important to note that Wendt is switching the referents of "legitimacy" and "political authority" relative to how the terms are defined by the book. Prior to this section, "political authority" has been used to refer to the permission to coercively enforce laws while "legitimacy" has been used to refer to the power to oblige via the issuing of edicts. By contrast, Wendt uses the term "legitimacy" to refer to political authority and uses "political authority" to refer to the conjunction of legitimacy and political authority. To avoid misrepresenting Wendt's argument, this section will adopt his definitions for the terms in question, but one should keep in mind that any subsequent appearances of the terms "legitimacy" and "political authority" correspond to different referents than the appearances of these terms in previous sections.

7.4 In Defense of Philosophical Anarchism

Wendt's argument against this position proceeds in two stages. First, he argues that the second and third theses are incompatible as a matter of definition: It cannot be the case that a state both lacks a permission to enforce certain kind of laws (i.e., it is not legitimate) while also being justified in enforcing those laws, as "having a [permission] not to do something simply means not having a duty not to do it" (533). In other words, because the illegitimate state *lacks* a permission to enforce the law, it has a correlative duty to *not* enforce the law, where this duty is incompatible with the philosophical anarchist's thesis that states are justified in enforcing the law.[13]

This incompatibility generates a dilemma for the philosophical anarchist. On the one hand, she can give up her contention that the state is justified in enforcing certain kinds of laws; however, to make such a concession is to abandon philosophical anarchism in favor of political anarchism, as one seemingly has reason to abolish the state if it is not justified in carrying out any of its law enforcement operations (535). On the other hand, the philosophical anarchist might insist that law enforcement is justified, but this would then force her to concede that the state is legitimate, which Wendt takes to be a form of statism rather than philosophical anarchism (532). Granted, the philosophical anarchist could avoid this conclusion if she revised her notion of legitimacy such that it did not refer merely to the permission to enforce the law but, rather, some other moral virtue, where this virtue (a) is not entailed by the permission to enforce laws and (b) is negated by the absence of political authority (536). However, this position is plausible only if some reason can be given for thinking that the state's lack of political authority is problematic enough to undermine the state's legitimacy (in this revised sense) but not so problematic as to render its enforcement actions unjustified (536). Given the apparent absence of such a reason, Wendt concludes that philosophical anarchism collapses into either political anarchism or statism.

There are two objections that can be made to this argument. First, one might contest Wendt's claim that a state cannot be both justified in carrying out enforcement actions and lack legitimacy, that is, a permission to enforce its laws. Wendt seemingly takes this to be a self-evident conceptual truth – one that follows from the similarly self-evident proposition that an action being justified implies a permission to carry out that

---

[13] Note that this sentence is simply negating both sides of the identity claim quoted in the previous sentence, as this transformation helps to clarify the logical relationship between the quoted claim and this section's exposition of Wendt's argument.

action (534). However, this entailment does not hold if one takes rights and duties to be merely *pro tanto* moral considerations such that a duty to ϕ does not imply that one ought to ϕ, all things considered. For example, one might think that even if P has a property claim against Q breaking into P's cabin, Q may still break in if doing so is the only way for her to avoid freezing to death.[14] In this case, Q's need does not negate her duty to remain outside, as evidenced by the fact that she would owe certain remedial duties to P in virtue of her action (e.g., a duty to compensate P for any damage or to at least apologize for using the cabin without permission). The persistence of this duty, in turn, implies that Q lacks a permission to break into the cabin, as one has a permission to ϕ if and only if one does not have a duty not to ϕ. Yet Q is, nonetheless, justified in breaking into the cabin (where a person is more generally justified in ϕ-ing if and only if it is not the case that she ought not ϕ).

Given this plausible view of the relationship between duties/permissions and justification, Wendt is wrong to assert that a justified action is one that a person has a permission to do (i.e., no duty not to do). This, in turn, implies that a state might lack legitimacy vis-à-vis some act of enforcement but also be justified in carrying out that act of enforcement. Thus, contra Wendt, one might maintain that there is no contradiction between the philosophical anarchist's second and third commitments, that is, the denial that the state is legitimate and the insistence that it might be justified in enforcing certain laws.

Alternatively, the philosophical anarchist might argue that Wendt's objection to philosophical anarchism is primarily verbal rather than substantive. To advance this argument, the philosophical anarchist would simply concede that the state is legitimate in the sense that it has a permission to enforce some of its laws. She would then contend that the core philosophical anarchist claim is that the state lacks political authority but sometimes has Hohfeldian permissions to enforce its laws; that is, it is legitimate but lacks political authority. Given that the denial that states possess political authority is compatible with those states also being legitimate, the posited position sidesteps Wendt's argument, thereby avoiding any collapse into political anarchism.

Wendt anticipates this argument, and his preemptive reply is that the concession that states are legitimate is an abandonment of philosophical

---

[14] This case is borrowed from Joel Feinberg (1978, 102). Feinberg also endorses the proposed account of the relationship between duties/permissions and what one ought to do, all things considered. For another explication and defense of this account of duties, see Thomson (1990).

7.4 In Defense of Philosophical Anarchism

anarchism in favor of statism (542). Here one might object that this reply still makes the dispute sound merely verbal, as nothing of philosophical significance hangs on whether one labels the position in question "philosophical anarchism" or "statism." However, Wendt argues that the disagreement is substantive, not verbal, as those who endorse the proposed position (i.e., that states are legitimate but lack political authority) "do not see themselves as anarchists. And they have good reason not to. A position that deserves the name 'anarchist' should deny that states are legitimate, and the position under consideration does not do this. As Simmons says, 'one central claim unites all form [sic] of anarchist political philosophy: all existing states are illegitimate. I take this thesis to be an essential, if not defining, element of anarchism'" (543).[15]

This reply is unconvincing for a few reasons. First, it seems to be no less of a verbal move than any of those it is supposed to support. So far, this section has granted that a state is appropriately labeled "legitimate" if and only if it has a permission to enforce some subset of its laws, with the term "political authority" being used to refer to a state's power to oblige. However, as noted in Footnote 12, this is an inversion of how these terms have been used by both this book and many other philosophers. Given that different philosophers assign different referents to the term "legitimacy," it is not clear that the denial of state legitimacy-as-Wendt-defines-it is the essential characteristic of an anarchist view as opposed to the denial of legitimacy-as-it-is-defined-earlier-in-this-book (i.e., the power to oblige). Indeed, when Simmons claims that the denial of state legitimacy is the defining feature of anarchism, he is using the latter sense of the term rather than Wendt's (1996, 106) – a point that Wendt, himself, recognizes (2020, 541). Thus, Wendt's appeal to Simmons' authority seemingly *undermines* his contention that the book's posited view would not qualify as a variety of anarchism.

Further, even if Simmons were referring to the permission to enforce rather than the power to oblige, it is not clear that one must accept his view as the correct one. As noted in Section I.1, it is difficult to answer the question of which philosophical positions deserve the "anarchist" label, and neither Simmons nor Wendt provide reasons for accepting their proposal that such positions must include the denial of state legitimacy (irrespective of what "legitimacy" refers to). Absent such reasons, one might assess this proposal by applying Section I.1's posited criterion of

---

[15] The "sic" indicates a slight mistranscription of Simmons' text by Wendt rather than an error in Simmons' original text being noted by Wendt.

what counts as an anarchist view: The anarchist position is that which the bulk of self-identified anarchists would accept given adequate philosophical reflection. Of course, as was noted there, it is difficult to determine whether a given position meets this criterion a priori. However, it was suggested that anarchists' post-reflection uptake of some position is a function the extent to which the position is independently plausible and the extent to which it coheres with their prior beliefs. Thus, to convincingly show that the posited philosophical anarchist position is not a genuine form of anarchism, Wendt would need to show that a position that assigns states a permission to enforce certain laws is either (a) less plausible than a rival view that does not assign such a permission or (b) is less coherent with other anarchist commitments.

It does not seem that Wendt would be able to demonstrate (a). Doing so would require showing that states lack a permission to enforce all and only those laws that any private individual would be permitted to enforce (e.g., a law against violent aggression). But this seems implausible. Why would a police officer lack a permission to stop an assault when a person standing next to the police officer possesses such a permission? Perhaps the answer to this question is that the state and its officers uniquely lack this permission due to the fact that the state should not exist at all. This answer would also support Proposition (b), as the political anarchist commitments of self-identified anarchists would then be incompatible with the state having a permission to enforce certain laws. However, first, even if the state should not exist, it is not clear that this negates its permissions to carry out many acts of law enforcement. Consider, as an analogy, the case of a trespasser who witnesses an assault occurring within the bounds of the private property she is invading. Presumably, she would be permitted to stop the assault even though it is also true that she should not even be positioned to stop the assault in the first place. This result suggests that an agent's permission to enforce certain rights can persist despite her failure to discharge other duties. Thus, more argument would be needed to show that the state's duty to dissolve itself negates the permission of its agents to enforce certain laws. Second, the discussion of the previous section has aimed to show that the political anarchist insistence on abolishing the state is misguided. If that conclusion is correct, then any (purported) incompatibility with political anarchism does nothing to diminish the plausibility of the posited position. Further, the incompatibility would not preclude anarchists from endorsing the position after adequate philosophical reflection, as such reflection would lead them to abandon any prior political anarchist commitments.

For these reasons, one should reject Wendt's claim that the proposed view is not an anarchist one.[16]

In sum, there is nothing inconsistent about the book's allowance that, although states lack the power to oblige, its agents sometimes act permissibly when they enforce their laws. Indeed, Wendt does not dispute this basic point. Rather, his only argument against such a position is that it is a form of statism rather than anarchism. However, he does not provide an account of which positions are anarchist in character, and the account proposed in Section 1.1 does not appear to vindicate his contention. Thus, there is no apparent problem with the social anarchist position's rejection of political anarchism in favor of philosophical anarchism.

7.5 Conclusion

So concludes the book's exposition and defense of social anarchism. The posited position is an unorthodox articulation of social anarchism *qua* political philosophy. However, this unorthodoxy allows it to attain various theoretical virtues such as a high degree of coherence and independent plausibility. The book has not attempted to compare social anarchism's advantages and drawbacks with those of rival views such as utilitarianism, Rawlsian liberalism, or other varieties of liberal egalitarianism. Instead, it has focused on putting dialectical pressure on libertarians, arguing that their position ultimately collapses into social anarchism. That said, its efforts to defend the independent (i.e., non-comparative) plausibility of the position – for example, by showing that it follows from a plausible meta-principle and does not generate unacceptable implications – have hopefully sufficed to show that social anarchism deserves a seat at the table alongside the more reputable political philosophies that have garnered the bulk of philosophers' attention.

---

[16] Wendt (private communication, 2022) pushes back on this argument by noting that the declaration that a state is *illegitimate* connotes that there is something morally problematic about the state that demands remedy. Thus, he suggests that an adequate account of legitimacy should entail that an illegitimate state is morally defective in a way that extends beyond it merely lacking the power to oblige. However, this point can be accommodated by appealing to the fact that existing states tend to *act* as though they do have the power to oblige, where the conjunction of this behavior and the fact that they lack said power is morally problematic. Given that states act in this way, pointing out that they lack legitimacy is a serious moral accusation, with the proposed account thereby satisfying Wendt's constraint on what counts as an adequate definition of "legitimacy."

References

Arneson, Richard. 1989. "Equality and Equal Opportunity for Welfare." *Philosophical Studies* 56, no. 1: 77–93.
    2011a. "Liberalism, Capitalism, and 'Socialist' Principles." *Social Philosophy and Policy* 28, no. 2: 232–61.
    2011b. "Luck Egalitarianism: A Primer." In *Responsibility and Distributive Justice*, C. Knight and Z. Stemplowska (eds.). Oxford: Oxford University Press.
Attas, Daniel. 2003. "The Negative Principle of Just Appropriation." *Canadian Journal of Philosophy* 33, no. 3: 343–72.
Baker, Alan. 2016. "Simplicity." In *The Stanford Encyclopedia of Philosophy* (Winter Edition), E. N. Zalta (ed.), https://plato.stanford.edu/archives/win2016/entries/simplicity/.
Bakunin, Mikhail. 1953. "Stateless Socialism: Anarchism." In *The Political Philosophy of Bakunin: Scientific Anarchism*, G. P. Maximoff (ed.). London: The Free Press.
Berkman, Alexander. 2003. *What Is Anarchism?* Edinburgh/Oakland, CA: AK Press.
Bookchin, Murray. 2004. *Post-Scarcity Anarchism*. Edinburgh/Oakland, CA: AK Press.
Bornschein, Peter. 2018. "The Self-Ownership Proviso: A Critique." *Politics, Philosophy & Economics* 17, no. 4: 339–55.
Braham, Matthew and Martin van Hees. 2014. "The Impossibility of Pure Libertarianism." *The Journal of Philosophy* 111, no. 8: 420–36.
Breakey, Hugh. 2009. "Without Consent: Principles of Justified Acquisition and Duty-Imposing Powers." *Philosophical Quarterly* 59, no. 237: 618–40.
Brennan, Jason. 2014. *Why Not Capitalism?*. New York: Routledge.
    2016. *Against Democracy*. Princeton, NJ: Princeton University Press.
Brennan, Jason and van der Vossen, Bas. 2018. "The Myths of the Self-Ownership Thesis." In *The Routledge Handbook of Libertarianism*, J. Brennan, B. van der Vossen, and D. Schmidtz (eds.). New York: Routledge.
Brilmayer, Lea. 1989. "Consent, Contract, and Territory." *Minnesota Law Review* 74, no. 1: 1–35.
Bryan, Ben. 2019. "Duty-Sensitive Self-Ownership." *Social Philosophy and Policy* 36, no. 2: 264–83.

Buchanan, Allen. 1987. "Justice and Charity." *Ethics* 97, no. 3: 558–75.
   2003. "Boundaries: What Liberalism Has to Say." In *States, Nations, and Borders: The Ethics of Making Boundaries*, A. Buchanan and M. Moore (eds.). Cambridge: Cambridge University Press.
Carter, Alan. 2013. *A Radical Green Political Theory*. New York: Routledge.
Casati, Roberto and Varzi, Achille. 2020. "Events." In *The Stanford Encyclopedia of Philosophy* (Summer Edition), E. N. Zalta (ed.), https://plato.stanford.edu/archives/sum2020/entries/events/.
Chartier, Gary. 2013. *Anarchy and Legal Order: Law and Politics for a Stateless Society*. Cambridge: Cambridge University Press.
Chisholm, Roderick M. 1964. "The Ethics of Requirement." *American Philosophical Quarterly* 1, no. 2: 147–53.
Chomsky, Noam. 2013. *On Anarchism*. New York: The New Press.
Christmas, Billy. 2020. "Ambidextrous Lockeanism." *Economics and Philosophy* 36, no. 2: 193–215.
   2021. *Property and Justice: A Liberal Theory of Natural Rights*. New York: Routledge.
Clark, John. 1978. "What Is Anarchism?" *NOMOS: American Society for Political and Legal Theory* 19: 3–28.
   1984. *The Anarchist Moment: Reflections on Culture, Nature, and Power*. Montreal: Black Rose Books.
Cohen, G. A. 1994. "Back to Socialist Basics." *New Left Review* 207: 3–16.
   1995. *Self-Ownership, Freedom, and Equality*. Cambridge: Cambridge University Press.
   2006. "Luck and Equality: A Reply to Hurley." *Philosophy and Phenomenological Research* 72, no. 2: 439–46.
   2008. *Why Not Socialism?* Princeton, NJ: Princeton University Press.
   2009. *Rescuing Justice and Equality*. Cambridge, MA: Harvard University Press.
   2011. "On the Currency of Egalitarian Justice." In *On the Currency of Egalitarian Justice and Other Essays in Political Philosophy*, M. Otsuka (ed.). Princeton, NJ: Princeton University Press.
Cruft, Rowan. 2019. *Human Rights, Ownership, and the Individual*. Oxford: Oxford University Press.
Davis, Lawrence. 1976. "Comments on Nozick's Entitlement Theory." *The Journal of Philosophy* 73, no. 21: 836–44.
Driver, Julia. 1992. "The Suberogatory." *The Australasian Journal of Philosophy* 70, no. 3: 286–95.
Dworkin, Ronald. 1981. "What Is Equality? Part 2: Equality of Resources." *Philosophy and Public Affairs* 10: 283–345.
   2000. *Sovereign Virtue: The Theory and Practice of Equality*. Cambridge, MA: Harvard University Press.
Epstein, Richard. 2009. "Property Rights, State of Nature Theory, and Environmental Protection." *New York University Journal of Law and Liberty* 4, no. 1: 1–35.

Ervin, Lorenzo Kom'boa. 2021. *Anarchism and the Black Revolution: The Definitive Edition*. London: Pluto Press.

Estlund, David. 2020. *Utopophobia: On the Limits (If Any) of Political Philosophy*. Princeton, NJ/Oxford: Princeton University Press.

Fabbri, Luigi. 1922. "Anarchism and Communism." *Northeastern Anarchist* 4, http://dwardmac.pitzer.edu/anarchist_archives/worldwidemovements/fabbrianarandcom.html.

Feinberg, Joel. 1978. "Voluntary Euthanasia and the Inalienable Right to Life." *Philosophy and Public Affairs* 7, no. 2: 93–123.

Feser, Edward. 2004. "Self-Ownership, Abortion, and the Rights of Children: Toward a More Conservative Libertarianism." *Journal of Libertarian Studies* 18, no. 3: 91–114.

   2005. "There Is No Such Thing as Unjust Initial Acquisition." *Social Philosophy and Policy* 22, no. 1: 56–80.

Flanigan, Jessica. 2019a. "Boundary Problems and Self-Ownership." *Social Philosophy and Policy* 36, no. 2: 9–35.

   2019b. "Duty and Enforcement." *The Journal of Political Philosophy* 27, no. 3: 341–62.

Fleurbaey, Marc. 1995. "Equal Opportunity or Equal Social Outcome?" *Economics and Philosophy* 11, no. 1: 25–55.

Foot, Philippa. 1978. *Virtues and Vices and Other Essays in Moral Philosophy*. Berkeley: University of California Press.

   1984. "Killing and Letting Die." In *Abortion: Moral and Legal Perspectives*, J. L. Garfield and P. Hennessey (eds.). Amherst, MA: University of Amherst Press.

Fressola, Anthony. 1981. "Liberty and Property: Reflections on the Right of Appropriation in the State of Nature." *American Philosophical Quarterly* 18, no. 4: 315–22.

Fried, Barbara. 2004. "Left-Libertarianism: A Review Essay." *Philosophy and Public Affairs* 32, no. 1: 66–92.

Friedman, David. 1989. *The Machinery of Freedom: Guide to a Radical Capitalism*. Chicago/La Salle, IL: Open Court.

Gaus, Gerald, and Lomasky, Loren. 1990. "Are Property Rights Problematic?" *The Monist* 73, no. 4: 483–503.

Gibbard, Alan. 1976. "Natural Property Rights." *Noûs* 10, no.1: 77–86.

Goldman, Emma. 1911. "Anarchism: What It Really Stands For." In *Anarchism and Other Essays*, 2nd revised ed. New York: Mother Earth Publishing Association.

Goodwin, Barbara. 2007. *Using Political Ideas*. West Sussex: John Wiley & Sons.

Guerin, Daniel. 1970. *Anarchism*. New York: Monthly Review Press.

Gustafsson, Johan E. 2022. "Bentham's Mugging." *Utilitas* 34, no. 4: 386–91.

Hanna, Jason. 2018. *In Our Best Interest: A Defense of Paternalism*. New York: Oxford University Press.

Hassan, Patrick. 2019. "Moral Disagreement and Arational Convergence." *Journal of Ethics* 23: 145–61.

Hohfeld, Wesley. 1913. "Some Fundamental Legal Conceptions as Applied in Judicial Reasoning." *The Yale Law Journal* 23, no. 1: 16–59.

Hopster, Jeroen. 2020. "Explaining Historical Moral Convergence: The Empirical Case against Realist Intuitionism." *Philosophical Studies* 177, no. 5: 1255–73.

Huemer, Michael. 2013. *The Problem of Political Authority: An Examination of the Right to Coerce and the Duty to Obey*. London: Palgrave MacMillan.

2016. "A Liberal Realist Answer to Debunking Skeptics: The Empirical Case for Realism." *Philosophical Studies* 173, no. 7: 1983–2010.

Hurd, Heidi M. 1996. "The Moral Magic of Consent." *Legal Theory* 2, no. 2: 121–46.

Hurley, Susan. 2003. *Justice, Luck, and Knowledge*. Cambridge: Harvard University Press.

Itō Noe. 2005. "The Facts of Anarchy." In *Anarchism: A Documentary History of Libertarian Ideas*. Volume 1, R. Graham (ed.). Montreal: Black Rose Books.

Jeffers, Matthew T. 2020. "Luck and the Limits of Equality." *Philosophical Papers* 49, no. 3: 397–429.

Jeske, Diane. 2014. "Special Obligations." In *The Stanford Encyclopedia of Philosophy* (Spring 2014 Edition), E. N. Zalta (ed.), https://plato.stanford.edu/entries/special-obligations/.

Knight, Carl. 2009. "Describing Equality." *Law and Philosophy* 28, no. 4: 327–65.

2013. "Egalitarian Justice and Expected Value." *Ethical Theory and Moral Practice* 16, no. 5: 1061–73.

Knight, Carl and Zofia Stemplowska. 2011. "Introduction." In *Responsibility and Distributive Justice*, C. Knight and Z. Stemplowska (eds.). Oxford/New York: Oxford University Press.

Kropotkin, Peter. 1995. *The Conquest of Bread*. Cambridge: Cambridge University Press.

Kukathas, Chandran. 2019. "Libertarianism without Self-Ownership." *Social Philosophy and Policy* 36, no. 2: 71–93.

Kymlicka, Will. 2002. *Contemporary Political Philosophy*, second ed. Oxford: Oxford University Press.

Lang, Gerald. 2015. "How Interesting Is the 'Boring Problem' for Luck Egalitarianism?" *Philosophy and Phenomenological Research* 91, no. 3: 698–722.

2021. *Strokes of Luck: A Study in Moral and Political Philosophy*. Oxford: Oxford University Press.

Lewis, David. 1973. "Causation." *Journal of Philosophy* 70, no. 17: 556–67.

1986. *Philosophical Papers: Volume II*. Oxford: Oxford University Press.

Lippert-Rasmussen, Kasper. 2008. "Against Self-Ownership: There Are No Fact-Insensitive Ownership Rights over One's Body." *Philosophy and Public Affairs* 36, no. 1: 86–118.

2015. *Luck Egalitarianism*. London: Bloomsbury Publishing.

Locke, John. 2005. *Second Treatise of Government*. Urbana, IL: Project Gutenberg, www.gutenberg.org/files/7370/7370-h/7370-h.htm.

Lomasky, Loren. 1987. *Persons, Rights, and the Moral Community*. New York: Oxford University Press.

Long, Roderick T. 2005. "Liberty: The Other Equality." *The Freeman: Ideas on Liberty* 55, no. 8: 17–9.

2018. "Anarchism and Libertarianism." In *Brill's Companion to Anarchism and Philosophy*, N. Jun (ed.). Leiden, NL: Brill.

Mack, Eric. 1976. "Distributionism versus Justice." *Ethics* 86, no. 2: 145–53.

1995. "The Self-Ownership Proviso: A New and Improved Lockean Proviso." *Social Philosophy and Policy* 12, no. 1: 186–218.

2002. "Self-Ownership, Marxism, and Egalitarianism: Part I: Challenges to Historical Entitlement." *Politics, Philosophy & Economics* 1, no. 1: 75–108.

2010. "The Natural Right of Property." *Social Philosophy and Policy* 27, no. 1: 53–78.

2015. "Elbow Room for Rights." *Oxford Studies in Political Philosophy* 1, no. 1: 194–221.

2018. "Robert Nozick's Political Philosophy." *The Stanford Encyclopedia of Philosophy* (Summer 2018 Edition), E. N. Zalta (ed.), https://plato.stanford.edu/archives/sum2018/entries/nozick-political/.

Makhno, Nestor. 1996. *The Struggle against the State and Other Essays*, A. Sirda (ed.), P. Sharkey (trans.). Edinburgh/Oakland: AK Press.

Malatesta, Errico. 1994. *Anarchy*. London: Freedom Press.

Mazor, Joseph. 2019. "Income Redistribution, Body-Part Redistribution, and Respect for the Separateness of Persons." *Journal of Ethics and Social Philosophy* 16, no. 3: 192–228.

McElroy, Wendy. 1991. "Introduction: The Roots of Individualist Feminism in 19th-Century America." In *Freedom, Feminism, and the State: An Overview of Individualist Feminism*, 2nd ed, W. McElroy (ed.). New York: Holmes & Meier.

McKay, Iain and unnamed authors. 2008. *An Anarchist FAQ, Volume 1*. Edinburgh/Oakland: AK Press.

2020. *An Anarchist FAQ*, Version 15.4, https://theanarchistlibrary.org/library/the-anarchist-faq-editorial-collective-an-anarchist-faq-full.

McKerlie, Dennis. 1989. "Equality and Time." *Ethics* 99, no. 3: 475–91.

McLaughlin, Paul. 2016. *Anarchism and Authority: A Philosophical Introduction to Classical Anarchism*. New York: Routledge.

Meinong, Alexius. 1972. *On Emotional Presentation*. L. S. Kalsi (trans.). Evanston: Northwestern University Press.

Mellor, D. H. 1995. *The Facts of Causation*. London: Routledge.

2004. "For Facts as Causes and Effects." In *Causation and Conditionals*, J. Collins, N. Hall, and L. A. Paul (eds.). Cambridge, MA: MIT Press.

Michel, Louise. 1896. "Why I Am an Anarchist." *Liberty* 3, no. 3, www.libertarian-labyrinth.org/anarchist-beginnings/louise-michel-why-i-am-an-anarchist-1896/.

Miller, David. 1984. *Anarchism*. JM Dent & Sons.
　2017. "Justice." *The Stanford Encyclopedia of Philosophy* (Fall 2017 Edition), E. N. Zalta (ed.), https://plato.stanford.edu/archives/fall2017/entries/justice/.
Moore, Margaret. 2004. *The Ethics of Nationalism*. New York: Oxford University Press.
Mulkeen, Nicola. 2019. "Rescuing Self-Ownership: Tackling the Pollution Problem." *Critical Review of International Social and Political Philosophy* 22, no. 6: 660–80.
Narveson, Jan. 1988. *The Libertarian Idea*. Philadelphia: Temple University Press.
　1998. "Libertarianism vs. Marxism: Reflections on G. A. Cohen's Self-Ownership, Freedom, and Equality." *The Journal of Ethics* 2, no. 1: 1–26.
Nine, Cara. 2008a. "A Lockean Theory of Territory." *Political Studies* 56, no. 1: 148–65.
　2008b. "Territory Is Not Derived from Property: A Response to Steiner." *Political Studies* 56, no. 4: 957–63.
Nozick, Robert. 1974. *Anarchy, State, and Utopia*. New York: Basic Books.
Okin, Susan Moller. 1989. *Justice, Gender, and the Family*. New York: Basic Books.
Olsaretti, Serena. 2009. "Responsibility and the Consequences of Choice." *Proceedings of the Aristotelian Society* 109, no. 2: 165–88.
O'Neill, Onora. 1981. "Nozick's Entitlements." In *Reading Nozick: Essays on Anarchy, State, and Utopia*, J. Paul (ed.). Totowa, NJ: Rowman & Allanheld.
Otsuka, Michael. 1998. "Self-Ownership and Equality: A Lockean Reconciliation." *Philosophy and Public Affairs* 27, no. 1: 65–92.
　2003. *Libertarianism without Inequality*. New York: Oxford University Press.
　2010. "Justice as Fairness: Luck Egalitarian, Not Rawlsian." *The Journal of Ethics* 14, nos. 3–4: 217–30.
Parsons, Lucy. 2004. "The Principles of Anarchism." In *Lucy Parsons: Freedom, Equality and Solidarity*, A. Gale (ed.). Chicago: Charles H. Kerr.
Pettit, Philip. 2012. *On the People's Terms: A Republican Theory and Model of Democracy*. Cambridge: Cambridge University Press.
Proudhon, Pierre-Joseph. 1876. *What Is Property?: An Inquiry into the Principle of Right and of Government*, B. R. Tucker (trans.). Cambridge: John Wilson & Son.
Railton, Peter. 2003. *Facts, Values, and Norms: Essays toward a Morality of Consequence*. Cambridge: Cambridge University Press.
Rawls, John. 1958. "Justice as Fairness." *The Philosophical Review* 67, no. 2: 164–94.
　1971. *A Theory of Justice*. Cambridge: Harvard University Press.
Reclus, Élisée. 1899. "Pourquoi sommes-nous anarchistes?" *La Société Nouvelle* 4, no. 2: 153–5.
Risse, Mathias. 2004. "Does Left–Libertarianism Have Coherent Foundations?" *Politics, Philosophy & Economics* 3, no. 3: 337–64.

Ritter, Alan. 1980. *Anarchism: A Theoretical Analysis*. Cambridge: Cambridge University Press.
Rocker, Rudolf. 2004. *Anarcho-Syndicalism: Theory and Practice*. Edinburgh/Oakland: AK Press.
Roemer, John. 2017. "Socialism Revised." *Philosophy and Public Affairs* 45, no. 3: 261–315.
Rose, Carol. 1985. "Possession as the Origin of Property." *The University of Chicago Law Review* 52, no. 1: 73–88.
Ross, Jacob. 2010. "The Irreducibility of Personal Obligation." *Journal of Philosophical Logic* 39, no. 3: 307–23.
Rothbard, Murray. 1978. *For a New Liberty: The Libertarian Manifesto*. New York: Macmillan.
  1982. "Law, Property Rights, and Air Pollution." *Cato Journal* 2, no.1: 55–99.
  1995. "Egalitarianism and the Elites." *The Review of Austrian Economics* 8, no. 2: 39–57.
  1998. *The Ethics of Liberty*. New York: New York University Press.
Sabatini, Peter. 1994–1995. "Libertarianism: Bogus Anarchy." *Anarchy: A Journal of Desire Armed* 14, no. 3: 6–8.
Sartwell, Crispin. 2008. *Against the State: An Introduction to Anarchist Political Theory*. Albany: SUNY Press.
Scanlon, T. M. 1998. *What We Owe Each Other*. Cambridge/London: Belknap Press.
Schmidtz, David. 1990. "When Is Original Acquisition Required?" *The Monist* 73, no. 4: 504–18.
  1994. "The Institution of Property." *Social Philosophy and Policy* 11, no. 2: 42–62.
Segall, Shlomi. 2010. *Health, Luck, and Justice*. Princeton, NJ: Princeton University Press.
  2013. *Equality and Opportunity*. Oxford: Oxford University Press.
  2016. *Why Inequality Matters: Luck Egalitarianism, Its Meaning and Value*. Cambridge: Cambridge University Press.
Sen, Amartya. 1992. *Inequality Reexamined*. Oxford: Oxford University Press.
Simmons, A. John. 1979. *Moral Principles and Political Obligations*. Princeton, NJ: Princeton University Press.
  1987. "The Anarchist Position: A Reply to Klosko and Senor." *Philosophy and Public Affairs* 16, no. 3: 269–79.
  1996. "Associative Political Obligations." *Ethics* 106, no. 2: 247–73.
  1999. "Justification and Legitimacy." *Ethics* 109, no. 4: 739–71.
  2001. *Justification and Legitimacy: Essays on Rights and Obligations*. New York: Cambridge University Press.
  2005. "Consent Theory for Libertarians." *Social Philosophy and Policy* 22, no. 1: 330–56.
  2016. *Boundaries of Authority*. New York: Oxford University Press.
Smart, J. J. C. and Bernard Williams. 1973. *Utilitarianism: For and Against*. Cambridge: Cambridge University Press.

Smith, Holly M. 2018. *Making Morality Work*. Oxford: Oxford University Press.
Smith, Michael. 1994. *The Moral Problem*. London: Wiley.
Sobel, David. 2012. "Backing Away from Libertarian Self-Ownership." *Ethics* 123, no. 1: 32–60.
  2013. "Self-Ownership and the Conflation Problem." In *Oxford Studies in Normative Ethics Vol 3*, M. Timmons (ed.). New York: Oxford University Press.
Spafford, Jesse. 2019. "Community as Socialist Value." *Public Affairs Quarterly* 33, no. 3: 215–42.
  2020a. "Does Initial Appropriation Create New Obligations?" *The Journal of Ethics and Social Philosophy* 17, no. 2: 228–38.
  2020b. "An Anarchist Interpretation of Marx's 'Ability to Needs' Principle." *The Journal of Value Inquiry* 54, no. 2: 325–43.
  2021a. "Explanation, Justification, and Egalitarianism." *Synthese* 193, nos. 3–4: 9699–724.
  2021b. "Social Anarchism and the Rejection of Private Property." In *The Routledge Handbook of Anarchy and Anarchist Thought*, G. Chartier and C. Van Schoelandt (eds.). New York: Routledge.
  2022. "Luck Egalitarianism without Moral Tyranny." *Philosophical Studies* 179, no. 2: 469–93.
  2023. "Gerald Lang, *Strokes of Luck: A Study in Moral and Political Philosophy*." *Ethics* 133, no. 3: 429–34.
Spencer, Herbert. 1851. *Social Statics: Or, The Conditions Essential to Happiness Specified, and the First of Them Developed*. London: John Chapman, https://oll.libertyfund.org/titles/273.
Steiner, Hillel. 1974. "The Concept of Justice." *Ratio* 16, no. 2: 206–25.
  1994. *An Essay on Rights*. Cambridge: Basil Blackwell.
  2000. "Original Rights and Just Distribution." In *Left–Libertarianism and Its Critics: The Contemporary Debate*, P. Vallentyne and H. Steiner (eds.). New York: Palgrave.
Stemplowska, Zofia. 2009. "Making Justice Sensitive to Responsibility." *Political Studies* 57: 237–59.
  2013. "Rescuing Luck Egalitarianism." *Journal of Social Philosophy* 44, no. 4: 402–19.
Sumner, William G. 1918. *The Forgotten Man and Other Essays*, A. G. Keller (ed.). New Haven: Yale University Press.
Taylor, Robert S. 2004. "A Kantian Defense of Self-Ownership." *The Journal of Political Philosophy* 12, no. 1: 65–78.
Temkin, Larry. 1993. *Inequality*. Oxford University Press.
  2011. "Justice, Equality, Fairness, Desert, Rights, Free Will, Responsibility, and Luck." In *Responsibility and Distributive Justice*, C. Knight and Z. Stemplowska (eds.). Oxford/New York: Oxford University Press.
Thaysen, Jens Damgaard and Andreas Albertsen. 2017. "When Bad Things Happen to Good People: Luck Egalitarianism and Costly Rescues." *Politics, Philosophy & Economics* 16, no. 1: 93–112.

Thomson, Judith Jarvis. 1971. "A Defense of Abortion." *Philosophy and Public Affairs* 1, no. 1: 69–80.
　1976. "Property Acquisition." *The Journal of Philosophy* 73, no. 18: 664–6.
　1985. "The Trolley Problem." *The Yale Law Journal* 94, no. 6: 1395–1415.
　1990. *The Realm of Rights*. Cambridge, MA: Harvard University Press.
　2008. "Turning the Trolley." *Philosophy and Public Affairs* 36, no. 4: 359–74.
Urmson, J. O. 1958. "Saints and Heroes." In *Essays in Moral Philosophy*, A. Melden (ed.). Seattle: University of Washington Press.
Vallentyne, Peter. 1998. "Critical Notice." *Canadian Journal of Philosophy* 28, no. 4: 609–26.
　2002. "Brute Luck, Option Luck, and Equality of Initial Opportunities." *Ethics* 112, no. 3: 529–57.
　2007. "Libertarianism and the State." *Social Philosophy and Policy* 24, no. 1: 187–205.
　2008. "Brute Luck and Responsibility." *Politics, Philosophy & Economics* 7, no. 1: 57–80.
　2011. "Nozick's Libertarian Theory of Justice." In *The Cambridge Companion to Nozick's Anarchy, State, and Utopia*, R. M. Bader and J. Meadowcroft (eds.). Cambridge: Cambridge University Press.
Vallentyne, Peter, Hillel Steiner, and Michael Otsuka. 2005. "Why Left-Libertarianism Is Not Incoherent, Indeterminate, or Irrelevant: A Reply to Fried." *Philosophy and Public Affairs* 33, no. 2: 201–15.
Van der Vossen, Bas. 2009. "What Counts as Original Appropriation?" *Politics, Philosophy & Economics* 8, no. 4: 355–73.
　2015. "Imposing Duties and Original Appropriation." *The Journal of Political Philosophy* 23, no. 1: 64–85.
　2019. "Libertarianism." *The Stanford Encyclopedia of Philosophy* (Spring 2019 Edition), E. N. Zalta (ed.), https://plato.stanford.edu/archives/fall2014/entries/libertarianism/.
　2021. "As Good as 'Enough and as Good'." *The Philosophical Quarterly* 71, no. 1: 183–203.
Van Fraassen, Bas C. 1980. *The Scientific Image*. New York: Oxford University Press.
Van Parijs, Philippe. 2000. "Real-Libertarianism." In *Left–Libertarianism and Its Critics: The Contemporary Debate*, P. Vallentyne and H. Steiner (eds.). New York: Palgrave.
Von Mises, Ludwig. 1998. *Human Action: A Treatise on Economics*. Auburn AL: Ludwig von Mises Institute.
Waldron, Jeremy. 1979. "Enough and as Good Left for Others." *The Philosophical Quarterly* 29, no. 117: 319–28.
Weber, Max. 1991. "Politics as a Vocation." In *From Max Weber: Essays in Sociology*, H. H. Gerth and C. W. Mills (eds.). Abingdon: Routledge.
Wellman, Christopher. 1996. "Liberalism, Samaritanism, and Political Legitimacy." *Philosophy and Public Affairs* 25, no. 3: 211–37.

Wendt, Fabian. 2015. "Justice and Political Authority in Left-Libertarianism." *Politics, Philosophy & Economics* 14, no. 3: 316–39.
  2020. "Against Philosophical Anarchism." *Law and Philosophy* 39: 527–44.
Wilson, Charlotte. 2005. "Anarchism." In *Anarchism: A Documentary History of Libertarian Ideas*. Volume 1, R. Graham (ed.). Montreal: Black Rose Books.
Wolff, Robert Paul. 1970. *In Defense of Anarchism*. New York: Harper & Row.
Zimmerman, Michael J. 2014. *Ignorance and Moral Obligation*. Oxford University Press.
Zwolinski, Matt. 2008. "The Separateness of Persons and Liberal Theory." *The Journal of Value Inquiry* 42, no. 2: 147–65.
  2014. "Libertarianism and Pollution." *Philosophy and Public Policy Quarterly* 32, no. 3/4: 9–21.

Index

abortion, 33, 42, 48
academic philosophy, 1, 13, 223
action/inaction distinction, 113
activists, 17
actual compliance, 190, 193–4, 202
actuality *desideratum*, 205, 206–7, 209, 212–13, 215
ad hoc, 45, 48, 66, 93, 144, 147, 164, 185, 207
advantage, 4, 18, 27, 29–30, 39, 50, 69, 71–2, 84–6, 90, 107, 109, 146–7, 155, 156, 169–73, 175–86, 188–201, 214
    appropriately distributed, 52, 176, 182, 184, 189
    lifetime levels of, 50, 57, 180, 184
    nontransferrable, 183, 185
    total, 181, 182, 184, 185, 189, 197, 199, 200, 201
    warranted expected distributed. *See* WEDA
agency, 32, 109, 111, 112–13
aggression, 222
aggressors, 46, 47–8
agriculture, 155
Albertsen, Andreas, 175, 197–201
aliens, 123
anarchism
    anarcho-capitalism, 2, 7, 140, 212–13
        a genuine form of anarchism?, 2–3, 7–9
    anarcho-communism, 2, 7, *see also* social anarchism
    canonical texts of, 1–2, 11
    market, 2
    philosophical, 2, 3, 6, 25, 92, 122, 123, 150–1, 203, 205–8, 212, 215, 217–22
        a genuine form of anarchism?, 221–3
    political, 6, 203–8, 210–20, 222–3
    relation between theory and practice, 16–17
    revisionary theories of, 12–13
    social. *See* social anarchism
    vs. socialism, 17–18
    as stateless political system, 2
    what counts as, 6–13, 221–3
    anti-essentialism about, 8
    essentialism about, 7–8, 12
    non-factualism about, 9
    quietism about, 9–10, 12
    social movement approach, 11–13
anarchist conclusion, 4, 5, 49–55, 58, 65, 91, 92, 97, 122, 123, 149, 151, 152–5, 157–9, 160, 162, 163, 164–5, 167–71, 173, 174, 175–6, 179, 185, 191, 193, 200, 202
anarchist enforcer case, 210–11, 214
anarchist self-ownership. *See* self-ownership; anarchist self-ownership
anarchists, 1, 21, 89, 173
    anarchist movement, 2, 11, 202
    political practices of, 16
    self-identified, 2, 10–14, 143, 203, 222
animal liberation. *See* rights; of animals
ant and grasshopper case, 84–6, 175
antifascism, 11
apologies, 60, 64, 220
appropriation. *See* initial appropriation
arbitrariness, 14, 31, 34, 37, 83, 91, 92, 144, 172, 207
aretaic theories, 70
argument from prudential choice, 74–6
Arneson, Richard, 51, 176, 195, 197, 199, 201
ASO. *See* self-ownership; anarchist self-ownership
assault, 33, 42, 58, 70, 210, 213, 222
Asymmetry Thesis, 102
Attas, Daniel, 27, 93, 104–5
autonomy, 11
    bodily, 143
auxiliary theories. *See* moral theorizing; auxiliary theories

Bakunin, Mikhail, 1
bargaining power, 95

baseline argument, 105–8
  revised version of, 107–8
beliefs, 10, 11, 29, 79, 156, 186–7, 200, 206–7, 208
benefits
  to citizens requirement, 140–1
  and special obligations, 126–7, 128
  supplemental, 37–46, 48, 55, 58–9, 99, 100–2, 117, 142, 144
Berkman, Alexander, 1
bicyclist case, 46–8
birthday case, 106–8
blasphemy, 46
bodies, 3, 5, 21, 32–3, 36, 61, 66, 93, 103, 112, 118–19, 142, 168, 171, 173
  contact with, 38–48, 55, 58–9, 63, 66–7, 100–1, 116–17, 142, 144, 145–7, 172
  moral control over, 145
  as parts of actions, 113
  relation to the self, 32
  unowned, 99–100
Bookchin, Murray, 1
borders, 122, 138
  open, 11
boring problem, 176–7, 195–6
Bornschein, Peter, 109
bottle-throwing case, 55–7
boxing case, 145–6
Braham, Matthew, 171
Breakey, Hugh, 132–3
Brennan, Jason, 45, 68, 80, 104
brick case
  hero variant, 197–8
  villain variant, 197
    modified version, 198–9
Brilmayer, Lea, 138
Bryan, Ben, 45
Buchanan, Allen, 138–41, 159
bucket of sand case, 110–11
  variation of, 114
Bundism, 11
bureaucracy, 213
buskers, 60

cabin break-in case, 220
capitalism, 2, 7, 11
car towing case, 175
catcalling, 60, 62–3
causation, 28–31, 38–43, 45–6, 48, 57–9, 71, 100, 156
  counterfactual theories of, 29, 39
charity, 176
child abuse, 116–17, 119–20
Chisholm, Roderick M., 77

choice
  rewardable, 200–1
  sanctionable, 51–2, 54, 56, 57, 67, 84, 85–6, 116, 153, 158, 163, 169–70, 173, 174–87, 189–97, 199–202
Chomsky, Noam, 1
Christmas, Billy, 49
citizenship, 25, 139, 213
Clark, John, 7
CNT/FAI, 11
coercion, 23–5, 122, 157, 206, 209–10, 214, 218
cognitive capacities, 34–5, 116, 117, 119–20
Cohen, G. A., 13, 16, 51, 71, 84, 86, 165, 171, 175
Cohen, Marshall, 207, 209
coherence, 79, 222, 223
  of left-libertarianism. *See* libertarianism; left-; coherence of
  of social anarchism. *See* social anarchism; coherence of
  as a theoretical virtue, 14–15, 19
coherentism, 80
collective action problems, 159
common good, 75
communication, 63
community, 144, 205
comparative advantage, 195
compensation, 70, 73, 88–9, 90, 156–7, 162, 169, 176, 220
compensation baseline, 107
competition, 213–14
  competition case, 87, 88
complaint
  basis for, 27, 62
consent, 22, 60–1, 72–3, 97, 145, 161, 166, 203, 204
  hypothetical, 61–3
  tacit, 63–5, 134
  theory of initial appropriation. *See* initial appropriation; consent theory of
  theory of legitimacy. *See* legitimacy; consent theory of
  theory of territorial legitimacy. *See* legitimacy; territorial; consent theory of
contextualism
  moralized, 178–9
  prudential, 175–9
control, 61, 82, 122, 129, 139, 143
conventions, 63–4
cooperation zones, 64
co-operatives, 21
costly rescue, 195, 197, 199, *see also* Mother Teresa case

counterfactuals, 43, 47, 71, 77, 85, 98, 99, 107, 108, 110, 112, 156, 181, 184, 191, 193, 197, 198–201, 212, *see also* full compliance
counterfactual analysis of legitimacy. *See* legitimacy; counterfactual analysis of
counterfactual theories of causation. *See* causation; counterfactual theories of
cross and compensate, 48
Cruft, Rowan, 70

Davis, Lawrence, 153
democracy, 68–9, 80
democratic theory, 140
dentist case, 75
deontology, 70, 75
  vs. utilitarianism. *See* utilitarianism; vs. deontology
desert, 51
disabilities (Hohfeldian), 71, 166
disability, 174
disadvantage
  creation vs. distribution, 197–201
distributive claims, 5, 50, 52–7, 65, 66, 116–17, 119–20, 122, 142, 150–1, 155–8, 166, 167, 169–73, 174, 179, 193, 195
domination, 7–8, 77–9, 80
doorway case, 100–1, 112, 113
drowning child case, 87–9, 176
drug use, 33, 123, 213
duties. *See* obligations
Dworkin, Ronald, 187

Earth, 131
edicts, 22, 23–5, 81, 122, 129, 133–7, 142, 146–8, 205, 206, 207, *see also* laws
education, compulsory, 11
efficiency, 50
egalitarian anarchism. *See* social anarchism
egalitarian proviso, 4, 26, 160
egalitarianism, 2, 14, 18, 19, 21, 26, 65, 68, 85, 86, 97, 151, 154, 157, 161, 170–1, 177, 179, 180, 185, 201–2
  all-luck, 187
  currency of. *See* distributive justice; currency of
  egalitarian presumption, 86, 170
  liberal, 223
  luck. *see* luck egalitarianism
  relational, 78
  strict, 6, 50, 84–6, 156, 169, 173, 174, 180
enough and as good, 3, 26, *see also* Lockean proviso
entitlement theories, 5, 25–6, 52–3, 97, 117, 153–5, 157–69, 171, 173, 202
  grounds of, 164
  revised version of, 161–3

environmentalism, 11
Epstein, Richard, 45
equality, 2, 50, 57, 84, 86, 152, 153, 191
  of opportunity, 4, 159–60
Ervin, Lorenzo Kom'boa, 1
Estlund, David, 194
events, 28, 38, 54, 153, 156, 168, 181–2, 184, 188, 190, 191
evidence, 186–7, 189, 192
exchange, 7, 95
  blocked, 165–6
  conditional, 144, 160
  productive, 111
exhibitionism, 45–6
expected value, 182–7, 190, 200, 201
explanation, 1, 9, 35, 43, 100, 103, 113–14, 157, 168, 177, 213
  demand for, 33
  explanatory power, 63, 79–80
  scientific, 79
exploitation, 68, 85, 87
extended mind, 32
extensional adequacy, 55, 56, 58, 62, 65, 66, 67, 69, 74, 87, 112, 119, 201
extortion, 87

Fabbri, Luigi, 1
facts, 145
  contingent, 25, 217
  empirical, 80, 85, 130, 133, 136, 216–17
  moral, 28–9, 99, 156
    responsiveness of beliefs to, 29
  non-factualism. *See* anarchism; what counts as; non-factualism about
  pre-social, 140
  social, 10, 138
fairness, 51, 85, 160–1, 174, 187
Faure, Sébastien, 21
Feinberg, Joel, 220
Feser, Edward, 26, 33, 93, 109, 120, 153
feudalism, 121
fish pond case, 95
Flanigan, Jessica, 37, 45, 48, 171
Fleurbaey, Marc, 177, 187
Foot, Philippa, 42, 43
foreseeability, 54, 69, 73–4, 76, 81–2, 85–6, 91, 109–10, 148, 157, 175, 177, 181–2, 186, 200
foundationalism, 80
free speech, 46
freedom, 11, 21, 78, 144, 165
  ability to limit. *See* domination
  moral freedom, 87
Free-thought Movement, 21
Fressola, Anthony, 171

Fried, Barbara, 14, 18–19
Friedman, David, 7
Friedman, Milton, 17
from each according to her ability to each according to her need, 11
fruit case, 98
full compliance, 4, 32, 54, 61, 69, 71–4, 76–8, 80, 81–3, 85–91, 94–106, 109–11, 115–16, 117, 118–19, 146–8, 156–7, 169–70, 171, 172–3, 175–86, 187, 189–95, 202
full ownership. See property rights; full
fur trapper case, 126
   modified version, 128

gangs, 209, 211
Gaus, Gerald, 132, 134
Goldman, Emma, 1, 21
Goodwin, Barbara, 7
Government of the United Mexican States, 206
gravity analogy, 11, 16
grounding *desideratum*, 204–5, 207–10, 211, 213–16
group agent, 23
Guérin, Daniel, 1
gun control, 126, 128
Gustafsson, Johan E., 87

hair growing case, 133
Hanna, Jason, 90
harm, 37, 69, 70, 95, 104, 106, 107, 115, 174
Hayek, Friedrich, 17
historical theories of justice. See entitlement theories
Hobbesian conclusion, 5, 97, 152–7, 168–9, 171, 172, 173
Hohfeldian incidents, 22, 25, 35, 54, 70–1, 86, 166, 171, 205, 206, 211, 220
holdings, 86, 136, 140, 152–3, 156, 157, 158–68, 173, 195
Huemer, Michael, 7, 138, 140, 212, 213–14
Hurley, Susan, 176, 195–6

ideological space, 12, 16
immigration, 212, 213
inaction baseline. See Lockean proviso; inaction baseline
incompatibilist argument, 157–60, 162–5
individuation, 9, 78
Industrial Workers of the World, 11
industry, 155
inequality, 2, 7, 50, 52, 54, 56, 84, 86, 153, 158–60, 162, 168, 169, 174, 176–7, 191, 195–6, 200–1, 202

initial appropriation, 5, 33, 53, 93, 94–108, 110, 111, 115, 121–2, 123, 130, 132–6, 137, 143, 148, 149, 152, 154, 156, 159–61, 171
   causal effects of, 28–30
   consent theory of, 122, 167
   constraints on. See Lockean proviso *and* egalitarian proviso
   justice in. See justice; in appropriation and transfer
   parental appropriation, 117–18, 119
   self-appropriation, 5, 33–7, 49, 55, 63, 65, 93, 99–102, 115–16, 119, 122, 141–2, 144, 146, 148, 154, 201
   unilateral, 2, 26
   vs. consensual, 82–3
insect case, 57
intellectual self-confidence, 16–17
intentions, 22, 38, 48, 113, 125, 211
   malicious, 69
internalization of costs, 180, 181–2, 186
intuitions, 12, 15, 57–60, 66, 73, 112, 117, 212
   libertarian, 146
Ito Noe, 1

Jeffers, Matthew T., 177
Jeske, Diane, 128
jurisdiction, 122, 138–9
justice, 6, 11, 17, 139–40, 161–8, 178, 194, 196, 203, 204–5, 206, 207–15, 216
   distributive, 4, 5–6, 16, 19, 50, 53, 66, 69, 117, 152, 170
   currency of, 50, 71, 180–1
   end-state principles of, 153
   entitlement theories of. See entitlement theories
   non-entitlement theories of. See non-entitlement theories
   patterned principles of, 153
   in appropriation and transfer, 153, 158, 159, 164
   rights' and obligations' relation to, 159, 163, 164, 165, 220
   social, 68
justification, 2, 14, 16–17, 19, 23, 34, 143, 158, 176, 191, 195–7
   vs. legitimacy, 150

kidneys
   purchase of, 146
   redistribution of. See redistribution; of organs
kissing case, 145–6
kitchen floor case, 41–2
Knight, Carl, 171, 186–7
Kropotkin, Peter, 1, 121
Kukathas, Chandran, 45

labor, 68, 84–5, 121, 153, 155, 165, 174, 180, *see also* sex; sex work
land, 3, 5, 49, 68, 95, 121–2, 129–32, 136, 138–9, 151, 152, *see also* territory
vs. objects, 122
Lang, Gerald, 196
laws, 2, 3, 22, 25, 122–3, 126, 140, 141, 203, 208, *see also* edicts
  enforcement of, 208, 218–23
  just, 150
legal systems, 74
legislative process, 208
legitimacy, 6, 121, 122, 203, 205–6, 207, 211, 216
  as a permission to coerce, 23, 218–21
  consent theory of, 3, 5, 22–5, 65, 80–3, 84, 86, 91, 92, 121–2, 123, 127, 129, 130, 132, 134–8, 139, 140–50, 151, 152, 173, 201, 203
    grounds of, 124
    Simmons' argument for, 124–7
    strong vs. weak, 82
    weaker version of, 143–4
  content independence of, 81
  counterfactual analysis of, 22
  exclusivity requirement, 23–4
  explication of, 22–5
  partial vs. full, 141
  scalar conception of, 23
  territorial, 121, 123–4, 127–32, 138, 140–5, 149, 150
    consent theory of, 121, 123–4, 127, 129, 136, 137, 141, 142, 146
    universal, 123
  tout court, 23
  unbounded, 123–4, 127, 128
  vs. political authority, 23, 218
  Weberian, 206–7
Lewis, David, 29, 39
liberalism, 46, 75, 89, 223
libertarianism, 4, 14, 21, 32, 37, 46, 49, 55, 56, 65, 68–9, 72, 74, 84, 87, 89, 92–3, 97, 116, 130, 132, 134–41, 142, 146, 152–3, 155, 160, 164, 169, 173, 174, 201–2, 216
  dialectical pressure on, 5–6, 15, 16, 18, 27, 49, 149, 151, 154, 170–1, 223
  and entitlement theories, 25
  left-, 4, 26, 52, 55, 159–60, 171
    coherence of, 18–19
  natural rights, 140
  radical right-, 26, 93, 108, 120
  right-, 3, 5, 19, 26, 27, 52, 86, 93, 135
    as a variety of egalitarianism, 171–3

liberties, 70
liberty, 68
Lippert-Rasmussen, Kasper, 51, 102
Locke, John, 26, 53, 83, 84, 171
Lockean proviso, 3, 4, 25–32, 36, 45, 49, 56, 62, 65, 80, 82–4, 86, 91, 92–111, 114–20, 121, 145, 148–9, 151, 152, 154, 156, 160, 167, 173, 201
  expected-compliance specification, 30–1
  full-compliance specification, 30–1
  inaction baseline, 108, 111–14
  natural interpretation of, 28
  non-appropriation baseline, 98
  nonexistence baseline, 28, 96, 98, 99, 100, 103, 107–9, 110, 111, 118
    emended version of, 115–16, 118
  Nozick's baseline, 103–8
  Nozick's interpretation of, 164
  preliminary/primary statement of, 32
  strong vs. weak, 82
  welfare specification of, 27
Lomasky, Loren, 104, 132, 153, 171
Long, Roderick, 7, 171
loyalty oath, 25
luck egalitarianism, 3, 5, 13, 50–2, 54–5, 56, 57–8, 64, 65, 66, 69, 92, 109, 117, 119, 142, 152, 157–8, 167, 169–78, 179, 184, 186, 191, 195–7, 199, 200–2, 203
  egalitarian baseline variant, 196
  motivation for, 84–7
  responsibility component of, 51, 80, 84, 86, 91, 201
  stakes of, 51

Mack, Eric, 26, 45, 68, 75, 83, 93, 109, 153, 163, 165, 168
Magón, Ricardo Flores, 68
Makhno, Nestor, 1
Malatesta, Errico, 1, 174
markets, 11
  private security, 212–14
  rejection of, 2
marriage case, 87, 88
mass, 131–2, 141, 143
maximin principle, 4
McElroy, Wendy, 171
McKay, Iain, 7, 8
McKerlie, Dennis, 181
medical procedure case, 73
Meinong, Alexius, 77
Meinong-Chisholm Reduction, 77
Mellor, D. H., 29
mere means, 75
meta-principles, 4, 16, 27, 65, 74, 79, 157, 173, 202, 223

Michel, Louise, 1
military, 7, 212
Milky Way Galaxy, 124
Miller, David, 159, 212
Millian liberties, 33
minarchism, 203
miner case, 200
Minyi Chu, 92
monarch case, 143
money, 50, 87, 146, 165, 195
Moore, Margaret, 140, 141
moral blackmail, 87
moral equality, 34–7, 53, 119–20, 171, 172–3
moral freedom. *See* freedom; moral
moral personhood, 33, 143
moral slavery, 118
moral theorizing, 67
    auxiliary theories, 63, 65, 92, 108
    comparative, 66, 223
    epistemic challenges of, 58, 63, 112
    holistic, 66, 80, 119–20, 146, 185
    moral tyranny constraint, 4, 5, 16, 27, 30, 51, 65, 69–74, 76, 77–91, 92, 108–9, 120, 142, 148, 149, 155, 156–7, 168–70, 171, 172–5, 176, 181, 182–6, 192, 193, 194–5, 196, 201–2, 223
    generalized version of, 110, 111, 112, 117
    laxity objection to, 87–9
    moral tyranny objection, 176, 177–80, 195, 196
    paternalism objection to, 89–91
    stringency objection to, 87
Mother Teresa case, 176, 195, 197
motorcycle case, 177–9, 187–93
Mulkeen, Nicola, 43, 45, 55
murder, 150
mutual aid, 212

Narveson, Jan, 26, 37, 93, 153, 171
natural duties, 124–6, 127, 128
    perfect vs. imperfect, 125, 128
    positive vs. negative, 125
natural resources, 2, 3, 5, 25, 49, 52, 55, 56, 65, 66, 82, 92, 93, 94–7, 98, 99, 103, 115, 116–17, 121–2, 130–1, 132, 142, 150–1, 152, 157, 159–60, 161, 166–9, 172–3, 174, 179, 191, 195, 200, 202
    improvement of, 94–5, 97, 155
    preservation of, 94–5, 97, 140
negligence, 69
Nine, Cara, 136, 138, 139–40
non-appropriation baseline. *See* Lockean proviso; non-appropriation baseline
non-entitlement theories, 153, 164–8

nonexistence baseline. *See* Lockean proviso; nonexistence baseline
nonexistence test, 98–101, 102
non-worsening constraint, 26, 31
norms
    gender, 11
    social, 17, 60
Nozick, Robert, 17, 26, 37, 45, 48, 74, 75, 84, 103–8, 111, 115, 117, 153, 158, 161–8, 207, 209
nuclear villain case, 89
nudism, 45–6
nuisance, 60, 64

O'Neill, Onora, 165
obligations
    and "ought" implies "can", 89
    conditional, 82, 123, 124, 127–8, 129, 132, 133, 135–6, 142, 144, 146
    conflicting, 24, 73
    directedness of, 52, 70
    filial, 125
    impersonal vs. agential, 77
    imposition of, 72, 78, 81–2, 86, 122, 132–4, 135, 137, 144, 205, 207, 218, *see also* legitimacy
    natural. *See* natural duties
    political, 122, 124–6, 127, 128
    positive vs. negative, 216
    pro tanto, 220
    promissory, 125, 128
    remedial, 88–9, 90, 156, 220
    special, 125, 126–9
        involuntary, 125, 126–7, 128
        voluntary, 125, 126–7, 129
    to rescue, 73, 88–9, 179
Okin, Susan Moller, 117
Olsaretti, Serena, 51, 175, 177, 178
omissions, 114
option luck, 187
Otsuka, Michael, 4, 33, 37, 45, 50, 85, 159–60
outstanding professor case, 132
overdetermination, 112, 114
ownership. *See* property rights

Parsons, Lucy, 1
paternalism, 89, 117, 119, *see also* moral tyranny constraint; paternalism objection to
patriarchy, 11
peanut farming case, 104
performances, 59–64
permissiveness objection. *See* self-ownership; anarchist self-ownership; permissiveness objection to
Pettit, Philip, 77–8

philosophical anarchism. *See* anarchism; philosophical
photons, 34, 44, 46, 59, 63, 66
physical force, 205
physical space, 131
physical space case, 133
pick up the tab, 85
planets, 11, 131, 132
plasma, purchase of, 146
police, 7, 68, 150, 212, 222
  abolition of, 11
political authority, 23, 206–8, 218, 219, 220–1
  vs. legitimacy. *See* legitimacy; vs. political authority
political institutions, 2
politicians, 17
pollution problem, 44–5, 48, 57, 59
possible worlds, 28, 32, 94, 96, 110–12, 118, 157, 204–5
poverty, 68, 155
power, 217
practical requirements, 133
pragmatic concerns, 204
prison abolition, 11
private property. *See* property rights
pro-attitudes, 62
probability, 217
  conditional, 182, 184–5, 189–90, 192
  objective vs. subjective, 186–7
production, 155
promises, 125, 128
promissory obligations. *See* obligations; promissory
propertarianism, 136–8
property rights, 2, 4, 8, 18, 53, 56, 82–3, 95, 122, 133, 134–8, 141, 144–5, 152, 155, 156, 157, 158, 159–64, 166, 167, 168, 170, 222
  anarchist rejection of, 3, 5, 7, 11, 18, 21, 49, 52, 56, 65, 91, 92, 96–7, 119, 121–2, 132, 142, 143, 146, 148–53, 168, 170, 173, 174, 201, 202
  as a form of legitimacy, 5, 121, 122, 129–30, 132, 134, 135–6, 138–41
  based theories of justice. *See* entitlement theories
  benefits of, 94, 104
  bundle theory of, 35, 53, 129
  collective, 49, 138
  full, 3, 26, 32, 52, 97, 164
  function of, 139–40
  in land vs. objects, 131–2
  initial acquisition of. *See* initial appropriation
  intellectual property, 52–3
  legal, 136, 139, 156

proporitionality, 210
protection agencies, 7, 140, 212–13
Proudhon, Pierre-Joseph, 1, 152
prudence, 155, 195–6, 209, 210
  prudential choice argument. *See* argument from prudential choice
  prudential contextualism, 192, 193, 195–6, 199, 201
punishment, 209

race case, 39
racism, 11
Railton, Peter, 45
Rawls, John, 74, 79, 223
reactive attitudes, 60
Reclus, Elisée, 1
rectification, 153
redistribution, 18, 52, 68, 85, 86, 109, 156, 161–2, 164, 165, 167, 175, 176, 179, 188, 189, 190–1, 195, 203
  of organs, 32, 42, 55, 66, 99, 100, 101
reductio ad absurdum, 18, 84, 165–8, 198, 201
reflective equilibrium, 31, 79–80, 87, 155, 157
regulations, 135, 149, 203, 206, 210, 212, 213, 214
religious believers, 46
republicanism, 77–9, 80
resentment, 60, 64
respect, 75
responsibility, 80, 84, 91, 92, 146–8, 157, 169, 170, 175, 176–7, 178, 179, 187, 195–6, 197, 200
  counterfactual analyses of, 115
  and foreseeability, 181–2
  holding responsible, 51, 85–6, 117, 169, 174–5, 176, 180, 185, 186, 196, 200, 201
  moral, 110–11, 112, 113–15, 117
  nonexistence comparison test, 110–13, 114, 146–7
  emended version of, 114–15
restrictiveness objection. *See* self-ownership; anarchist self-ownership; restrictiveness objection to
Right, the, 16–17, 86
rights
  to advantage, 178
  of animals, 11, 34, 36
  to assistance/rescue. *See* obligations; to rescue
  of children, 11, 34, 36, 93, 116–20
  conditional. *See* obligations; conditional
  distributive. *See* distributive claims
  enforcement of, 206, 208, 215, 222
    permission to enforce, 211, 212
    power to enforce, 210–11

equality of, 152, 171–3, 202
forfeiture of, 33, 34, 53–4, 86, 158, 170, 171, 177, 178–9, 180, 181, 184, 186, 191, 192–3, 194, 195
identical, 171–2
infringements on, 33, 37, 38, 39–48, 56–7, 59–60, 62–3, 73, 117, 156, 169, 172, 178
infringements vs. violations, 60
legal, 208, *see also* property rights; legal
power to transfer, 26, 32, 34, 37, 53, 54, 129, 136, 166–7
power to waive, 25, 31–2, 34, 37, 54, 61, 62, 63, 83, 96–7, 99, 101, 115, 118, 128, 129, 142, 148, 171
conditional, 144–6
pro tanto, 220
property. *See* property rights
symmetrical, 171, 172
violations of, 211, 214, 216–17
will theories of, 97
Risse, Mathias, 18, 160
Rocker, Rudolf, 1
Roemer, John, 51
Rojavan revolution, 11
Rose, Carol, 36, 103
Rothbard, Murray, 26, 37, 45, 68, 93, 153, 171
roulette wheel case, 196
rules. *See* edicts

scarcity, 94, 97, 145, 152, 167
scavenger case, 157
Schmidtz, David, 94, 104, 140
scientific theories, 79
secrets case, 133
security companies. *See* protection agencies
security provision, 212–14, *see also* markets; security
Segall, Shlomi, 187
self-appropriation. *See* initial appropriation; self-appropriation
self-defense, 33, 210
self-development, 21
self-ownership, 3, 49, 50, 55, 56–7, 98, 101, 116–17, 119–20, 141–6, 154, 173, 202, 203
acquisition of. *See* initial appropriation; self-appropriation
anarchist self-ownership, 37–49, 55–65, 92, 93, 98, 99, 101–3, 117, 119, 142, 144, 146, 148, 153, 154, 160, 172, 202
permissiveness objection to, 56–8, 65
restrictiveness objection to, 59, 65
weak version of, 144, 145

classical interpretation of, 37, 42, 44, 46–7, 59, 60, 65, 100, 101–2, 103, 142
grounds of, 120
native vs. acquired, 33–7, 143–4
self-ownership thesis, 3, 19, 32–3, 37–49, 55–65, 91, 92–3, 123, 142–3
grounds of, 98, 103
self-sovereignty, 142, 144, 146, 147–8
revised consent theory of, 147
Sen, Amartya, 171
separateness of persons argument, 74–7, 80
sex, 33
sex work, 146
sexism, 11
shares
appropriate, 52, 54, 64
entitlement to, 166
equal, 84, 86, 155, 160, 170, 172, 175, 183, 200
fair, 121
just, 51–2, 165, 214
Simmons, A. John, 23–4, 64, 81, 82, 84, 122, 132–3, 138, 150–1, 203, 221
simplicity
evaluative, 111
parsimony, 45, 116
syntactic, 45, 112
slavery, 33, 165
moral slavery. *See* moral slavery
Slice and Patch case, 194
Smart, J. J. C., 75
Smith, Holly M., 63
Sobel, David, 45, 55
social anarchism, 3–4, 6, 91, 92, 116, 119–20, 142, 152, 162, 169, 173, 176, 177, 201–4, 205, 223
coherence of, 6, 14–15, 49, 65, 91, 92, 98, 102, 120, 202
explication of, 22–41, 49–55
as moral theory, 1–2
plausibility of, 15
practical use of, 16–20
social design, 17
social insurance, 68, 80
social structures, 217
socialism, 1, 21, 49, 144, 202
core tenets of, 13, 51
relation between theory and practice, 16–17
socialist minarchism, 203
socialist philosophers, 4
vs. anarchism. *See* anarchism; vs. socialism
Socialist Party, the, 21
solicitation, 59–61, 63, 64–5
Spafford, Jesse, 120, 135, 144
Spencer, Herbert, 171

sphere case, 106, 107–8
spiteful destroyer case, 84, 86, 156, 173, 175, 180
Spooner, Lysander, 8
stakes. *See* luck egalitarianism; stakes of
state of nature, 152
state planning, 11
statehood, analysis of, 6, 22, 204–16
states, 1–2, 3, 6–7, 8, 22–3, 25, 68, 81, 122–3, 124, 126, 135, 136–7, 149–50, 202, 203–23
  abolition of, 6, 10, 17, 203–4, 205, 206, 212, 214, 216–17, *see also* political anarchism
  justified, 218–20
  state authorization, 209–11
  vs. property owners, 138–41
statism, 6, 205, 217, 219, 221, 223
Steiner, Hillel, 4, 33, 37, 45, 50, 153, 171
Stemplowska, Zofia, 175, 178
suberogation, 70
subordination, 138
Sumner, William, 68
Sun, the, 131
supererogation, 70
surgeon case, 105, 107
surrogacy, 146

tactics, 17
tax cheat case, 134
taxation, 4, 121, 179
taxpayers, 68
Taylor, Robert S., 37
telemarketing, 60, 62–3
Temkin, Larry, 51, 176, 181
tennis court case, 132–4
tennis racket case, 51–2
territory, 122–3, 127–32, 135–9, 140, 205, 209, 212, *see also* land
  transfer of, 140–1
Thaysen, Jens Damgaard, 175, 197–201
theft, 213
theoretical role, 104–5, 107, 113
theoretical virtues, 13, 15, 45, 48, 60, 65–6, 67, 79, 143, 146, 185, 223
Thomson, Judith Jarvis, 24, 26, 33, 37, 42, 44, 70, 220
threats, 210
touching, analysis of, 46–7
trade unions, 11, 21

transfers. *See* redistribution *and* exchange *and* rights; power to transfer *and* justice; in appropriation and transfer
trespass, 37
trespasser case, 222
Trolley Problem cases, 42–4
Tucker, Benjamin, 8
tyrants, 68, 74

United States Federal Government, 131, 205, 206–8, 211, 213, 214, 216
utilitarianism, 74–6, 87, 223
  vs. deontology, 75

Vallentyne, Peter, 4, 37, 45, 50, 51, 163, 187, 209
van der Vossen, Bas, 27, 45, 83, 104, 133, 135, 138, 153
van Hees, Martin, 171
Van Parijs, Philippe, 4
veganism, 11
violence, 150, 206–7, 209–11, 214, 222
  monopoly on, 205, 207, 209, 212
voluntariness, 72, 212, 214
von Mises, Ludwig, 68, 80
voters, 68

Waldron, Jeremy, 26
war, 11
waterfall pollution case, 96
Weber, Max, 205–6, 207, 209
WEDA, 179, 187, 190–4, 195, 196, 197, 199–201, 202
welfare, 4, 27, 50, 71, 159–60
well-being, 68, 121
  objective list theory of, 71
Wendt, Fabian, 209, 210–11, 217–23
White supremacy, 11
Wilson, Charlotte, 1
Wilt Chamberlain argument, 165–8
Wolff, Robert Paul, 82, 203
work. *See* labor

youth liberation. *See* rights; of children

Zapatistas, 11
Zimmerman, Michael J., 63
Zwolinski, Matt, 45, 66

For EU product safety concerns, contact us at Calle de José Abascal, 56–1°,
28003 Madrid, Spain or eugpsr@cambridge.org.

www.ingramcontent.com/pod-product-compliance
Lightning Source LLC
Chambersburg PA
CBHW072239160425
25273CB00008B/462